10,000
nights

10,000 nights

HIGHLIGHTS FROM 50 YEARS OF THEATRE-GOING

Marvin Carlson

UNIVERSITY OF MICHIGAN PRESS
ANN ARBOR

Published in the United States of America by
The University of Michigan Press
Manufactured in the United States of America
⊗ Printed on acid-free paper

2020   2019   2018   2017   4   3   2   1

A CIP catalog record for this book is available from the British Library.

ISBN 978-0-472-13050-4 (hardcover : alk. paper)
ISBN 978-0-472-12315-5 (e-book)

To Pat
Who shared the adventure

Contents

Prologue

By Way of Background

I was born in Wichita, Kansas, a city neither then nor since especially noted for theatrical activity, and my early exposure to theatre was not extensive. My aunt Velma, the "artistic" member of the family, performed regularly while attending Friends University, which had an ambitious theatre program in the 1950s, and the only professional production I remember from my Wichita years was a road show of *John Brown's Body*, directed by Charles Laughton and starring Judith Anderson, Raymond Massey, and Tyrone Power, which I saw in 1953, at the age of eighteen, and which left an indelible impression upon me. It was a staged reading, so scenic spectacle played little part in the effect, but the thrill of seeing those great actors at the top of their form was unlike anything I had ever experienced.

Fascinating as this experience was, when I enrolled that year as a freshman at the University of Kansas, I had no thought of majoring in theatre, but followed the more conventional course of a major in English. Still, I found myself more and more drawn to theatre, first as a spectator, then as an actor, and gradually in almost every other capacity as well. When I arrived in Lawrence, Allen Crafton, founder of the program and one of the pioneers of the American university theatre, was still active, and still full of the vision of the new stagecraft. Typically, he staged *Waiting for Godot* in 1955 shortly after its English-language premiere in London, and reveled in the confusion it aroused in conventional theatergoers. Crafton was followed by Lewin Goff, who brought both Broadway actors and foreign companies to Lawrence, considerably broadening my horizons. One of my warmest memories of Kansas was the opening of a major new theatre my final year there with a production of *Henry IV, Part I*. The Broadway actor and playwright Jerome Kilty was a guest artist, playing Falstaff, and I was delighted to play Gadshill, one of his companions.

By the time I was ready to begin my Ph.D., thanks to the inspiration of the program Crafton and Goff developed, I was totally committed to theatre. At that time, in the late 1950s, the preeminent theatre schools in the Midwest were Iowa and Northwestern, but I was determined to move into the New York orbit. The choices then were few. At Columbia and Yale I could have studied theatre but would have had to remain in English. I thus went to Cornell, which almost alone in the Ivy League offered a distinguished theatre program, established by Alexander Drummond, another visionary of the Crafton era. Coming to Ithaca from the Midwest, I naively assumed that New York was practically in the same neighborhood, but I soon discovered otherwise. The trains that used to regularly make this trip had disappeared a couple of years before my arrival, and flying was beyond the means of a graduate student. At least I had a car, a battered Renault, and so Pat, my fiancée, and I soon became accustomed to driving that long round-trip. Today, thanks to the building of the Southern Tier expressway, the driving time is about four and a half hours, but on the old narrow and winding Route 17, it was six or more, depending on traffic and the weather. Nevertheless, with graduate student energy and determination, we would often drive down on a Saturday morning, see three shows that day (a matinee in the afternoon and two shows in the evening, since at that time most off-Broadway theatres offered two showings Saturday evenings). When we could afford it, we would stay overnight, allowing us to include another matinee Sunday before returning to Ithaca. Otherwise we would return very late Saturday night and catch up on missed sleep on Sunday.

After graduating, in 1961, I was invited to join the Cornell faculty, and my improved finances allowed a more relaxed commute. Happily, at that time the New York theatre was alive with activities such as the first plays of Albee, the work of the Living Theatre and the Open Theatre, the arrival of the new British drama, of Brecht, of the French absurdists, of the new black theatre. It was a period of intoxicating variety and promise, and I couldn't get enough of it. Every week I would devour the newest edition of the *Village Voice*, my primary resource for what I might see. Productions of groups like the Living Theatre and Bread and Puppet combined the energies of the street and of the current political scene in the theatre in ways I had never imagined. The general level of excitement and innovation was so high that for a young man just getting a sense of theatre's possibilities, the total experience could not have been more stimulating.

Pat, now my wife, and I spent my first sabbatical leave in Paris, in the revolutionary year 1968, a time of enormous excitement and up-

heaval. There I received my first extended exposure to continental theatre, including Barrault's *Rabelais* and some of the earliest work, in the
Parisian suburbs, of Ariane Mnouchkine and Patrice Chéreau. Back in
New York, I found the theatre scene developing during the 1970s somewhat less politically charged (except for the striking emergence of the
new black theatre) but still pushing in stimulating new directions in the
work of artists like Richard Foreman, André Gregory, Squat Theatre,
and the Wooster Group.

In 1979 my theatrical and personal life took a major new direction
when I accepted a position on the faculty of Indiana University. During
the seven years I spent there, my theatre life became more diffuse,
though no less exciting. Bloomington itself had one of the country's
most ambitious opera seasons, and between that and the Chicago Lyric
Opera, I became more interested in that genre as well. Chicago was now
as close as New York had been, and I found not only the Lyric, but the
Goodman and the emerging and exciting Steppenwolf.

New York remained my theatre center, however, and my holidays
during the 1980s were spent either there or in Europe, where I spent my
second sabbatical in 1985, visiting theatres in London, Paris, Berlin, and
a variety of cities in West Germany. The following year, however, I was
invited to join the faculty at the Graduate Center of the City University
of New York, where I have remained ever since. Settled in New York, I
was at last able to attend the theatre as frequently as I had previously
done on trips to London or Paris. Thus, over a period of more than fifty
years of dedicated theatre-going, I am almost overwhelmed by the range
and richness of theatre it has been my privilege to experience. When I
decided to put together some kind of memoir of this experience, I cast
about for some time for an approach that would provide some sense of
that richness, without becoming overwhelmed by the potential size of
the project.

My solution was to look at a range of fifty years, beginning in 1960,
shortly after I began regularly attending the professional theatre in New
York, and for each of those fifty years to pick a single production, which
I would use to explore, in a short essay, some of the experience and impressions of theatre-going at that particular time and place. I have not
always picked my "favorite" show of a particular year nor the best-
known or most awarded production, but have instead picked productions that have remained in my memory and that I think reveal important aspects of the theatrical culture of their time. The examples, like

my theatre-going career, favor the New York stage, but also include a number of significant memories of productions in Europe and elsewhere. Deciding on which play to discuss from each year was rarely easy. In some years few obvious possibilities occurred, but more often a year would contain so many attractive possibilities, perhaps for quite different reasons, that choosing only one was a truly challenging process. There were certain artists whose work I enjoyed so much that it was hard not to include four or five of their works, but I resisted this temptation, feeling it more important to provide overall a range of material that would both be a more accurate indication of my actual theatre-going and a suggestion of how tastes and approaches to the art changed during this half-century. Despite the necessarily limited range of subjects, then, I hope that these reports from fifty years of the changing scene of the theatre in New York and elsewhere will provide the reader not only with the impressions of a dedicated theatre-goer but also with a firsthand impression of how the Western theatre world changed and evolved in the last part of the twentieth century. As I have recorded these memories, I have tried as much as possible to confirm them with written records, my own and others, from the period, but memory is a great fictionalizer and doubtless there has been some slippage, despite my efforts to present as accurate a record of my experiences as I could. For that I apologize, and hope that the authenticity of the experience will come across in any case.

The 1960s

The Fantasticks, 1960. Photo from the Billy Rose Theatre Division, New York Public Library Digital Collections. Used with permission.

1960 *The Fantasticks* at the Sullivan Street Playhouse

Although no one could have predicted in the spring of 1960 that one of the most innovative decades in the American theatre was beginning, there was clearly a change in the air, especially in the off-Broadway theatre, in those days centered around Sheridan Square. The pioneering Greenwich Village Theatre, located in that square, had closed years before, but its tradition had been carried on by the Sheridan Square Playhouse and the Circle in the Square. Just a few streets to the west, the even more famous Provincetown, created by Eugene O'Neill and his company in 1916, was still active, and significantly contributing to the spirit of the new decade by opening a double bill of Beckett's *Krapp's Last Tape* and Albee's *The Zoo Story* in January of this year. Macdougal Street, where the Provincetown was located, was during the 1950s the center of the beat generation, and much of that atmosphere remained by 1960, although many of the leaders of that generation had moved to San Francisco. Nevertheless, Macdougal Street, just to the south of Washington Square Park, was still lined with the bars, cafés, and bookstores where William Burroughs, Allen Ginsberg, Jack Kerouac, and others used to gather. Some of these, like the Caffe Dante or the Minetta Tavern, dated back to the days of O'Neill, and so had provided gathering spots for local bohemians for almost half a century by 1960.

My own favorite among these many Village gathering spots was the Caffe Reggio, which still is in operation at 119 Macdougal. When I first went there, in the late 1950s, it was already some thirty years old, having been opened in 1927 by Domenico Parisi, who served the first cappuccinos in New York. His original espresso machine, dating from 1902, still stands against the back wall of the café. Here a young Midwesterner could feel that he was in the heart not only of the New York's bohemia, represented then by the beats, but also in an international milieu. My favorite seat there was a bench from a Medici palazzo, where, surrounded by Italianate paintings as if you were seated in a museum, you could admire, across the room, a work from the school of Caravaggio.

Just one street west and one south from the Provincetown on quieter

Sullivan Street was the Sullivan Street Playhouse, one of several small theatres that opened this year, reflecting the growing interest in off-Broadway. It opened in May 1960 with a new intimate musical, *The Fantasticks*, by Tom Jones and Harvey Schmidt, which would become the longest-running show in New York theatre history. The two most popular types of productions off-Broadway at this time were experimental European works, especially from Brecht, Beckett, Genet, and Ionesco, and small musicals, inspired in part by the success of Brecht's *Threepenny Opera*, which by 1960 had been running for five years at the Theatre de Lys, to the west of Sheridan Square.

The show did not have a propitious beginning. The dean of New York critics, the formidable Brooks Atkinson of the *New York Times*, who had almost single-handedly ensured the success of the *Threepenny Opera*, did not much care for *The Fantasticks*, especially its dark second act, which broke with the conventions of the Rodgers and Hammerstein–style show. Michael Smith, in the *Village Voice*, which I already was beginning to rely upon for theatrical (and later political) guidance, was on the other hand warmly enthusiastic. Moreover, I had minored in French and my love of *Cyrano de Bergerac* had led me to read other Rostand plays, among them *Les Romanesques*, which I found quite delightful, and upon which *The Fantasticks* was based. Thus, undeterred by Atkinson's dim view, I attended this new work in June, less than a month after its opening.

I found that despite the *Times* review, every seat in the little theatre, about 150 of them, was full. Unquestionably this was in part due to the fact that an actor's strike that month had closed all the Broadway houses, a major boon for off-Broadway and particularly for the Sullivan Street Playhouse. Before the strike it had been playing to small houses, often fewer than the tiny cast. Thanks in large part to the strike, however, and to subsequent word of mouth, by the fall *The Fantasticks* was one of the most popular off-Broadway shows. The audience the night I attended clearly loved the production, and I was totally entranced, not only because I came already favorably disposed toward the play, but because as a theatre person I found the extensive use of theatrical quotations—the general commedia conventions, the aging Shakespearian actor, the masks, the vaudeville and Wild West routines, the cardboard sun and moon—quite entrancing. The intimacy of the space added to the effect, since the audience sat on three sides of the stage, and no one was more than two or three rows from the actors. Indeed the space was so small that some audience members had to cross the stage to get to their seats. I remember a pause after the opening number so that embarrassed latecomers could scurry across the stage to be seated.

I discovered that the show in its overall action closely followed the French original, but there were some striking changes. Rostand tells of a naive young couple fascinated by romances like that of Romeo and Juliet, especially since their fathers appear to be mortal enemies. They daydream of fanciful ways to resolve this problem, such as an attempted abduction of the girl being thwarted by the boy, resulting in a reconciliation of the quarreling fathers. Unbeknownst to them, however, their fathers are in fact close friends, who have pretended to quarrel so as to encourage the love of their romantic children. Overhearing the conversation of the young lovers, they decide to play out their imagined scenario. They hire a professional swashbuckler to stage such a fake abduction, which plays out as planned. Then, just as the young lovers are about to be united, their foolish boasting drives their fathers to reveal the plot. Disillusioned, the boy goes out into the world while the girl continues to seek a storybook romance. Later, both wounded by their experience and cured of their childish illusions, they reunite in a more mature relationship.

Clearly in terms of plot, *The Fantasticks* follows Rostand almost exactly, but from the opening moments I realized that Jones and Schmidt had created a very different actual theatre experience, one both more American and more consciously theatrical. The change was apparent as one entered the little theatre. The stage was a conscious evocation of a traveling show of the commedia dell'arte variety, a simple platform with poles at the two front corners, between which was draped a banner, bearing the name of the show. Probably no regular theatre-goer who saw this production during its opening months missed this echo of the commedia stage, since one of the most highly praised productions in New York that season was the touring production of the commedia classic *The Servant of Two Masters*, by Goldoni, staged by Italy's Piccolo Teatro, headed by Giorgio Strehler. This piece, the signature production of one of the most important international directors of the late twentieth century, was a dazzling display of theatrical vitality and virtuosity. I still remember it as one of my greatest theatre experiences, and in June 1960, when I had seen the Strehler production just two months before at the City Center, I seemed to see constant echoes of that production and that style in *The Fantasticks*. Everything in that production was marked by the commedia combination of theatricality, virtuosity, and simplicity. Most of the properties and occasionally some actors were produced out of a large upstage traveling trunk. Scenery was minimal and equally simple; a cardboard moon was hung on one of the downstage poles for the first act, to be replaced with a sun by the narrator at the opening of the harsher second act.

Strehler's *The Servant of Two Masters* was a part of one of the most outstanding elements of the New York stage at the beginning of the 1960s. Thanks to the impresario Sol Hurok, New York's City Center hosted at that time an offering of international companies never equaled before or since. The spring of 1960 saw not only the Piccolo Teatro but the Grand Kabuki of Japan. February of the following year saw a series of productions from the Comédie-Française and that spring The Old Vic and Gustaf Gründgens's *Faust* from Germany. The Moscow Art Theatre appeared a few years later. This astonishing display of major international companies has often been forgotten amid the widespread interest in the development at this same time of off- and off-off-Broadway.

In *The Fantasticks*, the narrator figure was one of the major changes from the original. Rostand's swashbuckler, Straforel, is clearly reproduced in El Gallo, but El Gallo has moved to the center of *The Fantasticks*, playing not only his own role, but introducing and stage-managing all the rest, with not a few echoes of Strehler's Arlecchino. Rostand's play opens in a conventional realistic way, with the boy reading to the girl from *Romeo and Juliet*. El Gallo opened *The Fantasticks* with a song, "Try to Remember," evoking the simple and romantic pleasures of young love. He then continued, rather in the mode of the stage manager in *Our Town*, directly addressing the audience and promising them a story: "You wonder how these things begin." The other major change in *The Fantasticks* was in El Gallo's entourage, those who help him tell the story. All of these reinforced the theatricalization of the narrative. First there was the black-clad mute, his movements suggesting classic mime, but whose function, as in the Chinese opera, was to provide El Gallo and others with the props and settings they required. Even more important were the characters El Gallo used to stage the false abduction. In Rostand this is an undifferentiated crowd of swordsmen, servants, torchbearers, and chariot bearers. In *The Fantasticks* these were replaced by two specific characters, well developed but still, like the children and fathers, traditional types. They, appropriately, emerged from the traveling trunk as part of the theatrical world conjured up by

El Gallo. The first was Henry, an ancient and emaciated traditional Shakespearian actor, exhibiting all the clichés of that tradition. His companion, Mortimer, was short and rotund, dressed as a cliché stage Indian, who, appropriately, was introduced as a specialist in dying.

Henry and Mortimer served in the first act to help El Gallo carry out the very funny and elaborately staged abductions, with highly theatricalized fake death scenes, but in the second, still serving as El Gallo's accomplices, they supervised the painful adventures of the boy in the world, placed offstage in Rostand, but here a memorable sequence performed to the music of "Round and Round," with the two guides, in what seemed a conscious quotation of the evil fox and cat who lead Pinocchio astray in Disney's popular film. Their stylized whippings and beating of the boy were watched by the girl, now under the dominance of El Gallo, who provided her with a mask whenever the action became painful, which converted it into a pleasant visual spectacle, one again reinforcing the production's constant negotiation between illusion and reality.

The narrator and master manipulator of the show, El Gallo, was created by Jerry Orbach, whose energy and spirit I still remember. It is today generally thought that this role launched his formidable career, but at that time he was already well known for his first off-Broadway appearances, first as the Street-singer and later as Macheath in *The Threepenny Opera* at the Theater de Lys, where I had seen and admired him the previous year. Several other members of that original cast went on to careers in New York, including Rita Gardner, who made her New York debut as the Girl in this production. She reappeared in my theatregoing experience much later in a surprising manner, to which I will return at the proper time. Orbach was the only member of this company, however, to became a major star. Within the production I most enjoyed him and Henry, the aged actor, played, according to the program, by Thomas Bruce. Only later did I discover that this was in fact coauthor Tom Jones, who had taken over the role when no suitable Henry appeared at the tryouts.

After its troubled opening months, *The Fantasticks* went from triumph to triumph, winning the Obie for best off-Broadway musical that year, and continuing to run, despite occasional announcements of its closing, until January 2002. It was revived in 2006 and at this writing, a decade later, is still running at a small theatre on West Fiftieth Street appropriately named for Jerry Orbach. I went back to it twice more in the intervening years and found it still as fresh and charming as it was when I first saw it. If anything, its charm increased as it brought back to me a time when I too was just entering the adult world and when the world in which I lived was just entering one of its most challenging and turbulent decades.

1961 The Living Theatre's *The Connection*

Although by the end of the 1960s the Living Theatre had a global reputation and for many was the central example of American alternative theatre, as the decade began it was a respected but hardly outstanding member of a handful but rapidly growing number of small, experimental companies mostly located in Greenwich Village. The Living Theatre was something of an outlier in that group, being located at the corner of Sixth Avenue and Fourteenth Street, which served as the northern boundary of the Village.

Although the company had existed since 1947, and gained a reputation for producing poetic drama and experimental European work, it was largely dormant in the mid-1950s until its founders, Julian Beck and Judith Malina, purchased a former department store on Sixth Avenue within which they constructed a performance space that opened in January 1959. Their first major success there was far from the poetic drama of their earlier years, however. It was Jack Gelber's rather notoriously naturalistic *The Connection*, which opened in July 1959.

The Connection had thus been running for more than a year when I saw it in January 1961, and it was not my introduction to the Living Theatre. Almost a year before, I had attended my first Living Theatre production, Julian Beck's staging of Pirandello's *Tonight We Improvise.* Although I was very pleased to see this rarely performed Pirandello, I had little interest in Jack Gelber's *The Connection*, then running in repertory with the Pirandello. There were too many classic revivals, interesting new European plays, and attractive new American works by dramatists like Albee for me to spend my precious trips to New York on a play and dramatist I did not know. Moreover, what I had heard about the play, that it was a slice-of-life depiction of the current drug scene, did not excite me. As the months passed, however, and the play continued to inspire commentary in the *Voice* and elsewhere, I finally decided that I should see it.

Although far from my most pleasant theatre experience of the early 1960s, this was certainly one of those I most clearly remember. The Living Theatre was one of the very few in the city pursuing the long-standing dream of American theatres, a continuing repertory. By early 1961 *Tonight We Improvise* was no longer on the bills, but *The Connection* remained, then in repertory with two plays indicating the Living Theatre's ongoing interest in European experimentation and poetic drama: *In the Jungle of Cities*, the first U.S. production of this early Brecht work, along with the first production of *Many Loves*, by the leading American modernist poet William Carlos Williams.

The Sixth Avenue space then occupied by the Living Theatre was far more impressive than that of most Village theatres, and seemed almost palatial compared, for example, to the tiny Sullivan Street Playhouse. One entered by a flight of stairs up from street level, coming out into a spacious (by New York standards) lobby, from which one entered the theatre itself. A similar spatial arrangement can be seen today (2014) at the La Mama Annex. Lobby and theatre were decorated in a minimalist, but very effective, style. The theatre, a conventional proscenium space, seated only 162, only a few more than the Sullivan Street Playhouse, but the more conventional layout, the capacious lobby, and the décor made it seem distinctly larger and more comfortable. The walls and ceiling of the auditorium were painted in alternative matte and glossy black stripes, becoming narrower as they approached the stage and thus increasing the apparent depth of the theatre, a visual trick the Becks very likely learned from Wagner's Bayreuth theatre, which employed a similar device architecturally.

When the audience entered the theatre the performance seemed already in progress. The setting represented a shabby, run-down Village apartment, with actors lounging about it, filthy and unshaven. On the left side of the stage a small jazz band (piano, bass, alto sax, and drums) was improvising. Beck and Malina, the founders of the company, were nowhere to be seen, although they had both performed leading parts in *Tonight We Improvise*, Beck as the pompous director, Hinkfuss, who spent most of the evening in the auditorium, and Malina as the tortured heroine Mommina, on stage. For *The Connection*, however, Malina served as director and Beck as designer. Reviewers tended to remark that the play recalled Beckett's *Waiting for Godot*, in that it showed characters unproductively passing time waiting, in this case for "Cowboy," who will bring them their "connection," a dose of the heroine to which they are addicted. The play was presented by its assumed author, but this was not in fact Gelber, but an actor, and presumably an addict, who in any case had little control over the production, breaking down in the middle of his own speeches and ranting at the band for disrupting the proceedings. In fact, the improvised jazz sequences provided much of the life of the evening, the actors sitting silently, wandering about, or engaging in small talk that, if not improvised, certainly appeared to be.

Two photographers came through the audience and went up on stage early in the evening, presumably to document this lifestyle for some journal, but they, like the "author," were listed as characters in the program, and no one had any doubt that they were actors simply playing intruders from the real world. Given that the company had so recently produced Pirandello, most of the audience probably felt, as I did, that this was another Pirandellian exercise, albeit much more gritty and contemporary. As the evening went on, however, this obvious interpretation gradually eroded, especially during the lengthy intermission, when the actors mixed with audience members in the lobby and pressed them for money to pay for their next fix.

My first reaction was that the production had simply taken Pirandello a step further, not only planting actors in the audience, but requiring them to actually interact with audience members as if they were in fact part of the audience. Indeed I remembered a Pirandello play that I had read but never seen, *Each in His Own Way*, where the "action" continues in the lobby during the intermission, and where Pirandello has written dialogue for a number of "audience members" who never appear in the play proper. To the best of my recollection, these actors mingled with the real audience as they carried on their conversation with each other but did not in fact specifically engage real audience members. It was clearly only a modest step, scarcely a break in convention at all, to send actors out among the audience without a written script, simply to improvise interactions with them.

These academic considerations were quickly challenged when I became aware that the unkempt, shaggy, disheveled, and barefoot figure soliciting me for money in anything but a deferential manner was emitting a strong and highly unpleasant odor, and not an unfamiliar one. As a frequent rider on the New York subway, especially the after-theatre trains to Brooklyn, I had become all too aware of the pong often emitted *stink* by sleeping vagrants on the trains, often enough to empty out the rest of the car. Suddenly I realized the total physicality of this unconventional and faintly threatening presence. Of course I knew that actors grew or removed beards, put on and took off weight for roles, but would they live in filth, not washing for weeks, to get that distinctive odor? Or was it possible that Beck and Malina had decided to actually scour the streets of the Village to find vagrants, preferably on drugs, to people their naturalistic drama? Another theatre memory came to me, that somewhere I had read that Stanislavsky at one point had tried bringing actual peasants on stage in his quest for a realistic presentation. Could that be what was happening here?

Often in the 1990s, when the use of nonactors on stage became common in many experimental companies, such as Rimini Protokoll in Berlin, I saw, and occasionally interacted with, these performers, but by that time the convention was established and the situation, though calculatedly ambiguous, was clear to everyone, and I never in such circumstances felt so unpleasantly destabilized in the theatre as I was that evening at the Living Theatre. Once I had accepted the possibility that this figure might in fact be a real vagrant, perhaps even a real addict, put on display by the Becks somewhat like the real drunken man Umberto Eco describes as being put on display by the Salvation Army, I faced a new dilemma. Raised in the proudly self-sufficient Middle West, in a state where liquor had been totally prohibited until 1948, I had been told that one never gave anything to panhandlers, as they would be certain to "spend it on drink." My Kansas soul shuddered at the possibility that I was being openly asked to support a habit not of liquor but heroin. Finally, essentially to escape, I emptied my pockets of change, but I was still pursued for the rest of the intermission by my tormentor, who insisted, not entirely unfairly, that "you college kids always have money to throw away."

I returned for the second act considerably shaken, and attempting, in vain, to witness something that would resolve the theatre/life tension on stage one way or the other. Finally, unlike Godot, the long-awaited "connection"—Cowboy—arrived, and the "actors" took turns going offstage to a bathroom to get their fix. Or did they? Only when they at length took a curtain call did I come to the guarded conclusion that they were in fact actors, and eventually I found that "Sam," my vagrant, was in fact an actor also and the money he collected was spent not on drugs but on property food for the production. Still the memories of that doubt and of the physical reality of that smell remain. Looking back later on that disturbing experience, I subsequently realized that it was on that evening that for me the theatre of the 1960s began, that the comfortable and predictable theatre I had known was being swept away, and that a rough and unpredictable, if fascinating journey lay ahead.

The success or at any rate the notoriety of *The Connection* earned the Living Theatre that spring an invitation to the Théâtre des Nations Festival in Paris. A prolonged and difficult fund-raising drive followed, but primarily due to the profits from an auction of manuscripts and works of art donated by fellow Village artists, they managed to go. They spent five weeks in Europe, performing in Italy, Germany, and France with the three plays in repertory they had been recently presenting in New York. As reports of this triumphant tour filtered back to New York, the Living Theatre began to be recognized as a leader among the off-Broadway companies.

Despite the better opportunities that the success of *The Connection* opened to him, Gelber returned to the Living Theatre in December 1961 with his second play, *The Apple*, which continued, although in a distinctly less threatening way, the mixing of art and life. The theatre was essentially converted into a coffeehouse, where the actors, under their own names but portraying exaggerated characters, interacted with the audience, but rather than panhandling them, served them coffee and cookies.

Despite the growing reputation of the Living Theatre, reinforced by Kenneth Brown's slice-of-life portrait of the U.S. Marine Corps in *The Brig*, the theatre experienced continued financial difficulties, and was being charged with evading taxes as early as 1962. In the spring of 1963 authorities padlocked the theatre, while some intrepid audience members managed to attend *The Brig* by using alternate entrances and even ladders from the street to the performance floor. Finally the theatre was closed, the furnishings confiscated, and the Becks convicted for nonpayment of taxes. Following this, in 1964, they went into self-imposed exile in Europe, which had welcomed them with enthusiasm in 1961. By then their antiestablishment message and challenge to the U.S. authorities added to their luster, especially in France, while back in the United States they came to achieve an almost mythic status among avant-garde companies. The interpenetration of art and life explored in *The Connection* took on new depths and new dimensions when it became also involved with their increasing politicization, their association with pacifism and anarchism, and their continued exploration of interactions of the personal and the public.

1962 Zero Mostel in *A Funny Thing Happened on the Way to the Forum*

In my early years of regularly attending theatre in New York, I primarily attended the rapidly developing off-Broadway theatre, which was then offering what seemed to be the most interesting new American authors, exciting new work from Europe, especially France and Germany, and excellent revivals of classic plays, such as the distinguished series of Ibsen and Chekhov revivals offered by David Ross at the little Fourth Street Playhouse. I attended many fewer Broadway productions, not because of the expense ($10 was in 1960 a common top price for Broadway, and standing room cost only $2.50), but simply because I found the classic and experimental fare downtown consistently more interesting.

When I went to Broadway it was also for the most part to European imports or revivals such as Anouilh's *Becket* or Delaney's *A Taste of Honey* in 1960, Bolt's *A Man for All Seasons* and Pinter's *The Caretaker* in 1961, and Dürrenmatt's *Romulus* and Felicien Marceau's *The Egg* in 1962. During these same three years I believe I attended only one Broadway musical, the return engagement of *West Side Story* in 1960. On the other hand I attended a number of the small musicals that were then flourishing off-Broadway, such as *The Fantasticks, Leave It to Jane, Little Mary Sunshine,* and *Ernest in Love.* I suppose I was reflecting the general feeling among theatre scholars in those pre-Sondheim days that Broadway musicals were merely light entertainment, not to be compared with a new play by Albee or a revival of Ibsen.

A Funny Thing Happened on the Way to the Forum was an exception for me for several reasons. First, it was a rarity among Broadway musicals in being based on a classic work of theatre, here the works of the Roman comedy author Plautus, and particularly his *Miles Gloriosus* and *Pseudolus*, with the two eponymous stock characters, the braggart soldier and the crafty slave. Knowing that Plautus had originally been presented with musical numbers, I was fascinated by the idea of bringing his work, of all places, to the commercial Broadway theatre. Second, having seen Zero Mostel the previous year in Ionesco's *Rhinoceros*, the first play from the contemporary French experimental theatre to be presented on Broadway, I was eager to see him in another role. His onstage transformation from a human into a rhinoceros, bringing into full play his great if surprisingly graceful bulk, and his astonishing facial mobility making us almost visualize an emerging horn, made this a sequence long remembered by theatre-goers of that era. The producer and director, although now recognized as among the leading names of late twentieth-century theatre, I scarcely knew. The director, George Abbott, was the more familiar to me, thanks to a series of musical comedy hits like *The Pajama Game*, *Damn Yankees*, and *Fiorello!* during the 1950s, but although I had cast albums of the first two, I had not seen any of his work. Both the producer, Hal Prince, and the composer, Stephen Sondheim, had been involved with *West Side Story*, but their names had not yet registered with me. It was during the 1970s that their collaborations brought them both very much into my theatrical consciousness. Sadly, the fact that this was the first musical with both music and lyrics by Stephen Sondheim was not in itself an attraction for me, although later in the century I would not have missed a Sondheim show. In the event, however, I was dazzled by the music and even more by the witty and daring lyrics of songs like the opening number, "Comedy Tonight," and the engagingly naughty "Everybody Ought to Have a Maid."

When I saw the show at the Alvin Theatre in the fall of 1962, it had been running since that spring, but it was still early in its long run, which lasted, despite moves to two other theatres, until the fall of 1965. The Alvin Theatre (today the Neil Simon) was a moderate-sized Broadway house (a bit over fourteen hundred seats). It was located on West Fifty-Second Street, near the northern edge of the rather confined Broadway theatre district (with the Billy Rose, which at this time was enjoying a great success with Albee's *Who's Afraid of Virginia Woolf?*, marking the southern edge). Although the major concentration of Broadway houses lay seven or eight blocks to the south, they were scattered fairly evenly northward, with two even beyond the Alvin, the ANTA Theatre, former home of the Theatre Guild, located just across Fifty-Second

Street from the Alvin, and the Broadway Theatre on Fifty-Fourth Street. Almost all of these theatres, like most Broadway houses, had been built during the 1920s, when the Times Square area had become the center of New York theatre. Going to a Broadway musical, in the Alvin or another of the larger houses surrounding Times Square, was for many visitors the essential New York theatre experience.

Most Broadway theatres, then as now, tend to be associated either with musicals or with spoken drama, the larger houses devoted to musicals. The two houses facing each other across Fifty-Second Street illustrated this division clearly. The ANTA had been built for the Theatre Guild, and when the American National Theatre and Academy took over the theatre in 1950, they very much carried on the Guild tradition of modern literary dramas. The Alvin, on the other hand, was from the beginning associated with the upstart new form of American musical comedy, a contrast noted by the leading critic Brooks Atkinson in his 1927 review of the first production there, *Funny Face*, where he described the new theatre as sitting "defiantly" across the street from the "scholarly" Theatre Guild. In fact, when I attended *Funny Thing* in 1963 I had already seen productions in both theatres, representative of the offerings of each: the revival of *West Side Story* at the Alvin in 1960 and at the ANTA Archibald MacLeish's retelling of the book of Job, *J.B.*, in 1959 and Robert Bolt's drama about Sir Thomas More, *A Man for All Seasons*, in 1961.

Whenever I attended theatre in this area in the early 1960s I would make a point of walking through Times Square, that dazzling center which I still recalled from my first visit to New York with my parents just after the end of World War II, when the Square was in one of its most spectacular periods. I still recall the remarkable billboards on the east side of the square, unequalled by anything there before or since. The centerpiece was the astonishing Bond clothing sign. The sign, on top of the Bond building, ran all the way from Forty-Fourth to Forty-Fifth Street, and at either end stood a fifty-foot nude statue (clothed in neon in the evening), one male, one female. Between them poured a fifty-thousand-gallon waterfall 27 feet high and 120 feet long. Above the waterfall was a huge digital clock and below it a zipper news band, one of several then in Times Square, imitating the original and most famous, running around the triangular Times building at the Square's south end. The other particularly striking sign matched the Bond sign in the next block south, between Forty-Third and Forty-Fourth. This was an almost equally large advertisement for Camel cigarettes, running across the facade of the Hotel Claridge. Near the north end was the huge head of a contented smoker, whose mouth was an open circle that every few seconds emitted a large, perfectly formed ring of smoke that drifted out over the Square.

The primary entertainment on Times Square then was the cinema, with a number of houses, some former "legitimate" theatres. Only two of these then remained on the Square, both of them later demolished, along with three other historic houses, to make space for the gargantuan Marriott Marquis Hotel. For me one of the most attractive locations in Times Square then was the Automat, located on the west side of the Square between Forty-Sixth and Forty-Seventh Streets. Here I ate whenever attending theatre in the area. Aside from the fascination of its futuristic serving of a huge variety of foods behind individual coin-operated glass windows, it was inexpensive (a dollar could buy a full meal) and yet full of atmosphere. Far from its fast-food descendants, the Times Square Automat was a virtual palace. Facing out onto the Square was a huge stained-glass window the full width of the building two stories high. Inside, the walls contained rows of small windows surmounted by beveled mirrors and surrounding a huge eating area with individual marble-topped tables on shining white-tiled floors. In the center of this area was a two-story carved column melding into the ceiling and a pattern of carved leaves and vines.

After dinner at the Automat, I went north to Fifty-Second Street, which, thanks to the proximity of the Alvin and the ANTA, was then the part of the Broadway theatre scene most familiar to me. Unlike many Broadway houses, the Alvin had a moderately spacious lobby of elegant black marble, and a more modest inner lobby before one entered the comfortable house, decorated in a fairly standard neoclassic style of pastel gray and blue, with ivory and gold columns and decorative detail. Downstairs, as in many houses, was a lounge, but that at the Alvin was particularly elegant and atmospheric, an "Old English" lounge with a large fireplace and carved wooden bar.

Today, half a century later, I most remember from this production the stunning comic energy and imagination of Mostel and the brilliant lyric imagination of Sondheim, then new to me. One of the most memorable sequences in the production was its opening. Mostel, in addition to playing the central figure of the slave, Pseudolus, also served as prologue, singing Sondheim's "Comedy Tonight," a marvelous riff on clas-

sic theatre conventions. At its conclusion he called out "Raise the curtain," upon which the curtain did not rise, but dropped to the floor and
then disappeared into a long slot just upstage of the footlights. Funny in
itself, this sequence held even more delight for a young theatre scholar
who had recently learned that in the Roman theatre curtains in fact did
fall into such slots, quite contrary to modern custom. The theatrical
joke, already elaborate, did not end there, however, but continued as
what was revealed was a vista full of classic temples, and agonized
masked figures shrieking in pain or passion. Apparently we had opened
by accident on tragedy, not comedy, and a proper curtain immediately
covered this catastrophe while Mostel apologized and took us almost
immediately (thanks to the wonders of rapid scene changing) into a totally contrasted comic scene of the play proper. This marvelous opening
sequence was not in fact conceived by Abbott, the director, but by the
enormously talented choreographer Jerome Robbins, who had been
brought in at the last minute (as he often was during those years) as a
kind of "play doctor" to provide an important extra boost to a production. Many years later I remembered this sequence when seeing a similar one in the parody musical *The Drowsy Chaperone* on Broadway in
2006. Here the unnamed protagonist plays records of a musical from the
1920s that comes to life as he listens. At one point, however, he acci-
dently puts on a record of a Meyerbeer opera and the stage is suddenly
filled with the unexpected and inappropriate spectacle of late nineteenth-
century grand opera, complete with elephants and warrior armies. The
appalled narrator hastily replaces the recording and the staggering vision abruptly disappears, just like the unexpected tragic production in
Funny Thing.

Although Mostel dominated the production, the company around
him provided a hilarious compendium of slapstick and burlesque routines. I still fondly recall the love-stricken old goat David Burns hoping
to restore his fading virility with an elaborate love potion (including
mare's sweat, which he brings with the memorable line "Would you
believe I found a mare sweating not two blocks from here") and an
equally elaborate ritual, requiring him to run around the city of Rome
seven times (allowing him through the rest of the production to stagger
across the stage when he has been quite forgotten to shout out "four" or
"five"). Then there was the old Shakespearian John Carradine playing a
sepulchral dealer in courtesans, Ruth Kobart as the domineering wife
who snarls at an attendant bearing a plaster likeness of her to "Carry

my bust with pride!," Ronald Holgate as the inevitable bombastic soldier, and of course a collection of beautiful and scantily clad slave girls, who posed decoratively for such antics as Mostel drawing tic-tac-toe games on their all-too-accessible exposed midriffs.

The show fondly looked back to the burlesque traditions to which the Broadway musical owed so much, in the antics and the routines of these master comics and gorgeous girls, but it also, especially in the ironic nostalgia that is so important a part of the Sondheim world, looked forward in his work and that of others to a different style of musical theatre, much more ironically self-reflective, which would develop in the years to come.

1963 Anne Bancroft in
Mother Courage

Not all of the productions that hold important places in my memory were great successes, like *The Fantasticks* or *Funny Thing*. Some were disappointments or outright failures, but they remain with me for their importance in the theatrical culture of their particular moment. Such is the case with two productions from this period, the 1963 Broadway revival of Brecht's *Mother Courage* and the 1964 premiere of Arthur Miller's *After the Fall*.

If one were looking for an initial moment when the theatre of the 1960s began for the academic world, an excellent choice would be the May 1960 issue of the *Tulane Drama Review*, which under that name and the subsequent *TDR* became the academic voice of the theatre of that decade. This issue opened with "The Theatre of the Absurd" by Martin Esslin, soon to publish the definitive work on that movement, and included a review by Eric Bentley of the two first major works on Brecht in English, Esslin's *Brecht: His Life and Work* (1960) and John Willett's *The Theatre of Bertolt Brecht* (1959). The inspiration of Brecht and the absurdists remained at the forefront of Western experimental theatre for a number of years to come.

Like most young theatre students of the time, I gained from these sources most of my knowledge about Brecht, whose work was still rarely seen on American stages. The one notable exception was the production of *The Threepenny Opera* at the Theatre de Lys (now the Lucille Lortel Theatre) in Greenwich Village, which by the early 1960s had achieved a near-legendary status. The show had opened here in 1954 and despite a considerable success, ran for only ninety-six performances before it had to close to make way for another booking. Public and critical demand, however, brought it back in the fall of 1955, and it ran through 1961, at that time a record-setting run for a New York musical (eventually to be surpassed by *The Fantasticks*, which overlapped *Threepenny*'s final year and a half). This was one of the must-see productions in my first years regularly attending New York theatre, and although when I saw it in 1960 it no longer featured Lotte Lenya, long the star of the production, it still had an energy and power that put to shame most of the other work that I saw at that time.

The success of *Threepenny Opera* and the appearance of the Esslin and Willett studies touched off a new interest in Brecht in the emerging off-Broadway movement of the early 1960s. The Living Theatre added to its growing reputation with a much-discussed though not entirely successful *In the Jungle of Cities*. Much better received was a collection of Brecht writings by George Tabori, *Brecht on Brecht*, which clearly sought to capitalize on the vogue of *Threepenny*, opening at the same theatre in November 1961. It was not highly theatrical, simply a semicircle of actors on stools delivering the material from behind music stands, but I remember being greatly impressed by the powerful vocal delivery of Lotte Lenya, whom I had missed in *Threepenny* and saw here for the first time.

In September 1962, two productions of *Mann ist Mann* opened on successive evenings, first at the Living Theatre and then at the Masque Theatre, in an adaptation by Eric Bentley. As theorist, translator, and director Bentley had clearly established himself, for good or ill, as the leading representative of Brecht and his work in the United States. Practically every New York paper ran comparative reviews of the two productions, giving Brecht's reputation a new boost. I saw both productions, Brecht now being obligatory viewing for dedicated theatre-goers in New York, but found both somewhat thin and cartoonish, possibly due to a perception at that time of Brecht as a kind of political cabaret artist, especially in quasi-allegorical works like *Mann ist Mann*. I did, however, very much like the two actors who played the leading role of

Galy Gay. At the Masque this was John Heffernan, whom I had recently seen as an impressive, quirky Polonius in the 1961 Donald Madden *Hamlet*. The Living Theatre version featured Joseph Chaikin. I had seen Chaikin in previous Living Theatre productions, but here for the first time he stood out, and gave clear promise of the ability that would make him a central figure of the New York experimental theatre in the coming years.

The attention stirred up by these productions at the beginning of the 1960s led to the first Broadway production of Brecht since the 1940s, a staging of *Mother Courage* that opened at the Martin Beck Theatre (today the Al Hirschfeld) in March 1963. Like most of the New York theatre-going world I looked forward to this major production of a key Brechtian work with enormous anticipation, but few viewers, myself included, found it met their expectations. I attended soon after the opening, and it was well I did so because reviews and word of mouth were on the whole so negative that the production closed after fifty-two showings. Even at the time many of the flaws of this failed production were clear. About the only positive element about which there was general agreement was the quality of the Eric Bentley translation. I, studying German at the time, was irritated by his toning down in his Brecht translations the most openly leftist comments (omitting, for example, the Russian source of the outlawed radio broadcasts for which the upstairs neighbor is denounced in *The Private Life of the Master Race*), but although we were now a decade after the fall of Joseph McCarthy, the Cold War continued and Bentley's caution was understandable.

I remember sitting in the balcony of the capacious Martin Beck and seeing Bentley presiding over the occasion from one of the side-boxes, which he may have done regularly. It is hard to imagine that he was pleased by what he saw. His text was faithfully followed, but in a production that seemed totally lacking in focus or energy. I wondered at the time if this resulted from a gross misinterpretation of Brecht's famous "alienation" as a calculated blandness in the production, but I gradually came to realize that the problems of the production came more from the people involved. The producers, concerned with filling a moderately large Broadway house, relied, as they still do, on casting a familiar star to attract the public. They selected Anne Bancroft, who the previous year had won both a Tony Award and an Academy Award for her stage and film versions of William Gibson's *The Miracle Worker*.

A better-known name could hardly have been offered, but Bancroft was both too young for the role and strongly committed to Lee Strasberg's approach to method acting, which was not well adapted to the rough, ironic edge of a Brechtian character. The production, as was common for Broadway shows at the time, had only four weeks of rehearsals (the time is not much longer today), adequate for actors working with familiar material and styles, but clearly not enough to find a unified approach to an unfamiliar style of dramaturgy, and Bancroft was surrounded by a cast playing in a variety of styles, some of them in harmony with her own and others clearly not.

A director with a clearer sense of Brecht's tradition, perhaps Bentley himself, might have been able to address this problem, but the same producers who looked to Bancroft as a reliable Broadway draw sought a similar reliability in the production's director. Jerome Robbins, like Bancroft, was much in the public eye in 1963, having won an Academy Award for his direction of the film of *West Side Story* in 1961 (even though he was fired after the photography was essentially complete) and scored a major Broadway success in 1963 with his work on *A Funny Thing Happened on the Way to the Forum*. Like Bancroft, however, he had no experience with the sort of theatre Brecht was creating, and his major attempt at "Brechtian" staging was to have the entire cast come downstage at the beginning of the production, announce their real names, and briefly introduce the characters they were playing. The ingenious opening of *Funny Thing* the previous year had successfully set that show off on a flamboyant pace that rarely if ever slackened. This opening had almost the opposite effect, setting a certain flat, untheatrical tone that was rarely disrupted as the evening continued.

Bentley's translation of *Mother Courage* was essential reading for theatre scholars at the beginning of the 1960s, and so I was familiar with the text when I attended the 1963 production. What most struck me in the composition of the work were the episodic structure, the use of scene titles, and the importance of songs. The first two were still utilized in this staging, but the music was surprisingly truncated. I assumed at first this was an artistic decision, but later discovered that it was an economic one. The production, already expensive and financially risky, could simply not afford to have more than forty-some moments devoted to music, since it would then be classified as a "musical" and required by the musicians' union to employ many more musicians, at considerable expense. The result of course was to further flatten an already rather static and unvarying production. Paul Dessau's music was used, but it did not always fit well with the rhythm of Bentley's lyrics, and so even those songs that were retained were often very difficult to understand. On a more positive side, the modest musical accompaniment was well suited to the minimalist style of the production. It consisted only of a piano, with thumbtacks in the keys to produce a tinny, cabaret sort of sound, with only a small ensemble, a trumpet and two or three others.

The designer, Ming Cho Lee, was unfamiliar to me, this being only the second of his twenty-odd Broadway productions, which made him the most prominent American scene designer of his generation, but I was struck by the stark minimalism of the set, clearly influenced by the Berliner Ensemble approach and far from the cluttered detail common on Broadway then and since. I remember the sensation of an empty stage with stark walls behind, and the major visual element, as in Berlin, Mother Courage's wagon. Unlike the Berliner Ensemble or any German theatre of comparable size, however, the Martin Beck, typical for a traditional American house, did not possess a built-in turntable. Constructing one, as many later musicals did, was unthinkable with the show's limited resources, so the major visual effect of the Berlin staging, scenery moving past the wagon, was not attempted. Instead the actors, and eventually Bancroft herself, simply dragged the wagon back and forth across the stage, with rather minor artistic effect.

The reviews were not savage, and a number indeed praised Bancroft, but the production was generally considered a failure. An even worse disaster, Christopher Plummer in a crudely cartoonish version of Brecht's anti-Hitler parody, *The Resistible Rise of Arturo Ui*, which opened and closed in November after only six performances, solidified the belief, among critics and public alike, that Brecht was really not suitable for the Broadway stage, and was best relegated to off- and off-off-Broadway production. In the half-century since these two productions, only the Vivian Beaumont, a special case among the so-called Broadway theatres, has attempted, on several occasions and with only modest success, to challenge this received wisdom.

Interestingly enough, Broadway did mount a German play the next season that made a strong political statement, and aroused tremendous controversy, though it is largely forgotten today. This was Rolf Hochhuth's *The Deputy*, a documentary drama suggesting that Pope Pius XII refused to acknowledge what was happening to the Jews in Nazi Germany. Bentley, doubtless relieved to see that a political drama could cause such a stir in New York, even if *Mother Courage* did not, published a book on the controversy, *The Storm over "The Deputy,"* with Grove Press in 1964.

1964 *After the Fall* at the ANTA Washington Square Theatre

Ever since the development of a serious art theatre in the United States early in the twentieth century, some visionaries have dreamed of establishing an ongoing repertory theatre for this country that like the Vienna Burgtheater or the French Comédie-Française would house an established company devoted to presenting a rotating repertory of the nation's most distinguished dramas. Among the most significant of these attempts were the Art Theatre of Winthrop Ames, begun in 1909, a number of seasons of the Theatre Guild in the 1940s, and most notably Eva LeGallienne's American Repertory Theatre in the 1930s. None of these, however, lasted even a decade.

In the late 1950s the theatre world, especially in New York, was astir with plans for a new attempt at this project. The monumental arts and urban development project that would become Lincoln Center was gradually taking shape. In the case of opera and music, existing institutions were to be moved there, but New York had no parallel in a state or city theatre, and at first theatre was not included, but before long a newly established repertory theatre was incorporated into the project, partly under the influence of European models, but also in recognition of the recent rapid growth of the regional theatre movement and the success in particular of the Stratford Festival in Canada. This opened a permanent theatre in 1957 with a thrust stage that was widely seen as a model for modern theatre arrangements and was strongly influential in the creation of the main stage in the Lincoln Center project.

The new theatre was planned to open in 1963, but as is almost invariably the case with large construction projects, there were many delays. The project director was Robert Whitehead, who had long championed a national theatre as a guiding spirit at ANTA, originally founded for that purpose. He felt the time pressure keenly, as he had a fledgling company of actors in training for the new venture and two plays commissioned from leading playwrights who were expecting production that year. Their selection for the opening season was perhaps the safest possible, commissioning two new works, one serious and one comic, from the most respected serious and comic dramatists in the American theatre during the previous quarter of a century, Arthur Miller and S. N. Behrman. With a company and plays ready, but with no space for them, Whitehead and the board of directors sought alternatives. An existing Broadway house was rejected, partly because of the expense but also because the planners were dedicated to the concept of a thrust stage in the Stratford model, and wanted to avoid a conventional audience arrangement.

Although the Stratford model clearly inspired a vogue for thrust stages during the 1960s, it should be noted that there was a much closer model at hand for the designers of the new Lincoln Center project, Theodore Mann's Circle in the Square. Mann, with the actor José Quintero, had founded this theatre in 1951 in Sheridan Square, in the heart of Greenwich Village, where, as its title indicates, it brought the then-new practice of theatre in the round to the New York professional stage. When the theatre moved to Bleecker Street in 1960 it introduced another new arrangement, the first professional stage in New York to seat audiences on three sides of the performing area, though it kept its now less accurate name. When I began attending theatre regularly in New York, I found the Circle in the Square one of the most exciting and innovative of the off-Broadway venues, producing such works as the stunning American premiere of Jean Genet's *The Balcony* in 1960, with Salome Jens as an unforgettably erotic Pony Girl, and commissioning a new set of plays in the increasingly fashionable absurdist style by Thornton Wilder, *Plays for Bleecker Street* in 1962.

Finally, in the spring of 1963, New York University agreed to lease a plot on its campus for a temporary structure, to be built at the expense of ANTA. Although the model of Stratford was rarely if ever openly evoked, the planners must have had that example in mind when they began referring to the temporary structure as a "steel tent." The Stratford Festival had famously started in an actual huge tent, whose form was strongly suggested in the recently erected permanent home. In fact, what was christened the ANTA Washington Square Theatre had nothing of the tent about it. It was a characterless steel box, about twenty feet high and more or less square, painted a mustard yellow and from the outside suggesting a warehouse or storage facility. The simple entrance had a marquee bearing the name ANTA.

Construction on this building began in the summer of 1963, and I often stopped by to watch its rapid progress on my way to other theatres in the area. The NYU campus is located in the center of much of the alternative theatre work in New York. The traditional heart of such work borders the campus on the west, in Greenwich Village, with the Sullivan Street Playhouse (home of *The Fantasticks*) and O'Neill's Provincetown Playhouse essentially on the borders of the University (much to their disadvantage, since the latter was demolished in 2008 to provide space for university expansion). By the 1960s, Village culture had extended to the south of the University as well, most notably along Bleecker Street, as the relocation of the Circle in the Square suggests. In fact the new ANTA Washington Square Theatre, while surrounded by university structures, was only one block north and two west from the Circle in the Square.

The ANTA Washington Square Theatre opened in January with Arthur Miller's much-anticipated new work, *After the Fall*, his first full-length play since *The Crucible*, ten years before. I attended the play early in February, in the midst of a bitter cold snap, reminding me that the new venture was not near any convenient subway. Thus walking was the most convenient way to attend the theatre. Located in the midst of a group of small streets normally serving only campus traffic, the new theatre was the center of a massive gridlock as hundreds of taxis, limousines, and private vehicles converged on it. I even noted a few motor scooters and bicycles parked near the entrance, in defiance of the bitter weather. The steel fortress-like exterior was even more forbidding in these circumstances, but the interior, designed by Jo Mielziner and Eero Saarinen, was surprisingly warm and attractive, though still very basic. The interior walls, seats, and floor coverings were blue, and the twelve hundred seats were wrapped around a thrust stage. One entered on a level with the back row of seats, some sixty feet from the stage, which was located fifteen feet or so below street level.

The much-publicized thrust stage was for this production far from the clear and simple configuration at Stratford. There was almost no scenery in the conventional sense, only a chair for the narrator/protagonist and a concentration camp tower. Mielziner had built up on the thrust stage a complex collection of irregular overlapping planes, like rocky outcroppings, providing an effective playing area for a play composed of the fragmented and overlapping memories of the protagonist, Quentin. Quentin was played by Jason Robards Jr., who had established himself during the previous decade as America's leading interpreter of O'Neill, in *The Iceman Cometh* and *A Long Day's Journey into Night*, both opening in 1956 and both directed by José Quintero. *After the Fall* was, not surprisingly, directed by Elia Kazan, then America's best-known director, who had first staged most of the major works of Williams and Miller, and who had now joined Whitehead as codirector of the ANTA Washington Square project. Kazan also directed the new Behrman play that closed this first season. Quintero, with his current close association to O'Neill, was selected to direct the third offering and the only revival, O'Neill's 1928 *Marco Millions*, not seen in New York since 1930.

The opening of this major new theatrical venture, the participation of many of the leading figures—directors, actors, designers, and dramatists—and the premiere of the first new work in almost a decade by the most honored living American playwright all would have made this production one of the most newsworthy theatre events of the decade, but all were in fact overshadowed by the content of the play, since Miller had decided to present a story with such detailed resemblance to his own life that it was essentially taken to be autobiographical. Quentin is a Jewish intellectual who begins the play by stepping out of the stage picture and moving directly down to the tip of the large stage and quietly addressing the audience as if speaking to a close friend (or perhaps a psychiatrist). In a series of nonconsecutive and overlapping flashbacks that make up the rest of the evening, he recalls and reflects upon his two previous marriages as he contemplates a third, to the German woman Holga. Many of the play's details inevitably recalled to audiences the best-known elements of Miller's life aside from his plays—his highly publicized marriage with the actress and sex symbol Marilyn Monroe during the 1950s and his refusal to name names during the anticommunist hearings of the House Un-American Activities Committee in 1956. Both details were prominent features of the play. In the play, the latter event is primarily reflected in the conflict between Quentin and his friend Martin, a Communist who does reveal his associates, outraging Quentin and ending their long friendship. Martin was universally seen as based on Kazan, who had had an identical falling out with Miller over exactly this issue. Clearly the rift was subsequently healed, though Kazan was left in the odd position of directing a play in which his avatar (played by Ralph Meeker, whom Kazan had directed a decade before as the replacement for Marlon Brando in *Streetcar*) is presented in a most unfavorable light. At the time of this production, Miller had already married his third wife, the Austrian-born photographer Inge Morath, who seems clearly to be represented by Holga in the play. Holga was created by Salome Jens, with a still palpable but much subdued trace of the sexual seductiveness she had shown as the Pony Girl in *The Balcony*. Kazan insisted that the characters in the play were absolutely not to be equated with anyone in Miller's real life, but virtually no one believed this then or since.

Nor did Kazan do anything to diminish the much more discussed feature in the play, the character Maggie. Her marriage to Quentin, drug problems, and eventual suicide were all closely reminiscent of Monroe, whose death had occurred only a year and a half before the play opened. On the contrary, Kazan cast Barbara Loden, another blond sex symbol, whose resemblance to Monroe Kazan was exaggerated by giving her a bouffant blond wig and highly revealing dress to wear and encouraging her (or at least not discouraging her) from performing in a husky voice and with mannerisms that, as several reviewers suggested, came close to parodies of those of Monroe, who had herself become a kind of self-parody during her later years. Her emotional disputes with Robards were the highlights of the long evening (the play, even after serious cutting, ran nearly three hours), but despite the quality of the acting, there was an inescapable air of somewhat tawdry voyeurism or even exploitation about it.

As for the repertory company itself, neither Whitehead nor Kazan remained associated with it even long enough to see it move from its temporary quarters to its permanent home in Lincoln Center. *After the Fall*, despite its mixed reception, was on the whole a success, but it was the only one. The other new work, S. N. Behrman's *But for Whom Charlie*, and the single revival, O'Neill's *Marco Millions*, received indifferent reviews and were poorly attended. Kazan's production of *The Changeling*, the company's first attempt at a classic work and the opening of the second season, was universally condemned. A new Arthur Miller work, *Incident at Vichy*, finally gained success, but it was too late. In December the board sought to replace Whitehead, and he resigned, soon after followed by Kazan. By the end of the year the new venture, still not in its new building, was drifting rudderless, a situation that would continue, with varying degrees of urgency, for the next two decades.

1965 Peter Brook's *Marat/Sade*

Ironically, in the spring of 1964, with the Lincoln Center company in Washington Square having presented the three plays of its first season, with two of them so indifferently received that they were not extended into the summer, Lincoln Center itself was host to one of the most outstanding theatre events of the season—the visit of the British Royal Shakespeare Company presenting Paul Scofield in *King Lear*, directed by Peter Brook. The Royal Shakespeare Company was just establishing an international reputation, thanks to Peter Hall, who became artistic director in 1960, and Peter Brook, who joined as resident director in 1962. Although both company and director were being much talked of among theatre people in 1964, *Lear* was the first time that I, and most New York theatre-goers, had been able to see the work of either.

The work for most of us was a revelation. The Shakespeare we had seen up until then, especially in major theatres, had normally been performed in a highly predictable traditional manner, what Brook himself famously characterized as "deadly theatre." *Lear* was so unconventional as to be almost an assault. The almost empty stage, the starkly presentational style, the turning on of the houselights during the performance, all likely influenced by the anti-illusionistic theatre of Brecht, kept spectators constantly off balance, and the bold and often almost overwhelming physicality of the production left a lasting impression. I had never seen such onstage violence as Lear and his soldiers destroying their dining hall, nor so stunning an effect as the giant metal sheets suspended in an empty stage and set vibrating to suggest the storm. *Lear*, already one of Shakespeare's darkest and most nihilistic plays, became even darker and more nihilistic in Brook's hands. As one example, the rebellion of the servant against Cornwall as he is putting out Gloucester's eyes, the only touch of humanity in that horrific scene, was cut. The bleak, empty landscape of the play and its aura of hopelessness was, as Brook admitted, much influenced by Jan Kott's recent writing on the play, which placed *Lear* in the world of Samuel Beckett. Appropriately, Kott's book, *Shakespeare Our Contemporary*, was on sale in the lobby of the theatre. The production was not given at the City Center, the traditional home for such international traveling shows, but at the newly completed State Theatre at Lincoln Center. The Vivian Beaumont, designed to house the spoken drama, was still under construction, and the State Theatre, designed for ballet, was soon discovered to have some of the worst acoustics in the city. In fact, with these sound problems and the sound and fury of the production itself, a good deal of the Shakespeare text was lost, but so powerful and overwhelming was the total effect that I left thinking, as did many, that Peter Brook would be a name to be reckoned with in the years to come.

It was with those memories in mind that the New York theatre received word that a new, and even more shocking Brook production, Peter Weiss's *The Persecution and Assassination of Jean-Paul Marat as Performed by the Inmates of the Asylum of Charenton Under the Direction of the Marquis de Sade*, would be arriving late the following year. Indeed in the early months of 1964 New York papers reported that Brook was working with a group of RSC actors and the American director Charles Marowitz in a new laboratory theatre exploring the performance implications of the writings of Antonin Artaud, the lab to be called the "Theatre of Cruelty," a much-debated central term of that author. Although Brook's production brought the name of Artaud into the mainstream of New York theatre discussion, those interested in experimental work had been aware of his writings since the late 1950s, when I began regularly attending New York theatre. The Living Theatre regularly evoked him as a major inspiration, and when the works of Genet began to appear in the early 1960s off-off-Broadway, knowledgeable critics frequently mentioned an Artaudian influence. Fortunately for interested theatre-goers who did not read French, an English collection of key essays by Artaud, called *The Theatre and Its Double*, appeared from Grove Press in 1958 and shortly became essential reading for anyone interested in current experimental work. During the next decade, just as students of contemporary theatre needed to read the *Tulane Drama Review* (changed in 1967 after its move to New York University to *TDR: The Drama Review*) they also generally built up libraries of central new dramatic works by collecting Grove Press publications. Grove Press began with editions of the French absurdists—Beckett, Ionesco, Genet—but continued with Pinter, Stoppard, Behan, Gelber,

Albee, and indeed most of the major new dramatists that emerged in the 1960s. It was by far the predominant press represented on my bookshelf of contemporary drama.

Although Brook's production brought the term "theatre of cruelty" into the critical mainstream, there was never much of a consensus concerning its exact meaning. Interpretations ranged from a kind of ascetic purity and rigor to a kind of Dionysian orgy. Despite Artaud's own warning that the term did not simply involve such matters as the shedding of blood, the sensational appeal of the latter tended to dominate public use of the term, and *Marat/Sade*, easily the most famous product of Brook's laboratory, did much to reinforce this view, with its apparently scarcely controlled displays of physical and emotional extremes. The production came with stories of considerable physical and emotional damage suffered by the company during the workshops and rehearsals, and the production on stage called up such extreme efforts on the part of the company that such reports seemed all too likely.

By this time, thanks to his previous *Lear* and glowing reports on *Marat/Sade* from Europe, interest in Brook's work was so great that the company was presented not in a venue like the clearly marginal New York State Theatre, but in the Martin Beck Theatre, on West Forty-Fifth Street in the heart of the Broadway theatre district. The production opened during the Christmas holidays of 1965 and was by far my most memorable theatre experience of that school vacation, or indeed for some time before and after.

Lear had prepared me for a violent and confrontational performance, for houselights unconventionally up, and for extreme physicality, but even so, *Marat/Sade* continually shocked in its extremes and dazzled in the originality of its images. Coulmier and his family came in through the audience and joined us, though in a slightly elevated box on the right-hand side, but other cast members were seated among us, and the most violent of the patients regularly seemed on the brink of directly attacking the audience. The stage was a fairly simple one, representing the asylum bathhouse, with appropriate pipes and fittings on the two side walls and a plain blank industrial wall at the rear. There was a frequently used pit downstage and upstage a circle of wooden platforms, slotted to allow the bathwater to drain away, out of which the actors would build crude replicas of scenic units, tumbrels, or guillotines. The large cast was in constant agitation (except the catatonic ones, who added their own disturbing note to the overall picture), and although they formed highly effective groupings for musical or physical choric numbers, total dissolution and chaos seemed always just moments away. One of the most disappointing aspects of the subsequent film, which captures many of the visual details, is that the sense of immediate physical danger, an essential part of the experience of the actual production, is completely missing. Of course the film medium itself inevitably removes all sense of physical immediacy, but Brook somewhat inexplicably increased this distance by placing the presumed real audience in the film behind a protective metal cage, as if they were not in the theatre, so the threat of the madmen breaking out was totally absent.

Along with the physical violence, there was a constant threat of uncontrolled sexuality. Perhaps this was most obvious in the "copulation round," where the entire company engaged in frantic mimed sexual activity to accompany a song equating revolution with sexual license. Still a mordant sexuality hung over most of the production. Duperret, the "true love" of Corday, described in the text as an erotomaniac, seized every opportunity to try to mount not only the heroine, but any female within reach. Corday, suffering from sleeping sickness, could only push him away with the greatest effort. The somnambulistic Corday was played by Glenda Jackson, who had joined the RSC for the Theatre of Cruelty season, and whom I will always associate with the brilliant RSC productions of the 1960s. Despite her passivity, Jackson's Corday was far from devoid of sexual interest. Her desire to stab Marat in his bath clearly came in large part from an erotic drive. Then, in one of Brook's most memorable visual innovations, where the text calls for her to whip the half-naked de Sade as he expounds his philosophy, Brook had her sweep the back of the kneeling de Sade not with a whip, but with her long tresses, as he gasped in erotic pain and pleasure.

The two other leading actors, Patrick Magee as de Sade and Ian Richardson as Marat, were also new to the New York stage, although much better known in England. Richardson had been for several years a leading figure at the RSC and Magee was closely associated with the work of Samuel Beckett, who in fact created *Krapp's Last Tape* for him. They provided a marvelous contrast, Magee cold and ironic, Richardson frantic and passionately agitated. In terms of the production's eroticism, de Sade of course provided constant ties between revolution and the erotic through his text, but Marat's physicality created an even stronger impression, and Richardson provided one of the most shocking moments of the production, when he emerged from his bath to move upstage, providing the audience with the first view of nude male buttocks ever displayed on a Broadway stage. During the next decade stage nudity became almost a cliché in the New York theatre, but this first example added distinctly to the overall sense of a production exceeding all previous boundaries.

I loved the quirky music provided by Richard Peaslee for the production, which used songs in a Brechtian manner, not so much to advance the action in the manner of the Broadway musicals of that time, as to comment ironically upon it. Probably the most memorable, however, were Brook's visual images—the actors advancing in ranks to be guillotined, then dropping into a pit and piling up so that their apparently separated heads formed a living pyramid facing the audience; the manically smiling member of the clown chorus pouring buckets of blood (red for the aristocrats, blue for the king, white for Marat) into a large onstage funnel after each death scene; the monstrous puppet figures representing the King, with a crowned cabbage for a head, and the personal and public monsters that appeared in Marat's nightmare. These latter figures for many in the audience suggested the creations of New York's Bread and Puppet theatre, just then coming to prominence as a major part of the anti-war movement. About them I will say more later.

The conclusion of the production was as original, as theatrical, and as disturbing as the production as a whole. De Sade's entertainment, always on the brink of descending into anarchy, finally apparently sprang out of control. The final choric number became more and more frantic, the scene turned into a riot, with nurses and the watching Coulmiers fleeing, and muscular guards wading into the melee beating the inmates with heavy clubs. Finally the stage was cleared and silence descended. The stunned audience joined in the silence, but after a moment or two burst into thunderous applause.

No actors appeared for some time while the applause continued. Finally they appeared, but still in character, escorted by the guards and nurses to line up across the stage and stare dumbly at the audience, without bowing or acknowledging the applause. Eventually the applause diminished, faltered, and stopped. The cast remained unmoving, staring out into the auditorium, alien and deeply disturbing in their immobility. At last the silenced audience began to leave, and as I reached the exit I looked back to see that line of passive lunatics still silently watching us depart, one final image to add to the many I still retain of this remarkable production.

1966 Bread and Puppet's *Fire*

By the year 1966 teach-ins, demonstrations, and various forms of protest against the escalating war in Vietnam had moved to the center of American concern, and nowhere more clearly than on the nation's campuses. Cornell was one of the centers of such activity, especially after the arrival of one of the most visible figures in the antiwar movement, the Catholic priest Daniel Berrigan, to join Cornell United Religious Work this year. Even before his arrival, however, Students for a Democratic Society (SDS) and other groups were a highly visible force on campus.

Then a young faculty member, I became increasingly involved in these activities, occasionally joining marches and demonstrations on my fairly regular theatre trips down to New York. I especially remember a mass demonstration there in March 1966, at which I was struck by the powerful theatrical presence of the Bread and Puppet theatre, which had become a regular participant in the antiwar demonstrations in the city. The grotesque but emotionally powerful robed puppets with their oversize masks and hands silently demonstrating the sufferings of innocent people under bombardment were the first examples I had seen of such politically oriented street theatre, and I found them fascinating. There were none of the towering puppet figures so typical of the group's later work, but still the effect was overwhelming.

At that time the downtown experimental theatre received little if any coverage in the major newspapers; indeed with the disappearance of the *Herald Tribune* in 1966, the city was left with only a single major daily, the *New York Times*. For those interested in the off- and off-off-Broadway scene, therefore, the essential source was the *Village Voice*. Here one found notices of currently running productions unannounced in the mainstream press as well as essays and reviews of these works by informed champions of this new theatre Jerry Tallmer and Ross Wetzsteon, who established the Obie Awards to call attention to off-Broadway achievements.

In the spring of 1966 I noticed a small ad in the *Voice* theatre section announcing the performance of a play, *Fire*, by the Bread and Puppet theatre, which both surprised and fascinated me since I knew them only as participants in demonstrations and protest marches. The play was presented on Saturday evenings only at an address on Delancey Street, and so on my next trip into the city, I sought them out.

Then, even more than now, Delancey was far from any established site of theatre activity in the city, and when I emerged from the Delancey stop on the subway I found myself in a totally unfamiliar part of the city. My only experience with New York below the Village was with the ethnic enclaves of Chinatown and Little Italy, both well to the west of the area where I now found myself. It was traditionally a working-class community of recent, primarily Jewish immigrants, and when I visited in 1966 still had much of the feeling of the previous century, rows of four- and five-story brick tenement buildings, most sporting metal fire escapes on the street side. Delancey being the main thoroughfare in the district, most buildings sheltered small businesses on the ground floor, shoe stores and food shops, but the upper floors were identical to the purely residential buildings on the surrounding scruffy streets.

The building that housed the performance (later torn down and replaced by a Holiday Inn) thus bore no resemblance to the off-off-Broadway theatres of the Village. One entered a standard tenement stair/hallway and walked up to the top, fourth floor, where the Bread and Puppet performance space was located. There was no proscenium arch, simply a large loft converted into a performance space by the addition of about fifty chairs to one part of the space, facing a simple closed curtain. There was no lobby, no box office, no tickets. Patrons simply filtered into the space and took chairs, several standing at the back and sides when the chairs were filled. A young woman, dressed in black, came out from behind the curtains carrying a stack of papers and under her arm a loaf of freshly baked bread. She moved through the audience, handing out the papers, which were hand-lettered programs, and breaking off bits of the loaf, which were similarly distributed. It was a delicious if rather coarse rye baked by the director of the company, Peter Schumann, who had begun his career as a dancer and baker in Germany. The breaking of bread, a traditional means of establishing a community, was a part of Schumann's quasi-ritual approach from the beginning and is of course memorialized in the company's name. Later I would recall this custom when I visited Ariane Mnouchkine's Théâtre du Soleil in Paris, where the director traditionally welcomes guests to a large public space in which a communal meal is served before each production.

There was no admission charge, but a container stood near the door for voluntary contributions to antiwar causes. The aura of war protest hung over the occasion. The production, we were informed by a black-robed actress as a kind of prologue, was dedicated to three American protesters, Alice Herz, Roger LaPorte, and Norman Morrison, three peace activists who, following the example of a Buddhist priest in Vietnam, had immolated themselves in protest to the war between March and November 1965. The title of the production clearly referred to these burnings, but the performance itself focused not upon the United States, either its actions or its protests, but upon the sufferings of war victims in general, creating a kind of ritual of mourning.

Fire was composed of nine brief scenes, almost tableaux, with powerful sound effects, but almost no speech. For each scene a bell tolled, the red curtain was pulled across the stage, as in the Kabuki theatre, and a group of masked and robed figures would be revealed. Of the bodies only the pallid masked faces and hands, both oversized and crudely distorted, were visible. Schumann himself called them Vietnamese villagers, and at the time that seemed the intended interpretation, but the white masked faces were not particularly ethnic, and suggested to me rather general human suffering. Their eyes were all closed, and the twisted expressions suggested mute pain and agony. The only other visible features of their bodies were white hands, the fingers resembling long twisted sticks. The only décor was a crude black-and-white cartoon drawing of huts, trees, and a hill on a curtain at the rear. At the side of the stage was a table with a sign announcing in one word the name of the scene, suggesting the announcing signs in traditional variety shows. The first seven signs were simply the days of the week. For each day the masked figures served as a kind of visual chorus, while one or more of them performed some simple, ritualized action. To me the week suggested the passion week, with one scene involving the serving of bread and a goblet to each of the figures, another showing the binding and freeing of a figure, the Friday scene showing a sheet drawn over this figure's prone body, the Saturday a frightening sound collage, swirling lights, and confused movement, and the Sunday the figures in meditation, one revealing a face covered in blood. Aside from the suggestion of the Eucharist and the modest echo of the Passion Week in the days, however, there was no attempt to suggest a particular Christian narrative, but rather a series of ritualized actions open to multiple interpretations.

The eighth scene made the most specific visual reference to external events. It was called "Fire." A huge red figure, the only example of the oversize puppets often associated with the company, was seen upstage. With huge wing-like arms it directed some of the onstage actors to wrap others in dark red bands of fabric, which with the scene title inevitably suggested the three martyrs to whom the production was dedicated. The last scene, called "End," also moved from the general suggestions of the opening scenes to a symbolic pantomime clearly tied to the U.S. actions in Vietnam. The chorus was seated, dimly lit, in the background with a single illuminated figure stage center, dressed all in white robes and with a mask clearly suggesting an ancient Oriental woman. Two figures, wearing masks of Western faces and dressed not in robes but in blue jeans and undershirts, brought in the materials—cinderblocks, poles, and fencing—to build a small enclosure around the woman. When they left, she produced a role of red tape (suggesting both blood and fire) and began slowly to bind her legs and her body and finally to cover her eyes and mouth. Finally, almost covered in red, she sagged lifelessly against the wire enclosure, which collapsed, some pieces scattering out to the feet of the closest spectators. A single actor entered, struck the bell a final time, and quietly spoke the words "The end."

This obviously concluded the performance, and the audience was plunged into darkness, but there was no applause, and when the lights went up no curtain call. Some may have thought the play, which was in sum quite short, was not really over, but clearly most of the audience felt that applause was inappropriate after an experience that had so much the feeling of a religious ritual. In fact a few people applauded when the houselights first came up, but they quickly stopped when the majority of the audience did not join in. Instead all moved quietly to the doors, without the normal conversation of postshow audiences. I remember going down the several flights of stairs and out into the unfamiliar surroundings of Delancey Street feeling even more than when I arrived that I had moved far from my habitual surroundings and experience.

Over the years that followed I saw the company many times (they are still active as I write this, half a century later) both in street performances, with the huge figures that became associated with them, and also in a wide variety of indoor venues, with an amazing variety of topics and of puppetry techniques. During the 1970s as Vietnam receded from the center of public consciousness, they turned to other themes, other wars, other oppressions, ecological concerns, but the production of *Fire*, in its simplicity and focus, remains in my memory more clearly than any other of their offerings. I saw them for the most part in New York, in indoor productions, primarily in churches, in outdoor shows, and in street parades, particularly in the Greenwich Village Halloween parade, where their huge puppets have been an annual feature for decades. They also appeared memorably once at Cornell while I was on the faculty there, in April 1970, for an event called the "America Is Hard to Find" weekend, celebrating the impending imprisonment of campus religious leader Daniel Berrigan, who had been sentenced for his participation in the burning of draft records in Catonsville, Maryland, in May 1968.

On the day Berrigan was to begin his prison term he left his office keys on a secretary's desk and disappeared. This was just over a week before the scheduled Cornell event, attended by some fifteen thousand people, myself included, as well as a number of police and FBI agents, seeking the now fugitive Berrigan, who was reportedly to appear. He did in fact appear and addressed the audience, but managed to slip away without being captured by the police, who only apprehended him several months later. It was eventually revealed that he had left Barton Hall inside one of the fifteen-foot-tall figures of the Bread and Puppet company, which was also a featured presence at the antiwar event. Like the Catonsville event itself (and the subsequent trial, which formed the basis of a widely produced docudrama, *The Trial of the Catonsville Nine*, written by Berrigan) the Berrigan escape within a puppet fascinated me as a key example of how closely intertwined performance and social action had become in the late 1960s.

1967 *Hair* at the Public Theater

During the 1960s few names were better known in the New York theatre world than that of Joe Papp, primarily because of his visionary program of offering free productions of Shakespearean plays in Central Park, which, by the time he built a permanent outdoor theatre, the Delacorte, in 1962, had already become a city institution. With Shakespeare in the Park established, Papp began to dream of realizing that elusive goal of the New York theatre, an ongoing repertory house in an indoor, year-around location. During the early 1960s he cast about for a location for this venture, and early in 1966 announced that he had found one, the long-abandoned Astor Library on Lafayette Street, just south of Astor Place.

The elegant building, opened just over a century before, was a major historical structure, one of the first to be preserved under the city's Landmarks Preservation Law, enacted in 1965. According to the law, the facade of the building must be preserved, but the interior could be redesigned, and Papp planned for a complex of theatres, offices, rehearsal rooms, and support areas, beginning with two theatres, one of 200 seats and the other of 800. Ming Cho Lee, who had been Papp's leading designer at the Delacorte since its opening, designed the small stage, the first to open, in the then-popular thrust form with the audience on three sides, smaller than but similar to that of the ANTA Washington Square project just two years earlier. During the summer of 1966 Papp, under financial pressure, scaled back to two small theatres, the first to be located in the elegant domed space on the top floor in what was originally the library's main reading room. This space, the most attractive in the building, was the first to be opened, in October 1967, and, Papp wanting to emphasize contemporary work, opened with a new musical, *Hair*, by James Rado, Gerome Ragni, and Galt MacDermot.

Although *Hair* went on to become for many the iconic theatre piece of the 1960s, it did not seem a particularly outstanding choice at the time other than to mark Papp's stated concern with new work. Like most regular New York theatre-goers, I had attended a number of the Shakespearean productions in previous summers at the Delacorte, and assumed that if and when Papp finally got a year-around downtown venue, he would continue with Shakespeare there, or at least other selections from the classic repertoire. As I have already mentioned, I was not yet a big fan of musicals other than the standard classics like Rodgers and Hammerstein; like many others, I was not converted until the 1970s, with the brilliant series of Sondheim works beginning with *Company*. If I was not especially excited by musicals, a production that billed itself as a "Tribal Love-Rock Musical" was even less appealing. Certainly at the University I was surrounded by rock music, which seemed to dominate my students' taste, and by 1967 was ever more conscious of the hippie counterculture that was also evoked by even the title of the work (I first heard the term "love-in" at Cornell this summer and hippie communities referred to as "tribes" about the same time).

My taste and experience in off-Broadway musicals had been formed by such early 1960s works as *The Fantasticks*, *Little Mary Sunshine*, and *Ernest in Love*, with *The Threepenny Opera* as outlier, and a hippie rock musical held little appeal.

Nevertheless, Papp's name and the event of the opening of a major new downtown venue took me to his new theatre in November 1967, and although I was by no means won over by the production, I found the occasion a memorable one. I am sure that I was never aware of the old Astor library before this time, indeed I am not sure I ever even walked past it, but Papp's new venture soon became the cultural center of the entire neighborhood. In reference to his long-standing interest in bringing theatre to a more democratic audience, Papp named this the Public Theater, suggesting even in the then unusual spelling of the name a more "populist" orientation than that of New York's traditional "theatres," especially those on Broadway. Later the Public became a kind of pivotal venture between the traditional off-Broadway district of the West Village, and the theatre district of the East Village that developed from the 1970s onward, but in 1967 the only significant theatre to the east of the new Public was Ellen Stewart's pioneering La Mama, then located in a loft several blocks east on Second Avenue, and at that time dedicated primarily to presenting the work of emerging new dramatists.

Although the elegant Victorian facade, still protected as a city landmark, remains the same today, the Public inside is much different than it was in 1967, or indeed than it was as recently as 2012, when the lobby areas underwent a major renovation. Before this recent renovation, one entered directly from the street, then up a short flight of stairs inside into the lobby proper. The renovation moved these stairs back outside (as they originally were), thus recapturing a significant amount of lobby floor space. Even before this, however, the lobby, with its large open space, high, modeled plasterwork ceilings, and classic columns, was quite palatial compared with other off-Broadway or even with most Broadway houses. In 1967 work was still going on in all the areas surrounding this lobby, and the only theatre then open was the Anspacher, on the third, top floor.

Although the landmark status required only the facade to be preserved, Papp decided to keep most of the architecture of what had been the library's main reading room, a kind of atrium with two levels of columns and a domed glass ceiling. Within this, Lee constructed the small thrust stage theatre. Behind the stage, two columns were stripped down to iron shafts to help support a light grid that extended out above the stage. The remaining columns were repainted white, their capitols outlined in gold leaf, and separated by red velvet curtains on the second floor. Soft lighting was installed behind the glass of the domed ceiling. Despite many donations, the project was an expensive one, and the free performances at the park gave way here to seats at $2.50.

Although the elegant physical surroundings and the red velvet seats were far from the rough surroundings of the Living Theatre that I had seen at the beginning of the decade, many things about this production brought me back again to my experience of *The Connection*. Although the performing space was far more upscale, I entered it noting the distinctive 1960s odor of marijuana and the ear-assaulting amplified contributions of a six-piece rock band, already performing when I arrived, both features of *The Connection*. Even more striking, ragtag figures were sprawled out in the seats or wandering about the aisles, confronting the arriving spectators. Although their hippie costumes were far more colorful and theatrical than the street-person rags of the wandering social outcasts who worked the audience at intermissions in *The Connection*, the main difference was that in the Living Theatre I was solicited as an audience member for money to buy dope, while at *Hair* I was offered a joint to share. It was, I thought, a striking illustration of the assumed society for the two productions and of the worldview they sought to project. The echoes were hardly surprising. Although the Living Theatre had at this time taken refuge in Europe, it continued to provide a powerful model of social protest, and of challenge to conventional norms regarding citizenship, sexuality, and drug use—all of which were central to the hippie aesthetic at the heart of *Hair*.

Hair also could claim a distinct theatrical lineage from the Living Theatre. A leading member of the Living Theatre, Joseph Chaikin, left that group in 1963 to found the Open Theatre, wishing to focus more on the work of the actor in experimental theatre and less on political activism. One of the authors of *Hair*, Gerome Ragni, left the Living Theatre with Chaikin and in fact coined the name "Open Theatre." He later met James Rado in the mainstream theatre and brought him into the Open Theatre. There, out of the improvised exercises that were at the core of that group's work, they developed the material that became the text for *Hair*.

The production clearly sought to provide a kind of physical, thematic, and musical collage of the experiential world of the current youthful counterculture, fearful of the draft and the ongoing nightmare of Vietnam, experimenting with pot, generally fairly well off, but disenchanted and directionless. Like most musicals, it had at its core a love story, but it was much more a musical reflection on the current mood among the most visible members of this generation. The youthful cast was talented, enthusiastic, and appealing, the rather gangly central couple (Walker Daniels and Jill O'Hara) rather suggesting to me the Boy and Girl of *The Fantasticks* (then about to celebrate its first decade in the West Village) suddenly finding themselves fast-forwarded into the late 1960s. Coauthor Ragni played Berger, the hirsute hippie buddy of the hero, and was one of the most striking members of the cast in his outrageous bespangled finery. The music, by Galt MacDermot, I enjoyed more than I expected, although only two of the songs really struck me— the title song, with its insolent, over-the-top celebrative feel, and "Aquarius," which I thought then, and still think, musically captures the note of precarious idealism of that time.

I remember few specific images or sequences, rather a sense of constant, often somewhat frantic, movement, dancing, singing, roughhousing, rather like a campus party in which everyone has had a bit too much to drink (or smoke) and is determined to have a good time, if for no other reason than to shut out the depressing outside world, with its unquestioning acceptance of bourgeois values and attitudes, and the ever-present threat of the draft and the war. In terms of collective memory, the sequence most associated with the show, the rather brief nude scene at the end of the first act, was not in fact part of the show when I saw it at the Public Theater. It was added to the Broadway production, perhaps to emphasize the uptown marketing of the show as daring and somewhat scandalous.

I did go back to see it uptown, and although it was rather more polished, with more music and even less plot, I was surprised how much difference the uptown move made. Not surprisingly, it became much more slick and professional, much closer to an uptown product. The already tenuous plot almost disappeared and new songs were added, giving the whole production much more the feeling of a traditional Broadway revue. Most striking, however, was the change from the distinct feeling at the Public that this was an intimate, casual product, almost like an ambitious community theatre project, a feeling completely missing on Broadway. Partly of course this was due to the shift from a

299-seat thrust stage to a proscenium theatre seating over 900—small for Broadway but still three times the capacity of the Anspacher. Cast members still wandered out among the audience, but at the Biltmore they seemed not really to share the audience's world as they did at the Public, and I am fairly certain no pot was offered.

Aside from these major physical changes, the Public was located in the very neighborhood that was the heart of the cultural world celebrated in *Hair*, with the hippie community of New York University immediately to the west and Fillmore East, the "Church of Rock and Roll" just to the east (on Second Avenue, a neighbor to La Mama). One had the clear impression that the performers in *Hair* at the Public, as well as the characters they played, all might have lived in that neighborhood. The appearance of one of the coauthors in an iconically central role, of course, reinforced this impression. Significantly, the Broadway producers removed Ragni, under protest, from the cast, and uptown the production became an import from another world. Unquestionably this added to its commercial appeal, but it created a very different reception dynamic. The move to a much larger commercial venue and the shift to a proscenium theatre made it far less intimate, despite the occasional forays of the cast members out into the house. Interestingly, a very similar dynamic was repeated almost thirty years later with the movement of the "bohemian" rock musical *Rent* from its East Village theatre of origin to Broadway, but that is another story.

1968 Jean-Louis Barrault's *Rabelais*

In 1968 I was eligible for my first sabbatical at Cornell and, my research having been centered on the French theatre up to that time, I naturally decided to spend the academic year 1968–69 with my family in Paris. As I was preparing for this trip, Paris erupted with the protests that are now remembered as the "Events of May." These began with student occupation protests against the rigidity and the capitalist orientation of the de Gaulle regime, and spread to factory workers, to whom the government reacted in an excessive and repressive manner. De Gaulle briefly fled France, and by the end of the month the country was on the brink of revolution.

Gradually in June and July, with the promise of new elections, the government reasserted its authority and the tumult gradually subsided. By August, when my family flew to Paris to begin my sabbatical, the Events were essentially over. Nevertheless most Americans, despite the social upheavals at home, still viewed France as in a far more precarious and dangerous situation. The TWA flight that we took to Paris was small by today's standards, seating somewhere between one hundred and two hundred passengers, but so unattractive was Paris as a destination that summer that our flight carried only six passengers, four of whom were my family.

Traces of the Events were still to be seen around the city, but already they were fading into history. If I had any doubts that the capitalist system had triumphed, they were dispelled when I saw stands in the streets in the Latin Quarter where one could buy souvenir cobblestones that had been pried up from the streets to form student barricades three months before.

The central theatrical event of the May events was the occupation of the Odéon, France's second national theatre, located in the Left Bank, just a few streets from the Sorbonne, where the uprising began. In the evening of May 15, a crowd of students and artists occupied the theatre, informing director Jean-Louis Barrault that this would no longer serve as an elitist bourgeois theatre, but would be converted into a continuous forum for political discussion. Julian Beck and Judith Malina, the leaders of the Living Theatre, led the crowds, and were reportedly welcomed by Barrault, who had some political sympathy with the protestors and much resented being cast in the role of representing the establishment. These sentiments rebounded upon him when the protests subsided, and in June the police reoccupied the by-then largely deserted Odéon at the same time as the nearby Sorbonne. By then, Barrault had already been removed from the directorship by the minister of culture, André Malraux.

No figure in the French theatre was better known and more respected nationally and internationally than Barrault at that time, and the prospect that I would miss seeing him in France was a big disappointment. It was with great pleasure, then, that I read in Parisian papers in the fall that his company was in fact preparing a major new work, called *Rabelais* and based on that author's sprawling classic *Gargantua and Pantagruel*, very much the kind of epic undertaking that Barrault had previously undertaken in *Le Soulier de Satin* and

Christoph Colombe, then the foremost examples of what he called "total theatre."

The production opened in December and although tickets were in high demand, I managed to get one for an early performance. So on a cold, dark, wintry night (the sun, when there is any, sets about mid-afternoon in Paris in December, a great shock to my American internal clock), I took the subway up to the Place Pigalle and walked along the boulevard to the Théâtre de l'Elysée-Montmartre, where Barrault's company had taken refuge. It was far from the center of mainstream Parisian theatre, in the heart of the city, and further still from the center of alternative theatre, then in the student area near the now-deserted Odéon. There the Théâtre de la Huchette had been presenting Ionesco's *The Lesson* and *The Bald Soprano* in permanent repertory for over a decade (the productions are still playing there today, almost fifty years later). In fact the area at and near the base of the Montmartre hill had been a major center of French entertainment since the late eighteenth century, and was the location of several major alternative theatres, including the first home of Antoine's Théâtre-Libre, Charles Dullin's Atelier, and the Grand Guignol. By the 1960s, however, it had lost much association with the theatre, and was known primarily for its night-clubs and cabarets (headed by the Moulin Rouge), and its wide variety of adult entertainment.

The boulevard leading from Pigalle to the Elysée-Montmartre resembled a carnival fairway—jostling crowds, garish lighting, a general festive if tacky air. The Elysée-Montmartre, formerly a ballroom and cabaret, had for some time become primarily a boxing arena and secondarily a strip club, but its more elegant past was suggested by its wonderful facade, a rococo confection a full story higher than the theatre itself and clearly dating back to the art deco period. On its upper part appears a cabaret dancer surrounded by swirling cloud-like forms. A series of doors opened into a comfortable lobby that in turn gave way to a huge rectangular hall surrounded by utilitarian columns. Even though it had a capacious stage at one end and an ornate balcony at the other, it still much more resembled a dance hall or even a gymnasium than a theatre. In the center of this hall, where recently a boxing ring stood, Barrault erected a stage for *Rabelais.*

The program of the production was decorated with remarkable grotesque woodcuts that within the program were attributed to Rabelais himself, although to me they bore a remarkable similarity to the demons that inhabit the paintings of Hieronymus Bosch. Rabelais scholars have since dismissed their attribution to that author, but they nevertheless created a remarkable and outrageous visual vocabulary for the production, whose costumes and scenic design were the work of the designer Matias, hitherto largely associated with the plays of Beckett. Matias created a striking but simple setting for the spectacle, a raised platform in the center of the hall, approached on each side by a walkway like the Japanese *hashigakari*, dividing the audience into four sections surrounding the stage. This simple arrangement set off the elaborate costumes, properties, and masques, displayed in a circus-like phantasmagoria of dances and processionals. In the second part the space was converted into a ship by the simple device of dropping ropes from the ceiling and hooking them to the sides of the central platform. One of the great scenes in the production is the re-creation of a storm that breaks upon this vessel and with lightning streaking across the ceiling, roaring wind, deafening thunderclaps, and the entire cast shouting out Rabelaisian text, the entire theatre becomes the storm-tossed ship, with Barrault, swaying back and forth, on its prow facing into the blast.

There was no direct reference to Barrault's recent conflict with the authorities, but the whole antiestablishment feel of the work showed clearly that Barrault continued to feel himself like Rabelais on the side of what would later be called the counterculture. Along with many references to the history of the French Renaissance, there were highly contemporary scenes. The opening of the second part, with half-naked couples stretched out on the ground, sporting long hair and beads, smoking and murmuring to each other, "Make love, not war" in English, could have come right out of *Hair* (a resemblance noted by several reviewers). The grotesque monster tyrant Picrochole, combining elements of Charlie Chaplin, Groucho Marx, Hitler, and a Kabuki samurai, and the huge red mask of the new-born Gargantua, held aloft with its avaricious lower jaw swinging open, would not have been out of place in a Bread and Puppet spectacle, a company that, like the Living Theatre, made its first appearance in Paris during this revolutionary year. At one point the young Pantagruel watches a heretic burned at the stake, a process described by the "master of the play," Barrault, while an actor mimes the death at the stake, calling out, "More wood, good people! More wood." The literary reference in Rabelais is to Jean de Cahors and other contemporaries of Rabelais who suffered this fate, but in 1968 there were echoes also of the Buddhist monks of Vietnam and the antiwar immolations. Almost certainly Barrault was also referencing another familiar image of martyrdom, Giles Corey, in Miller's *The Crucible*, who is pressed to death with stones as he cries out, "More weight." The play had then been familiar both to French theatre- and filmgoers for over a decade, as *Les Sorcières de Salem*, the film version having been adapted by Jean-Paul Sartre.

Musically too the production placed itself firmly in contemporary youth culture. Although the production was dominated by the stunning visual images of Barrault, its musical score was contributed by Michel Polnareff, at this time the leading representative in France of the contemporary Anglo-Saxon style of rock, which was marked not only by the music itself, but also by a distinct androgynous look and a championing of sexual liberty, all of which helped create a strong bridge between the notorious freedom on such matters of Rabelais and the contemporary youth movement. Polnareff was often portrayed in the contemporary French press as the personification of the beatnik, and a symbol of the decadence of the contemporary youth who had so recently nearly plunged the country into anarchy.

These contemporary echoes were by no means lost on the theatre's audiences. As the leading London critic, Ronald Bryden, noted in the *Observer*, Barrault was aware that Rabelais in his time had revolted against the rigid scholasticism of the Sorbonne and on these grounds "wrenched it into topical relevance, making the abbey of Thelme the 'first hippie commune,'" an observation proudly reproduced in the souvenir program I purchased in the theatre when I attended.

Nor were the sporting associations of the venue forgotten. The conception of Gargantua was staged as a professional wrestling match between King Grangousier and Gargamelle, who began on facing stools, like boxers, then met and grappled in the center in movements halfway between wrestling and sex, with the rest of the company surrounding the stage and cheering the action. Barrault himself appeared as both the director of the entertainment and the umpire, all under the watchful eye of the patron of the event, the god Silenus/Dionysius, sitting astride a donkey, who would soon transform into a Christ figure in a continually evolving carnivalesque shifting from pagan to Christian to secular references and transformations.

At the end Panurge, transformed into the god Dionysius, falls dying to the stage. Barrault, no longer the Master of Ceremonies, but an apparent representative from the audience, walks up to him to offer him final comfort, a white dove sitting on his hand, creating a final moment of great visual simplicity but enormous theatrical power. At that time one often heard quoted the remark made by Barrault when he joined the student protesters who occupied the Odéon: "Barrault is dead, but a living being remains before you." Barrault clearly saw himself, like the dying god, having come to the end of a major part of his remarkable career, beginning with this production to be reborn into the next phase. During 1972 he created a number of major productions on large flexible stages installed in a former railway station, the Gare d'Orsay, and when that space was taken over by the government to be converted into a museum, he moved his company and his flexible stage to the Rond-Point, a major performance space on Champs-Élysées, midway between the Arc de Triomphe and the Louvre. Here for the next decade Barrault returned to the sort of productions he had mounted at the Odéon—new French plays and international works. I remember seeing several of his productions there, especially a brilliant interpretation of Aristophanes's *The Birds* in 1985, utilizing stunning costume, puppets, and the usual Barrault skill at visual spectacle. Today the theatre, now a national house, fittingly bears the name of Salle Renaud-Barrault, honoring the director and his longtime partner.

1969 Jerzy Grotowski's
The Constant Prince

The journal *TDR*, under various names, was the primary source for the most important names and trends in the alternative theatre, nationally and internationally, during the 1960s, and it was there, in the mid-1960s, that I first read about the remarkable experiments of Jerzy Grotowski in Poland. His international fame grew steadily during this decade, to India, to France, and to various international festivals. He planned to bring three productions to the United States in 1968, but was denied entry by the State Department after the Soviet Union's invasion of Czechoslovakia. In Paris in September I was mailed a copy of a petition protesting this decision published in the *New York Times* and signed by sixty leading American theatre artists, among them Arthur Miller, Edward Albee, and Ellen Stewart.

By the time permission was granted for the company to come, I was myself back in the United States and eager to see this much-praised work. Grotowski was hosted by the Brooklyn Academy of Music, which had just (in 1957) come under the leadership of Harvey Lichtenstein, whose vision was to make this outpost of the New York theatre into a major center of modern dance and contemporary national and international performance, which he brilliantly accomplished during his three decades there. Grotowski was his first major international guest, but he proved a difficult one. Grotowski did not find the spaces available at the Brooklyn Academy suitable for the work, and Lichtenstein was unable to find a nearby space that was better. Finally Grotowski accepted an engagement at the Washington Square Methodist Church in Greenwich Village, in the historic heart of the American experimental theatre scene literally just around the corner from O'Neill's Provincetown Playhouse and only eight blocks from where Richard Schechner was editing *TDR*.

Not only was the neighborhood most appropriate to this venture, but so was the church itself. It was deeply involved in contemporary political and social movements, often referred to as the "peace church." All during the 1960s it hosted peace rallies and demonstrations, and its basement housed a draft-counseling center. Practically speaking, it allowed BAM to remove most of the fittings in the central part of the church, pews and all, to construct a small open theatre space there, an accommodation few other locations, especially churches, would have extended.

Seating, as was the custom with Grotowski, was strictly limited, with only forty to one hundred spectators permitted at each performance. I managed to get BAM tickets for the one-hundred-seated *Constant Prince* and the eighty-seated *Acropolis*, but the forty-seated *Apocalypsis cum Figuris* was already sold out when I inquired (though I did manage to see it in Paris four years later). The tickets were $10, surprisingly low by today's standards, but in 1969 equivalent to most Broadway admissions, and as the several-month run continued, they were reportedly being scalped for ten or even twenty times that amount.

My first ticket was for *The Constant Prince*, and my plan that pleasant fall evening was to go down to the Village an hour or so before the performance and have a light supper at my favorite village coffeehouse, the Caffe Reggio on Macdougal Street, very close to the church. As I walked down Macdougal, however, I looked up West Fourth Street and saw a crowd of twenty or thirty people already waiting in front of the church more than an hour before the show. I went up to them and found that they were there because BAM had oversold the performances and that on some previous nights, only the first one hundred patrons with tickets were admitted, while other ticket-holders were turned away at the door by Grotowski himself. Obviously I decided to skip my supper and join the crowd, and it was well I did so, because before the doors opened the street in front of the theatre was overflowing, with clearly well over one hundred would-be attendees. When the door opened indeed Grotowski himself stood with the ticket taker to count off the crowd. He was dressed in an elegant dark suit, white shirt, and tie, but from the neck up his wildly unkempt hair and beard seemed far more appropriate to these downtown bohemian surroundings.

Successfully past that checkpoint, I joined another, smaller milling crowd in the lobby, awaiting entrance to the performance space itself. The seating was highly ritualized. Each audience member was asked to remain silent, then escorted individually to a seat next to the performance space, which was unlike any I had ever seen. My guide took me into a dark cavernous space (the main sanctuary of the church with pews removed) in the middle of which was a large platform about four feet high, with steps leading up to it. A walkway about four feet wide on all sides of this platform surrounded an inner square made up of wooden walls about four feet above the platform. On all four sides of the platform simple wooden benches, with backs, provided seating, only one rank per side. Seated audience members could rest their arms and elbows on the top of this inner wall and look down into the square space. This space opened all the way to the actual floor, so that the playing area that we looked down into was about eight feet below us.

In it was a single piece of scenery, a low central platform, upon which the sacrificial victims of the play would suffer their torments. The blank wooden surrounding wall and the bodies of the actors provided all the other visual elements. In this space were six actors, five men and a woman. At the opening, one was lying face up, almost naked, on the podium, clearly suggesting a sacrificial victim. Around him were apparently the king (marked by a crown), his daughter, and his court, the men wearing heavy dark costumes, almost like judge's robes with knee-length boots and breeches. A grim sacrificial scene opened the production, with the court surrounding and poking at the unresisting Prince, all uttering nonhuman cries. A kind of ceremony developed during which the Prince was seemingly castrated and thus apparently eligible to join the surrounding society, which dressed him in robes similar to their own.

This grim scene served as a kind of prologue to the main action, in which the cruel court brought in another prisoner, a brother Prince to the first, but the new victim did not suffer the fate of the first. Instead of joining the court, he confounded their rituals by his passivity, leading at last to a state of ecstasy where he moved almost naked among the overdressed court members like a saintly figure in an El Greco paining. The court was at first dazzled by this vision, but then turned upon a figure so alien to themselves. In the most stunning and memorable sequence of the evening, the Prince was stretched out upon the podium and flogged, with his tortured cries played against a chanted litany by the others. Then came the most astonishing moment of all. The tortured cries of the Prince began to be supplemented not by the litany but by the unmistakable rhythms of a minuet, rather as if someone were making its sound through their nasal passages. Gradually I realized that although the court was now engaged in a ball around the Prince as his flogging continued, it was not they that were providing this music, but the Prince himself, somehow miraculously moaning in response to the lashes and simultaneously providing the ongoing minuet music. I was later informed that this astonishing technical feat come from Grotowski's development of different resonators located in different parts of the body, but whatever the technique, it was like nothing I have heard before or since. As the grotesque ball continued, the court put on hideous masks and moved in more and more contorted ways, eventually suggesting a kind of Witches' Sabbath conceived by Goya. Here and elsewhere one saw that while the Prince eclipsed the others, this was an entire company with extraordinary physical and vocal skills.

The Prince was played by Richard Cieslak, the leader of the company and not unreasonably considered by many to be the greatest actor of the late twentieth century. Certainly I never witnessed an actor with more total control of both his body and his voice. One had the impression that every muscle, virtually every neuron was under his control and pressed into service for the total expression of his inner being. Following his torture, the courtiers again swirled around him like a divine being, saintly or even Christlike, whose sacrifice could bring them along with him into a higher realm. In the final scene of the production the Prince seemed to reach a peak of both suffering and ecstasy and died amid the applause of the onstage actors, as if they were joining with the real audience in appreciation of the remarkable physical and indeed spiritual display they had just witnessed. Although I could not understand a word of the production, and the modest program provided gave only the barest outline of the action, the visual and aural elements of the evening were so overwhelming that these more discursive aids seemed almost superfluous.

There was a great deal of talk in the 1960s of bringing theatre back to its religious, sacramental roots, or of creating a modern theatre that could tap into those spiritual depths, but even though I was strongly moved by *Fire*, it was not until I saw Grotowski's *The Constant Prince* that I felt this was anything more than one of the many utopian dreams of that fevered decade. The previous year I had read one of the major theoretical statements of the decade, Peter Brook's *The Empty Stage*, which addressed this sort of work in a section appropriately entitled "The Holy Theatre." Brook cited Grotowski's theatre as a central example in such work, with a truly "sacred aim." Here, Brook said, the actor by technical mastery over his physical and psychic means seeks to achieve a kind of transparency that is also a ritualized "sacrifice" of himself, and "this sacrifice is his gift to the spectator." Brook like others saw a common concern between this process and the vision of Artaud, whose writings were central to him and many of the pioneering theatre artists of the 1960s. The chapter title, "The Holy Theatre," was, Brook noted, chosen by way of homage to Artaud.

One of the most often quoted phrases from Artaud's *The Theatre and Its Double* during the 1960s was his striking statement that condemned modern art as "dallying with forms," instead of being "like victims burnt at the stake, signaling through the flames." Like most informed theatre-goers of the time, I loved the apocalyptic vision of this image without being able quite to imagine how it could be translated into real theatre terms. When I saw Cieslak in this production, I instantly felt that at last I understood what Artaud was talking about. If not literally burning, he was, as Brook suggested, consuming himself in a sacrifice for us, the audience, producing a feeling close to religious awe.

I have from time to time as I think back over more than sixty years of theatre-going tried to think if I could pick any single production as the most outstanding in my memory, and have found this a hopeless challenge. If I were asked to name a single piece of acting that similarly stands out, however, I would unhesitatingly name this performance by Cieslak. It was for me the appropriate high note on which to conclude this fevered and visionary decade.

The 1970s

An unidentified actor and Charles Ludlam in the 1973 stage production of *Camille* by Alexander Dumas, adapted by Charles Ludlam. Photo from the Billy Rose Theatre Division, New York Public Library Digital Collection. Used with permission.

1970 Luca Ronconi's *Orlando Furioso*

During the late 1960s, the theatre district in New York underwent a profound change. The northern part of the district retained something of the show-business glamor from earlier in the century, but the southern part, especially Forty-Second Street, once the center of the New York theatre, became more and more a seedy, disreputable haven for drug dealers and pornography. Visitors to the dwindling legitimate theatres along the street had to move through an increasingly unattractive and dangerous area, and by the end of the decade the central two blocks between Sixth Avenue and Eighth Avenue had become almost a solid row of peep shows, adult bookstores, and pornographic cinemas, many of them former legitimate theatres.

At the eastern edge of this district was Bryant Park, occupying two-thirds of the city block behind the New York Public Library, facing Fifth Avenue. During the late 1960s, the park shared the urban decline of the neighboring Times Square area, becoming a haven for drug dealers, prostitutes, and the homeless, into which neither tourists nor most New Yorkers would venture either day or night. By the late 1960s plans and projects began regularly appearing for the "cleaning up" of Times Square, a monumental undertaking that took another three decades to carry out. Bryant Park, a much smaller and manageable area, however, was the object of a much smaller reclamation project carried out during the late 1960s by Mayor John Lindsay, Park Commissioner Thomas Hoving (much better known as the long-time head of the Metropolitan Museum), and a number of leading citizens and businessmen.

Protests about conditions in the park had been increasing for several years, but Hoving began a series of significant measures to improve it in 1966, first putting a fence around the park and clearing and closing it after 10:00 p.m., then instituting a series of regular events to attract New Yorkers back to the park—regular fashion shows, concerts, flower shows, and poetry readings. As this program developed, small theatre and dance groups began to appear from time to time among the frequent lunchtime offerings.

Bryant Park became for the first (and I believe only) time the venue for a major theatrical event in 1970, when the Italian director Luca Ronconi brought his internationally acclaimed production *Orlando Furioso* to the park, where it was performed under a huge inflatable bubble. Both production and venue broke new ground in the New York theatre. Major productions from abroad had for decades provided New Yorkers with highly polished traditional productions from theatres like the Moscow Art Theatre or the Comédie-Française, brought by entrepreneurs like Sol Hurok to large conventional venues like the City Center, but Ronconi was a quite different sort of visitor, very much a director of the late 1960s, inspired by the Living Theatre and the theatrical political demonstrations in France and Italy. Rarely did he work in conventional theatre spaces. *Orlando* was first presented at the Spoleto festival in a deconsecrated church, then in city squares in Bologna and Milan, in the cavernous empty spaces of the recently abandoned central markets in Paris, and on a boarded-over ice skating rink at the Edinburgh Festival before being invited to New York.

Mayor Lindsay saw the production as an ideal central offering for a project he was then pursuing to create a zone for the arts on the underutilized piers in Chelsea, a district bordering the Hudson River to the south of midtown. A producing organization was formed to bring the company, but the pier project fell through, largely due to protests from the Longshoreman's Union, objecting to the loss of shipping outlets. The *Orlando* project was then shifted to Bryant Park, a smaller and less controversial urban renewal project, and ground was cleared for the placement there of an inflatable tennis court bubble, filling the central part of the park.

The production was advertised as "Theatre in the Surround," and in many ways anticipated the kind of audience experience later called "immersive theatre." Theatre that mingled actors and audience in a common space, influenced by the Happenings of the previous decade, by the communal experiments of the Living Theatre, and by various political street theatre actions, was beginning to appear in the New York experimental theatre at this time. Probably the best-known example was the work of Richard Schechner at the Performing Garage in Soho, such as *Dionysius in 69*, which he called "environmental theatre." Experiments in mixing audiences and actors were still fairly uncommon, though, and in any case the scale and visibility of the Ronconi work was something quite new and for many quite shocking.

The main entrance to the large rounded structure was from Forty-Second Street. When one entered the large performance space, one had rather the impression of attending some sort of public rally or political event. There were no chairs, and the several hundred spectators milled about in the essentially open space, not even knowing which way to face, there being a rough stage with a large, hand-painted cardboard curtain in front at either end of the space. The production began with Astolfo, the magician who serves as a kind of master of ceremonies, appearing in the center of the crowd in a brilliant carnivalesque costume, partly medieval, partly high fashion, partly fantastic, to introduce the other major characters. Orlando appeared first, dashing in upon a machine that was part wagon, part mechanical horse, pushed at breakneck speed through the audience by his attendants.

Suddenly a whole set of similar wagons appeared, bearing other major characters—Rinaldo, Bradamante, Angelica, and others, coming from all directions, chasing and confronting each other, shouting, dueling, whirling about, while the audience scattered in all directions, often avoiding one chariot only to find themselves unexpectedly in the path of another. Every part of the area was in motion, and no place sheltered or safe. The curtains opened on the two stages at the ends and scenes from the romance were performed simultaneously in a variety of styles—operatic, commedia, Brechtian, melodramatic, naturalistic, but what coherence they offered was almost impossible to follow because of the variety of other stimuli coming from all sides.

A huge scaffolding suggesting a tower transported an actress from one of these stages to another; a machine suggesting a giant whale on wheels attacked one of the women and was in turn set upon by Orlando, in a kind of parody of Perseus, but he broke it open only to have it revolve and engulf him in turn. Mechanical contrivances of this sort filled the action, but always had an improvised, rough-hewn quality about them as if they had been rapidly assembled out of whatever material was at hand.

The production lasted about ninety minutes with, of course, no intermission and scarcely a moment of relaxation. Indeed the action seemed to increase steadily in tempo and complexity. There were often five scenes unfolding at once, two on the raised stages, two on the other side walls, and one in the center, overlapping and flowing into each other, with audience members caught up in a tempest of interwoven dialogues, shouts, cries, and lines heard out of context from some other part of the theatre, pure sounds, and passing actors (there were over fifty in all) and machines.

Barrault often referred to his approach as total theatre, and certainly there were some striking relationships between his *Rabelais* and Ronconi's *Orlando Furioso*, both monumental productions hewn out of vast sprawling national epics and both created in large, nontheatrical spaces offering unconventional actor/audience relationships. But although Barrault placed his action among his spectators, performance and viewing spaces remained almost entirely distinct, and the audience could watch his sometimes violent and complex action in personal tranquility. For him, total theatre meant an overwhelming theatrical experience, using every visual and aural strategy the art offered. Ronconi's production, however, was truly total, engulfing the spectators physically in a multifaceted world that far exceeded whatever part of it was within their immediate experience.

Toward the conclusion the pandemonium of the production began to move toward a more unified series of actions, drawing the audience into something closer to a common experience. One of the visions earlier in the production had been the magical iron castle of the sorcerer Atlante (a rather whimsical program, itself full of jokes and puzzles, provided explanations of some fragments of the action). This "iron castle" was composed of a series of cages holding various knights and ladies in thrall to the sorcerer's illusions. Near the conclusion the cages were reassembled on one of the platforms to represent the castle of Charlemagne, besieged by Moorish knights on their mobile horses, which, along with battling infantry, carried out a conflict that engulfed the entire theatre. Orlando, in his final madness, fought against himself in a space like a small boxing ring cleared for him in the center, while fragments of other stories popped up here and there amid the continuing conflict that surrounded him. The cages, now open, were removed from the platform and distributed around the central space, where they formed a fence-work labyrinth enclosing both actors and audience. This provided an opportunity for the actors to confront individual spectators and provide them with monologues (in Italian of course) presumably designed to clarify or convince, but in fact only creating an overwhelming mosaic of sound as the dozens of simultaneous stories were delivered all over the theatre by the impassioned performers.

Suddenly a figure appeared overhead, flying across the performance space with the aid of a giant crane ending in a crude construction suggesting a winged horse. This was the hippogriff upon which the quasi-narrator Astolfo departed for the moon, his escape from Orlando's mad world ending the performance. The cages were rolled and carried away and the stunned audience was free to return to their own world, where even the tawdry raucousness of Forty-Second Street now appeared as a relatively sedate environment.

The Ronconi production, with its cartoonish mixture of visual and dramatic styles, its sensual and physical assault, and most of all its creation of an environment in which no two spectators could possibly have anything like the same experience and of which no spectator could possibly gain any total or unified idea, went much further in these directions than most of the radical attacks on conventional theatre seen off-off-Broadway during the previous decade, and by the standards of Broadway, on the fringe of which this production took place, it was truly revolutionary. Not for several decades, until the radical productions of Reza Abdoh, and subsequently, certain works in the immersive theatre movement, did the mainstream theatre in New York see work that similarly disrupted conventional audience expectations.

Few productions of this season so sharply divided audience and critics as this, and critical response very clearly reflected the differing standards of uptown establishment critics and those of the downtown alternative writers. In the sacrosanct pages of the *New York Times*, Clive Barnes and Mel Gussow fulminated against the production's lack of focus and content, and proudly distanced themselves from European critics who had praised it. Not only the confusion of the audience was noted but also its discomfort. On the other hand, critics more open to downtown work, such as Jack Kroll in *Newsweek* and especially John Lahr in the *Village Voice*, were almost as extreme in their praise for the imagination and theatricality of the production. I personally considered it the boldest use of scenic space I had yet seen in New York.

1971 The Manhattan Project's *Alice in Wonderland*

Almost everything about *Orlando Furioso* was as overwhelming as its physical presentation, with a cast of fifty, gargantuan, if rough-hewn set pieces, and a venue that could accommodate up to three thousand audience members. Far more critical praise, however, was heaped upon another production running at the same time in a tiny space twenty blocks to the south, seating only one hundred, with a cast of six providing most of their own visual spectacle. This was the stage adaptation of Lewis Carroll's *Alice in Wonderland* by André Gregory's Manhattan Project. Indeed, it was so popular that I was not able to get a ticket until early in 1971, several months after its opening.

The first thing that struck me about this production was, rather surprisingly, how much it reminded me of Grotowski's *Constant Prince*. It was partly that the performance space had been erected within a church, although in fact off- and off-off-Broadway have been utilizing spaces in churches ever since the 1960s, when Al Carmines at the Judson Memorial Church on Washington Square was a key figure in downtown theatre. Churches offering space to theatrical production were then as now scattered about the city, and while the Polish Lab Theatre had performed in the heart of the Greenwich Village theatre district, Gregory's company appeared at the Calvary Church on Park Avenue South in the Gramercy Park area, a location about the same distance from midtown but with nothing of the performance world about it.

Still the Manhattan Project, like the Polish Lab Theatre, had not simply arranged chairs and a platform in an open room but built a specific theatrical space inside a room within the church. Although both had strictly limited seating, the audience was not admitted one at a time to *Alice*. Even so Gregory, like Grotowski, welcomed us at the door and even helped hand out programs. These two built environments were also markedly different. For *The Constant Prince*, scaffolding was erected with a much larger room around the pit-like performance area, distinctly separating audience from performers. For *Alice* also the audience entered a large room with a smaller area inside it, here a square the walls of which were made up entirely of old, mismatched doors. Instead of being escorted directly to their seats, the audience was provided with a much more casual experience, left to mill about outside the performance enclosure. Against one wall sat a table with cookies and lemonade, with crude lettering on the doors above it saying "eat me" and "drink me" with arrows pointing to the refreshments. Just before the show began, a small door, about three feet high, opened in one wall and the audience was allowed to crawl through this improvised "rabbit hole" into the actual performance area, to the accompaniment of one of the few music cues of the evening, *The Sheik of Araby*, playing in the still empty performance area on an old Victrola. An enclosed area made of the rough wooden door/walls enclosed both actors and audience. Inside, the audience could either sit in chairs on rough bleachers on two sides of the acting area or sit on the stage floor, next to the actors. Despite the intimacy, however, there was no interaction with audience members. In theory, chairs were $6 and floor seats were $3, but there was no reserved seating and people in fact sat wherever they wished.

The production too was in certain ways reminiscent of the work of Grotowski, and not surprisingly, since Gregory and his actors, like many experimental groups in New York at that time, had been profoundly influenced by the reading of *Toward a Poor Theatre* and by the firsthand experience of seeing the three works the Polish Laboratory Theatre brought to the city in 1969. The extent of this influence remained unknown to me until the appearance two years later of the collection of photographs of the production by Richard Avedon with interviews conducted by Doon Arbus early in 1971, just when I saw the production. Both interviews and a section of the photos, showing company member Gerry Ammon doing a Grotowski exercise, "The Plastiques," revealed how important this influence was.

Of course the Manhattan Project evolved its own style, a deadpan grotesque approach somewhat reminiscent of American silent films, but their work, like that of the Polish Lab Theatre, was highly physical, stretching bodily capacities while maintaining tight control, and relying almost exclusively upon the body for theatrical effects, with minimum use of scenery, properties, lighting, or sound. A long table, like the platform in *The Constant Prince*, and a few neutral chairs were the main set pieces. Aside from these, the highly trained bodies of the actors provided everything necessary.

The company was composed of two women and four men. Only Angela Pietropinto, who was Alice, played a single character. The others each played fifteen to twenty characters, shifting scene to scene. The second woman, Saskia Hegt, took on most of the other female parts, while the others each did one or two major supporting parts (the White Knight, the Cheshire Cat, Humpty Dumpty, the Caterpillar) and a variety of smaller roles (gardeners, gravediggers, King's Men, trees, walls, water spirits, etc.). On a few occasions they combined their bodies into a single being or object.

The production began with the stage empty. The lights went out and then the entire company burst onstage through a paper curtain, entwined in a confused bundle of bodies with protruding legs and arms, topped with a black umbrella and representing the Jabberwock, the first part of whose verse tale, shouted by various actors in the tangle, opened the production. During the poem, Alice managed to disentangle herself from the others and for the rest of the evening she remained separate, confronting the others singly or in groups. Most of the familiar scenes from the Lewis Carroll book were present, along with a few scenes and characters from *Through the Looking Glass.* Although the dialogue came almost entirely from these books, its staging and delivery very much reflected the youth culture of the period, especially in the frequent sexual overtones and in altered states of consciousness. The association of the latter with drugs was made particularly clear in one of the production's most memorable scenes, Alice's encounter with the Caterpillar, played by Larry Pine seated on a mushroom created entirely with other actors' bodies. The remaining four actors created the Caterpillar's mushroom by facing in four directions and bending over at the waist with their butts touching while Pine sat atop them cross legged, his hookah created by reaching down, pulling up the arm of one of the others and using its thumb as the mouthpiece of the hookah. The croquet scene was similarly anthropomorphized. Carroll himself imagined the wickets as formed by soldiers bending over with their hands to the ground, and the actors followed this suggestion, also rolling through the human wickets as human croquet balls instead of the hedgehogs imagined in the original.

One of the most striking and original of these bodily manipulations occurred early in the production, when Alice altered her size by sampling the food and drink she found on the glass table. Here she was guided in these actions by an actor standing in for Lewis Carroll. When it was time for Alice to grow in size he blew on her thumb as if it were the valve to an inflatable balloon. As she "grew" he sank to the floor at her feet. Then, seeking to provide a companion for this "balloon princess," he similarly inflated himself, towering up beside her. Alice hit him, apparently puncturing him, and he spun about the stage, imitating remarkably a rapidly deflating balloon with its air escaping.

The few properties utilized were simple, neutral, and generally put to multiple uses. The black umbrella that crowned the Jabberwock at the opening was echoed by four others later in the play when the non-Alice actors covered their head and shoulders with partially closed umbrellas to represent a forest. Another umbrella with slits in its top was placed over the only light on stage, creating a filtered forest-like effect. Later an actor twirled this umbrella in front of the light to create a strobe-like effect while the other actors opened their umbrellas to form the walls of a shop around Alice.

Humpty Dumpty's wall was created by stacking several chairs rather precariously on top of each other. One actor balanced on top while the others pantomimed holding ropes to support him. At the end of the scene he smashed a real egg against his forehead and toppled from the "wall" while the others released their imaginary supporting ropes. The most frequently used prop was the table, which like the umbrellas was employed in a variety of ways. It was used in a fairly conventional way to support the antics of the participants in the Mad Tea Party, but with chairs at one end to suggest a chimney, it became the Duchess's house, with the Duchess, the Cook, and the Cheshire Cat crouched beneath it. At another point, turned on its side, it served as a wall for chalk graffiti: "Alice eats mushrooms," "T. Dum and T. Dee" (who did not appear in the play) inside a heart, and "Lewis likes Liddell girls."

The latter inscription suggests a tone of barely repressed sexuality that ran through the production. Lewis Carroll's interest in prepubescent young women was a recurring motif, developed most clearly in the production's final major scene, between Alice and the White Knight (from "Through the Looking Glass"), played by Garry Bamman, the tallest actor in the company, who towered over Pietropinto's Alice. The frequent suggestion of "Eat Me" in the play rarely occurred without the distinct implications of a wink to the audience.

The rough-and-tumble costumes worn by the actors distinctly added to the impression that the production had grown out of rehearsal improvisations, as indeed it had. Like the properties and the doors that surrounded the acting area, these had a distinctly used and patched-together feeling, some apparently made from quilted blankets and comforters, others of scraps of old clothing and quilts. Two of the men (the White Knight and the Caterpillar) wore rough quilted coveralls without shirts. The Lewis Carroll actor, who also played the Cheshire Cat and other roles, wore a ragged quilted jumpsuit with stripes and bars faintly suggesting a Harlequin costume. Only a few accessories were added to these basic outfits. The Red Queen wore a crown, which appeared to be an upside-down lampshade, while the Dormouse at the Mad Tea Party sported a battered World War I helmet, but those were the only such additions. Alice's costume, though of the same material as the rest, was the most conventional in appearance—white sleeves and long stockings, dark slippers, and a dress of rough material with a black belt at the waist.

The Manhattan Project *Alice in Wonderland* toured widely during the following year and was revived several times in the early 1970s in New York. The company also presented several revivals, included Beckett's *Endgame* and one new play, the first by Wallace Shawn in New York, *Our Late Night*, at Joseph Papp's Public Theater in 1975. Later in the century Shawn and Gregory became among the best-known artistic collaborators in New York, but there was no hint of that future in the mid-1970s. Gregory apparently gave up theatrical production and went to Europe to work with Grotowski. The Manhattan Project continued on for a few years without him, but for some years *Alice in Wonderland* remained a much-admired, but rather isolated event in the American experimental theatre.

1972 Ariane Mnouchkine's *1789*

During the winter break of 1972–73 I returned to Paris, to find important changes in the theatre world there. Among these was the growth of important experimental theatres in the city's suburbs. During my earlier visit I traveled into the northern suburbs to Sartrouville to see the early works of Patrice Chéreau, to the federally funded Théâtre de l'Est, where Guy Rétoré offered such politically oriented drama as the work of Armand Gatti and Peter Hacks, and to the Théâtre de l'Ouest, in my own neighborhood, Boulogne-Billancourt, whose huge Renault factory had been one of the centers of the 1968 uprisings and where in the later months of that year still frequently offered Soviet-style agit-prop dramas and visiting, politically engaged opera troupes from North Vietnam, presenting condemnations of the ongoing American war there.

All of these suburban ventures were still thriving when I returned in 1972, but several new ones had been added, by far the most praised of which was Ariane Mnouchkine's Théâtre du Soleil. In fact I had seen the Soleil production of Arnold Wesker's *The Kitchen* in 1968, which was performed for an audience mostly of workers in the Renault Factory on the Île Seguin, about a mile south of my Billancourt apartment. I was impressed by the detailed naturalism of the staging and acting, but remember little to suggest that this would before long become the most honored of European companies.

Four years later that promise was much clearer, largely due to the enormous success of the company's collective meditation on the French Revolution, *1789*, which premiered at the end of 1970 and during the following year became a huge international success. Since my first book had been a study of the theatre of the French Revolution, seeing this production topped my theatre wish list in the early 1970s. Happily the production was revived in the fall of 1972, playing in repertory with the closely related subsequent work, *1793*, and I was fortunate to have a Parisian friend, whom I had met in 1968, who was able to get me tickets to the almost totally sold-out performances.

By this time the company was settled into what has been their home ever since, the Cartoucherie, to the east of Paris. The company discovered the Cartoucherie in 1970 when looking for a large empty rehearsal space. In 1972 when they returned to Paris after a triumphant opening of *1789* in Milan, unable to find a suitable venue in Paris, they decided to convert this space into a permanent home. It was a difficult choice, not only because the site, a long-abandoned ammunition factory, was in extreme disrepair, but even more, its location was anything but promising.

A location in the middle of a vast wooded area, the Bois de Vincennes, with no habitations or even other buildings anywhere nearby and far from public transportation, was perhaps ideal for an ammunition storehouse, but truly difficult for a theatre. Nevertheless, the space was cheap and available, and with no clear alternative, the company prepared the space as best they could and opened *1789* there at the end of 1970.

When I first visited the Cartoucherie two years later it had become, despite its remote location, one of the centers of the Parisian theatre, and even the difficulty of access had become part of its lore, as if it were a kind of pilgrimage site. Then, as now, most visitors approached the theatre by riding to the eastern end of Line 1, the first subway line opened in Paris and running through its center east to west. The final station was Château de Vincennes, named for the fourteenth-century castle that still dominates this area. Emerging from the subway, I was inevitably first aware of its massive bulk towering behind me against the night winter sky. In front was a large bus depot, where commuters from Paris transferred from the subway to one of the many busses fanning out to suburbs to the east. On one edge of this large area was a small wooden bus stop bearing the legend "Navette Cartoucherie," where one caught a shuttle bus into the depths of the woods that stretched eastward from the castle. I have subsequently walked to the theatre through the woods, about a forty-minute hike. On a summer evening it can be quite lovely, but not in the dead of winter, and the shuttle was clearly the vehicle of choice.

The shuttle deposited its passengers before the main gate of the Cartoucherie, but we were still some distance from the theatre itself, which occupied only a few of the larger buildings at the far end of the complex (since that time a number of the smaller buildings have been occupied by other experimental companies, so that the area is now a kind of small theatrical enclave in the woods). Proceeding through the stone gate and passing between two buildings, we came out into a large open area with buildings on three of its sides and Mnouchkine's venture in the far corner to our right. The Soleil public area was composed of three attached buildings, each really simply a very large, long shed, rather like a small aircraft hangar, the narrow side facing onto the open area at the center of the complex.

Then, as now, the audience entered the most distant of the three buildings, which was essentially a huge open hall that served as a foyer. As the audience came into this foyer, they were greeted by Mnouchkine and members of the company, as all milled about in the common space. Having been already welcomed personally to their productions by Grotowski and Gregory, and now by Mnouchkine and experiencing in these and other productions in recent years new and more informal actor/audience relationships and productions based more clearly and directly upon improvisational work, I began to feel that a new era in theatre was dawning. Looking back, however, I realize that much of this sort of work came to a peak in the late 1960s and early 1970s, and though it has never since entirely disappeared, it has diminished or turned in other directions, such as the recent vogue for "immersive" theatre.

The lobby, basically still a rough-hewn space, also served as a display area for material on the French Revolution and on the history of the Soleil itself, so that the audience had an opportunity to begin to orient themselves toward the production they were about to experience. This practice has in subsequent years become one of the hallmarks of the Soleil, with this massive lobby decorated to provide a visual introduction to the world of the work offered, including even simple meals also themed to the production, with Mnouchkine herself often among the servers.

From the lobby we entered the other two adjoining hangers, separated by iron pillars but essentially one huge performance space. The walls were plain brick, the floors stone. Coming in from the lobby, we first passed a large raked seating area, with a control booth above it, facing out into the performance space. Under this area (as in subsequent Soleil productions) the company was seated before mirrors applying makeup and preparing for the performance, in full view of the passing spectators. Seating was unreserved, and so I took a spot not too far up in the bleachers, but high enough to have a good view out over the playing area. This was composed of a large rectangular open area in the center, surrounded by five small wooden platform stages, each about five feet high and accessible by stairs on several sides, and with elevated runways connecting the end platforms with one side platform on one side and with two on the other. As the bleachers filled, a smaller number of audience members remained in the center of the performance section, becoming embedded, as in *Orlando Furioso*, a part of the action, surrogates for the citizens of Revolutionary Paris.

The production presented a carnivalesque series of scenes creating a kind of popular or folk history of the Revolution. Sometimes the spotlights picked out a single figure, like Marat, and at others scenes were being played simultaneously on all five platforms, under general lighting, giving rather the impression of an immersive fairground experience. Such sequences recalled *Orlando Furioso* to me, especially when actors would descend from the platforms and push their way through the standing audience members to reach another platform. More impressively, there were scenes where the actors would consciously engage the spectators, most notably in spreading word of the fall of the Bastille. Here individual actors gathered small groups of spectators around them, some even coming up into the bleachers, each rather quietly but excitedly reporting what he or she had seen at the storming. Gradually the volume, excitement, and enthusiasm built until the entire theatre was engulfed in a riotous celebration, with flags and banners flying, drums rolling, tumblers, acrobats, and audience members mixed together dancing and celebrating both on the platforms and throughout the house.

A stunning variety of popular entertainment forms were utilized, offering a constantly shifting theatrical experience. There were puppets of all sizes, from small marionettes, with their manipulators clearly visible, to gigantic figures representing the King and Queen in the style of Bread and Puppet or the nightmare figures in Brook's *Marat/Sade*, to actors dressed as and imitating puppets (a device that would become central in Mnouchkine's 2001 *Tambours sur la digue*). Many of the scenes on the platforms were played before crude canvas backdrops, and in exaggerated makeup and tawdry but obviously symbolic costumes clearly suggesting the tradition of European street performers for centuries. Sometimes the backdrops were used as illustration boards in the manner of other street performances, with an actor explaining events by pointing out items painted on the canvas. A few scenes were almost naturalistic, most notably one in which four peasant fathers, on different platforms, murder their own starving children, but on the whole the style was bold cartoonish, and full of exuberant energy.

In the latter part of the production, as each new faction comes to power, one of its representatives would shout, "The Revolution is finished." The last group to appear was the triumphant bourgeoisie, who entertained themselves with a final puppet show demonstrating their own victory over the nobility and the clergy. As they were leaving the theatre, satisfied by their own miniature version of *1793*, the unrepentant revolutionaries Marat and Babeuf appeared in spotlights on two of the small stages, demanding that the Revolution continue until its goals of liberty and equality are truly met. Immediately after this, triumphant music was heard from all directions, the houselights flared up, and the company came running in from all sides, up onto the platforms, and began bowing to the audience.

They continued smiling, bowing, blowing kisses to the spectators and dancing with those in the central area while others (including myself) came down from the bleachers to join in the celebrations. Others remained at the seats, but all were standing, cheering, and applauding. The sense of universal celebration was almost the exact opposite of the overwhelming of the audience response at the end of Brook's *Marat/ Sade*, but after five minutes or so the music faded away, as did the actors, and the spectators began to gather up their coats and depart. The excitement and glow of the experience still remained, but so did the final grim words of Marat and Babeuf. Could we really be content with converting the dreams of the Revolution into Guignol entertainment?

Perhaps the end the production left many viewers with the same sense of a still unfulfilled social vision that darkened the conclusion of *Marat/Sade*. Certainly these questions gave a more solemn edge to my general mood of excitement and exhilaration as I boarded the shuttle and headed back through the dark woods to Paris, a glittering example of the triumph of the bourgeois culture that the production showed emerging triumphant from the Revolution.

1973 Charles Ludlam's *Camille*

Except for Andy Warhol, whose challenges to traditional high art made him one of the best-known cultural figures of the mid-1960s, I had almost no knowledge of the performance subculture that gave rise to the Ridiculous theatre until I saw the production of Ronald Tavel's *Gorilla Queen* in 1967. This wildly freewheeling amalgam of parody, camp humor, pop culture references, and outrageous sexual jokes was so praised by the reviewers, particularly by the alternative presses, that the initial run, at the Judson Poets' Theatre, was sold out almost at once, before I had a chance to see this new sensation.

Fortunately it was very quickly moved more uptown to the still quite small Martinique Theatre on Thirty-Second Street, where I was able to see it in the spring of that year. Basically the musical play was a burlesque of King Kong and Tarzan movies, with a chorus of glittering and singing orangutans, a transvestite ape god, a witch doctor, and a sacrificial maiden, but this only provided a framework for an exuberant three-ring circus entertainment in which costumes, acting style, and script were all pushed to the most outrageous extremes.

Long a fan of the lunatic humor of the Marx Brothers films, I was delighted by this theatrical fun house, even more expansive and clearly reflective of the more open society of the late 1960s (*Hair* opened later this same year). I eagerly awaited the next production of Tavel's company, Play-House of the Ridiculous, but Tavel moved on, and when I attended an apparent reorganized company, now called the Ridiculous Theatrical Company, that fall, its head and leading dramatist was

Charles Ludlam, who over the next twenty years would become not only the name most associated with this theatre, but one of the best-known and most beloved artists of the late twentieth-century American avant-garde.

Although the first Ludlam play I saw, *Big Hotel*, was even more formless than *Gorilla Queen*, composed essentially of a series of encounters in a hotel lobby, I enjoyed it even more, largely because in addition to the freewheeling slapstick and gags, the script drew upon an astonishing variety of literary and pop culture references. In college I had discovered James Joyce's *Finnegans Wake*, which fascinated me with a similar web of wildly wide-ranging references. When Ludlam, parodying Greta Garbo playing Norma Desmond in *Sunset Boulevard*, opened the production with the line, "I weel kiss thy lips, O Magic Mandarin, I weel kiss thy lips," simultaneously parodying the Strauss opera, the popular hair gel, and one of the most memorable lines from Oscar Wilde's *Salomé*, I was totally converted to his work.

Over the next five years I saw several other Ludlam productions, which continued to delight and impress me with their manic energy as well as their range of comedic styles and literary references. Even so, I was unprepared for the achievement of Ludlam's *Camille* in 1973, indisputably among his most remarkable and daring creations. In 1973 the Ridiculous Theatrical Company had not yet found a regular home, and *Camille* was first presented at a small theatre on West Thirteenth Street, which had only opened the previous year, one of its first offerings being Ludlam's previous show, *Corn*. The theatre, which still exists today, was a tiny standard off-off-Broadway space, converted from the basement floor of a narrow townhouse. One entered down a flight of stairs, passing through a small lobby with box office and bar and then into the theatre filling the far end of the space, with around sixty seats between the two side brick walls of the building, with a prosceniumless stage at the far end.

Although the comic energy and imagination of this production were no less than in earlier Ludlam shows, they took a rather different, and more daring, direction. For the first time, Ludlam did not create a new collage text, but followed closely, scene by scene, a long-familiar text in the popular theatre, Dumas fils's *Camille*, a great favorite of such Ludlam icons as Bernhardt and Garbo. Moreover, without departing from his commitment to the tradition of farce-comedy, he undertook and astonishingly succeeded in maintaining the play's traditional pull at the audience's heartstrings. With only a small measure of irony, he called his production *Camille—a Tearjerker.*

Ludlam's entrance was one of his most famous. At first glance it was almost as if the legendary Garbo had come back to life. Ludlam had exactly copied her style of dress, the dark ringlets that framed her pale-white face, its color reflected in the white carnation above her forehead, even the striking dark eyebrows and lashes, and the carefully sculpted thin red lips. Scarcely had this impression registered, however, before one noted that his plunging neckline revealed a hairy and distinctly masculine chest. The stunned audience, almost all male and clearly Ludlam fans, were delighted at this challenge to drag performance itself and greeted this vision with cheers and wild applause. Those who expected a camp send-up of Dumas's play were soon surprised to find that Ludlam did nothing to stress this incongruity, but played the role with such conviction and passion that all were soon drawn into the emotional manipulations of the original story.

Throughout the evening Ludlam kept the audience balanced on the knife-edge between the serious emotional situations in which the play abounds and sudden bursts of comic incongruity, which, astonishingly, did not destroy the sentimental appeal of the piece, but somehow deepened and enriched it. There was much less physical comedy here than in previous pieces, although the heightened acting and vocal style of precursors like Garbo were often evoked. This gave to the whole performance a whiff of parody, but the mood was really more one of a shared delight in old-fashioned heightened theatricality, an important aspect of modern reception of films like the Garbo *Camille* themselves.

The clearest echoes of previous Ridiculous productions were thus not physical or visual, but verbal, and even here, *Camille* showed a rather different side of Ludlam's dramaturgy. Although the production was itself a continual exploration of lines and situations from the French original, the sort of freewheeling intertextuality found in earlier (and most subsequent) Ludlam works was little in evidence here, and indeed would have pulled audiences out of the re-creation of the nineteenth-century melodramatic world of the play, the emotional appeal of which Ludlam was seeking to evoke.

When Ludlam inserted examples of his explicit sexual humor or bizarre literary references, these were carefully worked into the texture of

Dumas's play. Thus the somewhat risqué story Saint-Gaudens tells in the first act Ludlam simply made more sexually explicit and set it in the Opera so that he could inset the typically Ridiculous title of the work being performed: *Zinnia, the Mute Girl of Cincinnati.*

The most memorable such elaboration, both perfectly suited to the situation and yet an excellent example of Ludlam wit, occurred at the beginning of the final act, where the dying Marguerite lies huddled in her bed in poverty in an unheated bedroom early in the morning of a cold New Year's Day, with snow blowing past the window. In Dumas's play the thirsty Marguerite awakens and asks her faithful nurse Nanine for a cup of tea. At this point Ludlam added a second request. "I'm cold," she says to Nanine. "Throw another faggot on the fire." The drowsy Nanine, played by Everett Quinton, Ludlam's partner and a leading figure in the company, responded helplessly, "There are no more faggots in the house." Whereupon Ludlam, rising feebly from the bed, looked plaintively out into the audience, repeating in a wondering voice, "No faggots in the house? Open the window, Nanine. See if there are any in the street." This exchange, delivered to an audience that, like most of the Ridiculous audiences, was composed in large part of gay men who enjoyed nothing more than a joke about gay sexuality, caused near pandemonium, especially since these two seasoned comedians knew how to ride the laughs so that each line built the reactions to new heights.

And yet, despite this memorable comic opening, Ludlam remained for most of the remainder of this emotional act surprisingly faithful to Dumas, sequence by sequence and often line by line, he and his fellow actors playing with the utmost sincerity but also with enough of the emotional exaggeration within the material itself to keep the audience constantly vacillating between the comic and the seriously sentimental. The last five minutes or so of the production followed the original word for word and clearly produced in much of the audience something very close to the emotionality of the original "tearjerker," which was clearly Ludlam's intention. Only in the very last line did Ludlam make a tiny but telling adjustment. Quinton, as the faithful Nanine, kneeling beside the body of Marguerite, repeated Dumas's own closing line, "Much will be forgiven you, for you loved much," but then, in a final, deft touch, added a surprising coda: "Toodle-oo, Marguerite," which provided no small jolt to the many audience members, myself included, who had indeed been brought to the point of tears by the death scene.

Ludlam was said to have often had thoughts of his own mortality, one of the many things that reportedly attracted him to this role, and indeed his life was tragically short. He died in 1987, just fourteen years after his first major triumph, in *Camille*, though during those years he created another twenty works that solidified his position as one of the great comic geniuses of the American theatre.

His obituary appeared on the front page of the *New York Times*, and the *Village Voice* devoted a full page to his passing.

Ludlam's funeral service was held in St. Joseph's Church, in Greenwich Village just one block away from the theatre on Sheridan Square that had housed the Theatre of the Ridiculous since 1978 and which is most associated in my mind with that company. After attending the service I walked by the theatre and found that a makeshift memorial shrine had already appeared before its doors—candles, letters, cards, and of course flowers, recalling the lavish bouquets of *Camille*. Sheridan Square, like many of the so-called squares in New York, is not at all square in shape, but is in fact two not quite connected long triangles. The site of the Stonewall riots is on the northernmost section and the bottom of the southernmost section is a short street, really an extension of Barrow Street, where Ludlam's downstairs performance space was located. Later this short street was officially renamed "Charles Ludlam Lane" by the city (although I recently noted that the single street sign is now gone).

The Church of St. Joseph was packed for Ludlam's funeral, even the sides and back and balcony filled with standing as well as seated crowds. In addition to a mass, with the clergy in elaborate robes and the sanctuary filled with incense, as Ludlam doubtless would have loved, friends and associates read Bible passages and in the manner of such observances, recalled personal and professional memories. The final eulogy was delivered by the playwright Leon Katz, who concluded his remarks with an evocation of the climax of Camille. He concluded his eulogy with that final line: "Much will be forgiven you, for you loved much. Toodle-oo, Marguerite." The church erupted in laughter, a standing ovation, and then shouts from all sides of "Toodle-oo, Charles," the most fitting and moving tribute to a departed artist I have ever heard.

1974 Richard Foreman's *Pain(t)*

In the fall of 1972, one of the most talked-about productions off-off-Broadway was the musical entertainment *Dr. Selavy's Magic Theatre*, a multimedia event presented at the Mercer Arts Center, which had recently opened as a home for video art, installation art, and mixed-media work of various kinds. Its contribution to the New York experimental scene was short-lived because the building that housed it collapsed in 1973, and its programs and mission moved further uptown to The Kitchen, where they continue today.

Dr. Selavy somewhat suggested to me the work of Ludlam in the nearby West Village, primarily in its surrealistic mixture of elements from everyday life, pop culture, film, and theatre, with a kind of Marx Brothers disregard of, irreverence for, and dismissal of coherent structure. Ludlam's palimpsest text was notably absent here, however; the only words in *Selavy* were the amusing but calculatedly banal lyrics of the songs by composer Stanley Silverman. I was sufficiently intrigued by the whimsical visual effects and the rather Brechtian presentational style of the performers, however, to follow director Foreman's work, which he announced in the program as taking place in what he called his "Ontological-Hysteric Theatre."

I had already missed the first productions of this venture, but I did attend the next two, *Sophia=(Wisdom)* early in 1973 and *Particle Theory* a few months later. Although each of these three productions was performed in a different space, an underlying similarity of approach was strikingly clear and was quite unlike either that of the Theatre of the Ridiculous or any other experimental work in New York at that time. Foreman, like many experimental artists of the early 1970s, built up his creations within an empty space, often with the walls visible or only partly hidden by dark hangings. He also quite disregarded the conventions of the realistic drama, both in the unconventional movement and posing of his actors, and in the use of simple and often clearly artificial set pieces, exposed lighting instruments, and signs providing information to both actors and audience, all devices that connected him to the traditions of Brechtian staging. The rather Brechtian signs and the live but bodiless voice of some unseen commentator were quite different from what might be found in Brechtian productions, however. While

Brecht in *Galileo* or *Mother Courage* provides short scene summaries or the location and date of a scene, Foreman's signs (and the projected voice, which was his own) gave instructions to the actors ("sit down" or "leave the room") or posed questions to the audience ("Can you imagine a body like that?" "Do you remember what she said before?") or even asked them to participate imaginatively ("Imagine a curtain here").

Other elements of his approach were even more untraditional. Perhaps most striking was his use of white ropes and strings, stretched across the playing area to create alternative perspectives or areas of focus. Houses and properties appeared in diminutive size, often making it difficult to judge scale or position accurately. The actors, who had basically the same neutral names in each of these plays—Max, Rhoda, Ben, Sophia—did not attempt to create characters or coherent lines of action. They simply presented a series of actions, some dictated by the voice or signs. Instead of a traditional theatre narrative, then, the audience was presented with a series of stage actions, rather more resembling a living artwork than a conventional theatre piece. Clearly the intention was essentially a phenomenological one, to make the audience aware moment by moment of the physical process of participating in this presentation.

By the time I attended Foreman's *Pain(t)* in the spring of 1974 then, I was already generally familiar with his approach (though none of his illuminating manifestos had yet been published). By that time Foreman, like Ludlam, had created a core audience that was familiar with his aesthetic and tended to form the basis of his repeating public (as they continued to do in the future). Thus, although each new production took up different themes and concerns, the memory of previous Foreman work soon became, as it did for me, a central part of the experience. An important aspect of *Pain(t)* was that it was the first production Foreman mounted in a theatre space he created himself, which was located on an upper floor of what was essentially an apartment building at 141 Wooster Street. At this time the area known as Soho (SOuth of HOuston Street) was becoming a center for experimental theatre work, thanks in significant measure to the pioneering efforts of George Maciunas, a cofounder of the Dadaist experimental group Fluxus, who purchased the building at 80 Wooster Street in 1967 and divided it into small performing spaces and residences for artists. The main performing area was Jonas Mekas's Cinematheque, which not only showed experimental films, but provided performance space for Fluxus events, Happenings, and the first productions by Foreman. Just around the corner from the Cinematheque, on Spring Street, Robert Wilson had a loft where he performed his first solo piece, *Baby Blood*, in 1967. A year later, Richard Schechner opened the Performing Garage, also on Wooster, just one block south of the Cinematheque.

Although the other major center for experimental theatre in this concentrated area, the Ohio Theatre, did not arrive until the mid-1980s (to a space just a few doors south of the Cinematheque), I was already familiar with this area as a new home of experimental work thanks to both the Cinematheque and the productions at the Performing Garage like Schechner's *Dionysus in 69* when I first visited Foreman's new home on Wooster.

The space was slighter larger and deeper than he had at his disposal in previous venues, about 30 feet wide and 150 feet deep, but its organization was much the same. The areas for staging and seating were approximately equal, the seating six or seven rows of basic and fairly uncomfortable wooden bleachers, the top one so high that the heads of taller seated audience members almost touched the ceiling. There was no raised stage; the performing area began on the same level as the front row, but in the middle of the row Foreman sat in a small enclosed area, back to the audience, with a microphone, to provide a regular voice-over commentary. I was reminded of this effect years later when I saw the work of Polish director Tadeusz Kantor, who, though he did not speak, watched each of his productions from a highly visible onstage chair.

From time to time one could see the side walls of the stage area, but they were usually hidden, mostly by drapes and curtains, but sometimes by simple scenic units. There was no proscenium, but two floor-to-ceiling supporting Doric columns, perhaps fifteen feet apart, gave the suggestion of a frame. As always, white ropes crossed the visual field, one horizontal, between the pillars, just above head-height and others swooping down from the flies. As usual, a miscellaneous collection of lighting instruments was clearly visible above the stage, along with two small period chandeliers (a favorite decorative element for Foreman), one near the flies on the left, the other about shoulder height on the right. Signs were less used here than in earlier works, but were still present, and sometimes individual letters making up a word were brought on by the actors.

The characters in *Pain(t)* bore the same names as in earlier Foreman works, but brought no other individual context with them. Indeed except for Rhonda, played by Kate Manheim, Foreman's wife, none of these parts were played by the same actors I had seen the previous year in *Sophia=(Wisdom) Part 3*. In *Pain(t)* Rhonda is or maybe was a famous painter, sought out for a portrait by Max and alternately inspiring admiration and jealous hatred from the other women, as potential rivals. In fact the production, unlike earlier Foreman pieces, focused almost entirely upon two characters, Rhonda and Eleanor, played by Manheim and her younger sister Nora, who had not previously worked with Foreman. Although female artists were the presumed subject of the work, in fact, as feminist critics like Jill Dolan pointed out, the production was primarily concerned with the male gaze. Although Rhonda did appear in her studio in a typical artist's smock, she far more often appeared in the nude, as she had in previous Foreman productions. This was hardly a major surprise in New York theatre in the early 1970s. Tom O'Horgan, the director of the phenomenally successful Broadway production of *Hair* with its famous nude scene, remarked in a later interview that for the next six months every new show that opened in New York had an obligatory nude scene in it.

Despite this hyperbole, the next few years did see a flood of nudity, on-Broadway, where the cast of Kenneth Tynan's 1971 *Oh! Calcutta!* opened each performance by all displaying their nude bodies to the audience, and off-Broadway, where Richard Schechner's 1969 *Dionysus in 69* presented nude Bacchic revels in the very laps of his audiences. Seeking neither the erotic nor the ecstatic, Foreman's nudity was in fact much closer (as was especially appropriate of course in *Pain(t)*) to the nudity in classical painting. Although one can never remove a certain eroticism from the display of the body, Foreman's overall visual approach encouraged a more abstract reception, treating the body, like the physical properties and the other elements within the scenic field, as simply a part of an overall composition, a stimulus to perception and reflection.

This seemed to me particularly clear in the very careful and planned visual balance within most of the nude scenes. As I have noted, the production relied heavily on confrontations between Rhonda and Eleanor, and very frequently they would mirror each other's positions within the overall stage composition, but with Rhonda completely nude and Eleanor fully clothed. Kate Davy's often-reproduced photograph of the production shows a scene with them in those contrasting positions, the pale body of Rhonda surrounded by a soft white drapery, the white ropes leading visually to her and beneath the high chandelier to the left and Eleanor in a contrastingly rigid black framing box to the right, next to the lowered chandelier. In such arrangements I was strongly reminded of a very similar scene in *Sophia=(Wisdom) Part 3* where Rhonda and her counterfigure, Sophia, were seated at two ends of a very long, waiting room-style bench parallel to the audience seats. Their rather slumped postures, turned slightly toward each other, were almost identical, but Rhonda was totally nude and Sophia in a rich fur coat with an elaborate fur neckpiece. The visual echo of Titian's famous allegorical painting *Sacred and Profane Love* was so striking that I remain certain that Foreman was inspired by it. This is not at all to suggest that the quotation of works of visual art is a part of his technique, indeed I cannot recall of any other instance as clear as this one, but it does emphasize how much closer his work has always been to painting than to traditional theatre.

After *Pain(t)*, the Ontological-Hysteric Theatre moved to its first permanent home, a few blocks away, a loft on Broadway, where it remained for the next decade. It then offered works at a number of major off-off-Broadway locations, including La Mama, the Public Theater, and at its old neighbor, the Performing Garage, before settling in 1992 into its current home in the East Village in Saint Mark's Church-in-the-Bowery, where in addition to presenting its own works, it has provided performance space for a wide variety of younger experimental companies.

1975 Giorgio Strehler's *King Lear*

My sabbatical in 1968 in Paris had whetted my appetite for European theatre, and from that time onward my wife and I tried when possible to spend all or part of the usual January winter break seeing European theatre. Generally at this time of my life that meant primarily the theatres of London and Paris. In January 1975 we could easily and happily have spent the whole time in London, where we were able to enjoy such rich fare as the Royal Shakespeare Company, in winter residence, presenting Stoppard's *Travesties* and a dazzling Ian McKellen appearing in the title roles of both Marlowe's *Dr. Faustus* and Wedekind's *The Marquis of Keith*. We decided, however, to spend a few days in Milan, partly, to be honest, to seek a break in the grim London midwinter weather but more importantly, to see something by Giorgio Strehler. James Clancy, my Cornell colleague with a strong international interest, often spoke of Strehler's *Servant of Two Masters*, which he had seen in Paris in the early 1950s, as the greatest theatre piece he had ever witnessed, and Strehler's productions of Brecht were widely considered among the best on the continent. Like Barrault, Strehler had been challenged as an establishment figure by the protestors of 1968, and like Barrault this confrontation led to his leaving the theatre, although in Strehler's case willingly. He created a new politically engaged company that he headed for the next six years until 1972, when he was urged by the authorities in Milan to resume directorship of the Piccolo. His first new production there was *King Lear*, and I decided to travel to Milan to witness this major new work.

I was quite astonished by my first view of the Piccolo Teatro. Based on its reputation for experimental work and its name, I had expected a modest performance space, not similar to an off-off-Broadway loft of course, but more one of the more established off-Broadway houses, seating perhaps three to four hundred people. In fact I found the theatre was a monumental building, on a commanding corner location just two blocks from the Duomo, and of a size rivaling or surpassing most Broadway houses. The interior was no less impressive. The auditorium followed the traditional European pattern with balcony seating extending around the sides of the auditorium, and the interior had a rather more sleek and modern feeling than most Broadway houses (many built in the 1920s), while the interior was completely rebuilt in the late 1940s, having been totally destroyed in the war. Even with this somewhat different seating configuration, however, it was clear that the capacity of the so-called Piccolo rivaled that of major Broadway houses.

The first image of the production was Tino Carraro as Lear, standing alone in a downstage spotlight, a commanding, and yet somewhat caricatured figure, enveloped in billowing gilded robes, wearing a simple and clearly fake golden crown, his face and short-cropped beard in clown white makeup resting upon a large white ruffle collar. Scarcely had he promised to express his "darker purpose" when a stagehand rapidly separated him from the audience by pulling across the stage in front of him a transparent curtain. I immediately recognized this as one of the standard staging devices in Strehler's theatre, which I had seen in a number of illustrations. This traverse downstage curtain was a direct borrowing from Brecht's Berliner Ensemble, indeed often called the "Brecht curtain," tall enough to hide the actors behind but not the upper parts of the scenery. It was normally, as in this case, drawn manually across the stage along a quite visible line. Here the curtain, although transparent, had traced upon it an outline map of Lear's kingdom, and on which the King, standing upstage of it, indicated his divisions. When Cordelia failed him, he first literally drove her into outer darkness, into the area between the Brecht curtain and the audience, where she remained as a silent silhouette, and then later, he slashed his sword through this curtain and its map, leaving the two halves on the floor for Goneril and Regan to fold up and carry off like the weekly washing after his departure.

Once the curtain had been sliced open, the acting area behind it and the assembled company became more visible, although this scene, like most of the production, tended to keep the actors in a pool of light center stage. Essentially the stage was open and empty, suggesting the approach of Peter Brook, or more likely, of Brecht, but while both of these tended to favor open neutral spaces, Strehler's setting, when fully illuminated, was much more in the tradition of realism. It was revealed to be in fact the interior of a huge circus tent, with ropes hanging down on the sides. The entire acting area was surrounded by a traditional circus ring and the area within it not a traditional floor, but a more yielding surface of earth, mixed with sawdust or sand. In the middle of the ring were a series of small raised platforms and ramps that provided the actors with solider footing, some slight elevation, and, occasionally, planking that could be used for balancing and acrobatic movements. Although Lear was the visually dominant figure, the rest of the company, partly in shadow, reinforced his appearance. The royalty wore gaudy but faded and worn robes, resembling the contents of an old theatrical storage bin. Gloucester's sons, and indeed most of the male younger generation, wore black tight-fitting leather jackets and breeches rather like those of biker gangs. Both daughters had exaggerated hair treatments, Goneril a white bouffant style like a fright wig and Regan equally exaggerated flowing waves of dark red.

The makeup, like the costumes, was theatrically exaggerated. Tino Carraro as Lear in particular was clearly recognizable as the traditional white clown, typically the leading clown of a circus company.

Gloucester was portrayed as a lesser Lear—billowing but simpler cloaks, a build similar to that of Lear, but, most strikingly, similar close-cropped hair and white clown makeup. The conventional opposing figure to the white clown is the Auguste clown, the least intelligent clown who traditionally plays the zany fool. These two figures, their traditions, and their routines were particularly familiar to me at this time because only a few years earlier I had seen in New York the documentary/fantasy film *The Clowns* by Federico Fellini, Strehler's great countryman, which had focused upon this traditional pair.

Gloucester had no countering Auguste, although later in the play Edgar as "Mad Tom" provided a similar contrasting figure. Obviously, in the case of Lear it was the Fool who was costumed and made up as his Auguste counterpart, with heavy face painting, a red nose, baggy trousers, a green, well-worn sequined tailcoat, and a battered black top hat. Most importantly, Strehler followed a tradition often employed in this play and going back, some have argued, to Shakespeare's own times, casting the same actor (in this case a young actress, Ottavia Piccolo) as both Cordelia and the Fool. Often the routines between these two characters were delivered in such a way, both physically and verbally, as to suggest circus routines. Another clear echo called up by this relationship was that of the clown-like tramps in Beckett's *Waiting for Godot*. Since the appearance of Jan Kott's enormously influential *Shakespeare Our Contemporary* a decade before, suggestions of Beckett had become common in new interpretations of *Lear*, beginning with the famous Beckettian production by Peter Brook that I had seen at Lincoln Center soon after Kott's book appeared.

Like circus performers, also, the actors frequently acknowledged the presence of the audience. Edmund in fact was seated among the spectators for the opening scene, and when the sisters left the stage, he jumped up, leaped over the footlights, and then turned to present his opening soliloquy. The Fool devoted almost as much attention to the audience as he did to Lear, sometimes actually leaving the stage to discuss the situation directly with the spectators, and Lear himself often seemed to appeal directly to the public. This casual acceptance of the theatricality of the performance allowed stagehands to move easily on and off the stage to adjust the modest scenic arrangements. Probably the most striking example of this blending of onstage and offstage activity occurred in the sequence where Lear appears with his full entourage at Goneril's home. The company being much too small to represent a stage full of knights, much of the backstage crew filled out their numbers, still in their casual work clothes.

In an evening of memorable images, I found those of the final sequence the most powerful, building as they did upon all that had gone before. Strehler speeded up and condensed the final scenes of the play so that everything from the duel of the brothers to the ending consisted of one continued action. He emphasized the disguises of both brothers by staging a duel in which they were both blindfolded within an enclosed space of waist-high walls, each armed with a knife and seeking each other out by sound and feel. The sisters and their husbands watched from behind this wall, and when Edgar triumphed, he removed his own blindfold and then that of his dying brother. Instead of leaving the stage to kill herself and her sister as in Shakespeare, the stricken Goneril threw herself over the wall to come closer to him and plunged a knife into her own breast, falling as her poisoned sister collapsed over the corral on the opposite side. Edmund, revealing he had wooed both sisters, pulled their two bodies to join him in the center, then, revealing his plot against Lear and Cordelia, he fell backward, knocking down the walls of the corral and leaving the stage essentially clear.

Then came a moment of unforgettable theatricality. The back wall of the cyclorama tent, up until then enclosing the universe of this play, was ripped open with a frightful tearing sound, recalling, but in far greater intensity, Lear's ripping apart of the downstage curtain at the opening, and the pale face of the dead Cordelia emerged from the center of the tear, as if the womb of the universe had ripped open to give birth to her. She was, however, in fact carried in the arms of Lear, who bore her slowly downstage as he delivered his famous "Howl, howl, howl, howl!" He bore her body to the center of the stage, where already the corpses of Edmund and her sisters were stretched out, and placed her parallel to the footlights in front of them, kneeling over her to deliver his final lines.

Traditionally these lines are given with Lear surrounded by the sympathetic figures of Albany, Edgar, and of course the faithful Kent, but Strehler elected to have Lear die in isolation, except for the body of his daughter, upon whom was his entire focus. There was no interchange with the other characters, who retreated into the dark areas at the sides of the stage, and on "Pray you, undo this button" Lear himself ripped open his collar as if preparing himself for lying down in death next to his daughter.

Once these two new lifeless bodies were added to those already on the stage, the other figures slowly and quietly made their way in from the shadows. As in Shakespeare, Kent removes himself and the sorrowing Albany and Edgar speak the final words. Significantly, Strehler gave them mostly to Edgar, whose gradual maturing to a wise and temperate leader was one of the important subactions in this interpretation. Strehler also slightly but significantly altered the final line from the neutral "We that are young / Shall never see so much, nor live so long" to a much more dedicated "We that are young / will not permit / such tragic events to occur again." Thus the fatalism that makes this one of Shakespeare's darkest plays was mitigated, if only to a limited extent, by Strehler's determined belief in the possibility of social progress.

1976 Ntozake Shange's *for colored girls* . . .

One of the most striking developments in the New York theatre in the decade between 1965 and 1975 was the Black Arts movement and the new generation of African American theatre artists that came to prominence with it. The dominant and most controversial theatre artist in that movement was surely LeRoi Jones, who in 1967 changed his name to the Muslim/African Amiri Baraka, to mark his personal and professional reorientation toward African American cultural expression. During that decade black theatre artists, almost all men, were presented in many off-Broadway theatres, but the two theatres most devoted to their work were the New Lafayette Players in Harlem and the Negro Ensemble Company, located on Second Avenue, just a block north of what was then the home of Ellen Stewart's La Mama. Indeed these two nearby ventures were the pioneers of the shift in off-Broadway theatres from the old Sheridan Square area (the West Village) to what was then beginning to be called the East Village. At these two theatres I followed the developing careers of artists like Ed Bullins and Douglas Turner Ward. I even made one trip out to Newark to attend a Baraka play at his cultural center, Spirit House, but found a very different welcome there. An imposing black doorman strongly advised me that I should "get my white ass back to New York," which advice I thought it best to follow.

I recall seeing only one African American play during those years at the Public, but it was a significant one, Charles Gordone's *No Place to*

Be Somebody, which won Gordone the Pulitzer Prize in 1970. The next African American play I attended at the Public was seven years later, on a summer evening in 1977, and it offered a totally different experience. This was Ntozake Shange's *for colored girls who have considered suicide / when the rainbow is enuf.* The performance had transferred to the Public from a new addition to the black theatre scene, Woodie King's New Federal Theatre, which had opened in 1965 at the rather remote Henry Street Settlement House on the Lower East Side. Its move to the Public brought it, however, to the center of the off-Broadway world, since Joseph Papp had during the past decade become the dominant new figure of the New York stage. When I had attended *Hair* almost a decade before at the intimate Anspacher stage (where *for colored girls* was also presented), the Anspacher was the only performance space open in the still unfinished building and Papp's theatre ventures included only the Anspacher, the Delacorte Theater, where he offered free Shakespeare in Central Park, and the Mobile Theater, which extended his offerings to more remote areas of the city. Now a decade later, Papp's empire had reached its greatest extent, with no less than thirteen venues around the city presenting his projects. The Delacorte and the Mobile Theater remained quite active, but his base was now the Public Theater on Lafayette Street, with five operating performance spaces. In 1973 the troubled Repertory Theatre at Lincoln Center closed after nine seasons and two failed directorships and Papp was invited to establish a new organization there. This brought two more major theatres under his administration. To complete the range and importance of his work at this time, the Public had moved two of its productions to Broadway, *A Chorus Line* and Dennis Reardon's *The Leaf People,* and was coproducing with another leading off-Broadway organization, the Manhattan Theatre Club, *In the Vine Time* by Ed Bullins, another leader of the Black Arts movement.

For colored girls attracted an audience with many more African Americans than one normally saw at the Public then or since, although it was still far from the predominantly black audiences seen at the New Lafayette in Harlem, or even at the nearby Negro Ensemble, which had during its first decade built up a substantial and faithful black audience. What was striking at the Public, however, was the large number of young black women, a group not at all well represented in either of those other two venues, and obviously the group most directly addressed by Shange's new work.

The title provided a clear indication that this new work would depart distinctly from normal theatrical expectations, as did the official description of the work as an unfamiliar genre, a "choreopoem." The previous examples of black theatre I had seen were for the most part either fairly traditional social dramas with black characters, like *No Place to Be Somebody*, or rather more direct and strident works, often with a sardonic, absurdist edge, like Baraka's *Dutchman* or Ward's *Day of Absence*. The surrealistic nightmares of the only major female dramatist so far to appear in the Black Arts movement, Adrienne Kennedy, offered a very different dramatic vision, but *for colored girls* was something quite new, as distinct from Kennedy as it was from Gordone or Baraka.

Visually, the work was quite different not only from all of these earlier examples of black theatre but indeed from almost anything on the New York stage at that time. The stage was totally devoid of any properties or setting, simply an empty space for the movement of the costumed bodies of the actresses. As such it much more resembled a dance space than a conventional theatrical one. The lighting was also more like that of a dance work, providing focus and defining the constantly changing performance area. The work had no through narrative, although a number of disparate narratives were embedded within it. Overall it had something of the shape of a coming-of-age story, beginning with childhood memories, continuing through a high school prom and a loss of virginity, and proceeding onward through other trials and disillusionments without ever totally losing a hope for something better. This general shape, however, was woven out of fragments of memory and pieces of stories that overlapped, deepened, and enriched each other, picking up and developing themes in a quite musical (or poetic) fashion as the evening progressed. The performers were seven young black women, identified only by the color of the clothing they were wearing: the Lady in Red, the Lady in Brown, the Lady in Yellow, the Lady in Purple, the Lady in Green, the Lady in Rose, and the Lady in Orange, the last played by Shange herself.

The text was composed of twenty poems of varying lengths, but even though certain poems contained short narratives and were fairly self-contained and even though on the whole each poem was primarily presented by one of the ladies, all seven actresses were on stage throughout the evening and were often in verbal or physical conversation, adding their own comments or observations to the main line of the narration, interacting with, sympathizing with, or even mocking or parodying the lady currently presenting the main text. The Lady in Brown introduced the evening, evoking childhood memories and speaking directly to the audience, who throughout the evening were treated as a silent witness to the ongoing soliloquies and conversation. The others were at first unmoving, but gradually joined in her childhood games and songs ("Mammy's Little Baby" and "Sally Walker") and provided brief geographical introductions (all were "outsiders"—"I'm outside Chicago," "I'm outside St. Louis," etc.).

For the next sequence the evocations of childhood changed to those of puberty—the playground games were replaced by youth dances of the 1960s—the Swim, the Pony, the Nose Dive.

Against this background the Lady in Yellow told the story of her loss of virginity at her graduation dance. Sexuality played a central role in the lives represented in the piece, and although the young women were well aware of the pleasures of sex, they were even more conscious of how sex was commonly used as a force for domination and exploitation by uncaring males. All of the material being presented being from the women's point of view, the males were seen from outside and never really sympathetically, except when they were presented as imaginary projections of the desires of the young women, such as the idealized sweetheart cousins in the prom sequence, the often promised but never actually appearing Willie Colon, or the spirit of rebellion Toussaint Louverture, whom the Lady in Brown discovered in the adult reading room of the public library and who became the secret lover of her dreams.

The real men in the play, named and unnamed, almost invariably shattered such dreams, much more often becoming the feared rapist (not the deranged stranger of the popular imagination, but a presumed friend) than the longed-for sexual and social partner and equal. This dynamic was most powerfully expressed in the penultimate poem/sequence in the play, "a nite with Beau Willie Brown," which is also the most detailed and extended narrative section of the work. The Lady in Red recounts the chilling story of Beau Willie and his girlfriend Crystal. Although unmarried, the couple have two children, but Beau Willie, a disturbed Vietnam veteran, becomes so physically abusive to both Crystal and the children that she obtains a police restraining order to protect them. Beau Willie nevertheless returns and demands that Crystal allow him back, marry him, and accept him as head of the house, backing up his demands with threats and new physical violence. When she continues to refuse, he seizes the two children, carries them to the window of their fifth-floor apartment, and threatens to drop them if she does not submit. Then, as she stands frozen in horror at the situation and her children's screams, Beau Willie drops them.

This chilling narration was followed by a choric poem of redemption, led by the Lady in Red, called "a layin on of hands." Although the laying on of hands is a process associated with healing and spiritual solidarity in many religious traditions, it has been a widespread practice in the African American church and so joins the other cultural expressions—sung, danced, and recited—from which so much of this play was built. Here both of these central functions, healing and mutual spiritual support, are clearly present as the "colored girls" seek a means of survival and enrichment in their difficult lives.

This laying on of hands, the chorus explains, is not the sexual laying on of bodies offered by men and still leaving something missing, nor the material bosom and womb of the mother, who can offer only infantilization, but the finding of a god in oneself and learning to love that god. Finally the chorus sang, first to each other, and then, gathered in a tight circle, out to the audience, the opening phrase of the title "this is for colored girls who have considered suicide," but, reflecting upon the new insights of this final passage, concluded with the hopeful "but are movin to the ends of their own rainbows," no longer accepting what exists as "enuf."

At the time I experienced *for colored girls* as a moving and beautiful evening, somewhere between theatre and dance, but not really closely related to any other current work with which I was familiar. It had almost nothing in common with the work of current black male dramatists, and seemingly even less with the dream visions of Adrienne Kennedy. It was not until the next decade that I came to feel that although few others used the specific technique of this play, it clearly anticipated a type of work that become highly visible and important in subsequent years, the feminist search for an expression of identity. The hitherto silent "colored girls" to whom Shange gave theatrical voice were followed by many others of many ages and ethnicities given voice by the dramas of the years that followed. A significant number of these followed Shange in offering a collection of different feminine voices as a kind of anthology of experience, though these were for the most part presented by a single artist. The poetic weaving together of such a set of discourses with such success and power remained a singular achievement of this remarkable precursor.

1977 Andrei Serban's
The Cherry Orchard

Although more than a decade after its founding the Lincoln Center Theater was in one of New York's most modern theatres and headed by Joe Papp, one of the city's most honored directors, the high hopes of its original supporters had never come close to fulfillment. Elia Kazan and Robert Whitehead, the original directors, were gone even before the venture moved from the temporary home in Washington Square to the new Vivian Beaumont Theater uptown two seasons later. Herbert Blau and Jules Irving, the directors of the outstanding San Francisco Actor's Workshop, opened the new venture, still devoted to the concept of a major ongoing repertory theatre in New York, but they had such a disappointing first two seasons that in 1967 Blau resigned. Irving struggled on alone, but never managed to get the board of directors to provide the financial support needed for this scale of repertory theatre, even after an open letter complaining of this parsimony by Arthur Miller to the *Times* and other papers.

Finally Irving too resigned, in 1972, and the board, after considering simply turning the theatre into a rental house, hired Joe Papp, a proven downtown success, to become director but to give up entirely the idea of repertory. Papp approached the task with his customary enthusiasm and imagination, but after trying several alternatives with mixed success, he too was forced to abandon the ill-fated Beaumont.

Papp's first plan for the theatre was to present new American plays, but after two generally unsuccessful seasons he decided to change to the classics, beginning conservatively enough with Shaw and Pinero, directed by previous Public Theater directors Gerald Freedman and A. J. Antoon. Then he took a bolder step, presenting more challenging classics directed by more experimental downtown directors from theatres other than the Public. The first such offering was the most surprising, a *Threepenny Opera*, directed by Richard Foreman, his first work outside his own theatre and his own texts. Although more conservative critics were negative, the production was generally highly praised, and Raul Julia emerged as a star with his interpretation of Macheath.

After Foreman, Papp turned to another highly innovative downtown director, Romanian-born Andrei Serban, whose productions of a series of Greek tragedies at La Mama during the 1970s had made him one of the most highly praised of young experimental directors in New York. *The Cherry Orchard* was a new experience for Serban, who had done no modern classics and who had worked with his own group of actors at La Mama, while the Beaumont production featured big name stars like Irene Worth and Meryl Streep. Serban did, however, bring his regular music director, Elizabeth Swados, and his scenic designer from La Mama, Santo Loquasto, already beginning to be recognized as a major figure. For the first time here he worked with lighting designer Jennifer Tipton, who also was developing a major reputation and had done the lighting for *for colored girls*. Both designers won their first Tony Awards for their work on *The Cherry Orchard*.

I had attended a number of productions at the Vivian Beaumont Theater, beginning with Herbert Blau's ambitious but ill-fated *Danton's Death* in 1965, but Loquasto's design for the Chekhov was both simpler and more impressive than anything I had yet seen there. The large thrust stage has always presented a challenge to designers, but Loquasto accepted it as the center of his acting area, covering it with a huge white carpet, upon which were a few isolated toys and items of furniture, with no walls, doors, or windows, only three or four small trees in blossom forming a row at the rear, and behind them a huge curtain, upon which various realistic and suggestive symbolic images appeared during the evening. Despite the light tone of the acting, the stage was often dark, with pools of light in the acting areas. A new translation, very contemporary and idiomatic, was provided by Jean-Claude van Itallie, whose *American Hurrah* in 1966 was one of the outstanding experimental works of that decade. He began a series of much-praised Chekhov translations in 1973 with *The Seagull* (which Serban directed later at La Mama), and followed *The Cherry Orchard* with *Three Sisters* in 1979 (later directed by Serban at the American Repertory Theater) and *Uncle Vanya*, which Serban premiered at La Mama.

At that time I had seen only one professional production of *The Cherry Orchard*, directed by Eva Le Gallienne in 1968, and had acted the part of Firs in a summer theatre production, and although I knew that Chekhov himself had described the play as a comedy, at times almost a farce, Serban's production revealed that aspect of the play for the first time to me. In fact, although there were many scenes of almost frantic physical action, what I remember most were slow and quiet scenes, often without lines, that had an incredible visual power and emotional intensity. Central to these, and to the production, was Irene Worth as the mercurial Madam Ranevskaya. Fittingly, it was her face, framed with blossoms and against falling snow, that was used on the posters for the show. Two scenes I particularly recall—the first was when she receives the letter from Paris. Worth took it far downstage and sat there trying to decide whether to keep or destroy it, for several long silent moments before finally resolutely and very slowly tearing it to pieces. The second was even more unconventional and powerful. Just before leaving the house for the last time, she made a slow circle all around the large empty stage, trying to fix its details in her mind for the last time. But when she met her brother Gaev, played by George Voskovec, at the door, waiting to escort her out, she only briefly touched his hand, and then rushed past him to make a second sweep around the stage at a faster pace and then, marvelously, a third, at almost a full run, ending with her sweeping off-stage, one of the most effective exits I had ever seen.

A distinctly different note and one much closer to traditional farce was struck by Meryl Streep as the lustful maid Dunasha and Ben Waters as her target, the self-centered valet Yasha. Their various encounters, tumbling about the stage, over furniture, and entangled with various items of clothing, came close indeed to the physicality of a Feydeau romp. These boisterous scenes came back to me twenty-five years later in 2001 when I saw Streep in another Chekhov, *The Seagull*, in Central Park, in one of her most famous moments, turning cartwheels as Arkadina to demonstrate the youthful ability of both actress and character.

Raul Julia was probably the other dominant figure of the production, his Lopakhin an unusual blend of rather endearing, bumbling deference, and a distinct streak of angry frustration, possibly intensified in the audience's impression by the memory of his very recent Macheath in *The Threepenny Opera*. Certainly his most striking and memorable scene was that after the sale, when the exultant new owner in his enthusiasm damages a piece of furniture, and covers his clumsiness by announcing he can pay for any damage. In most productions that is the end of the matter, but here Julia allowed Lopakhin's new sense of power to carry him away, and his accidental error led to a frenzy of destruction, reducing most of the furniture in the scene to wreckage.

Serban made much of the fact that the key interior in the play is the nursery, and a few ancient toys, a model train, and a shrouded and much-worn rocking horse clearly stirred up childhood memories in the family members and indeed led them to revert to childlike moments when they encountered those objects. In the final scenes, as the rocking horse, unshrouded at last, was carried bobbing out of the room along with other furnishings, its triumphant departure perfectly captured the combined joy and sorrow of the moment.

One of the most striking and unconventional visual elements of the production was a sweeping curtain upstage upon which Loquasto projected large and often more suggestive than distinct images, some of them suggesting the actual physical setting of the scene and others, more frequently, offering symbolic comment. One of the many memorable visual moments in the production came when early in the evening Worth recalled her memories of spring, and the curtain, illuminated in a glowing light, ascended to reveal row upon row of trees in cold white blossom, suggestive of both life and death, like the final line of A. E. Housman's "Loveliest of Trees."

For most of the evening this large curtain was either washed with light, somewhat in the manner of a Robert Wilson background, or was the field for huge rather hazy projections that mixed realistic and symbolic elements, often somewhat distorted, as in act 2, which provides an outdoor vista with telegraph lines, as Chekhov suggested, but also a group of peasants pushing a huge ancient plow. Often these backgrounds hinted of the coming Soviet industrialization and oppression, especially when Trofimov, played by Michael Christopher in a costume with red lapels that clearly was meant to suggest a Soviet army overcoat, spoke of the bright future that lay ahead for Russia. In cruel visual irony, the background presented a rather undefined but distinctly menacing dark industrial landscape under a blood-red sky. Although Christopher did not gain the critical praise accorded to Worth and several of the other actors in this production, this was a memorable year for him, since his play *The Shadow Box*, which opened on Broadway soon after *The Cherry Orchard* opened at Lincoln Center, won both the Pulitzer Prize for Drama and the Tony Award for Best Play for this year.

The final scene, with Firs left alone in the deserted house, blended reality and fantasy. Firs entered the almost empty playing space by pushing aside the back curtain, where the glowing white of the cherry orchard had been replaced by the gloomy industrial sky of a menacing future. Firs curled up into a fetal position on a central stage sofa, the one bit of furniture left on stage, and as he lay there unmoving, a young girl came up behind the sofa, bearing a bough of cherry blossoms, as a kind of funereal offering to the passing of the last member of a dying era.

The image in fact reflected far more than the end of the dreams of the fictional Ranevskaya household; it also reflected the end of the most recent and by far the most ambitious dream of creating a permanent repertory theatre in New York. Despite a general critical success and good attendance at *The Cherry Orchard*, Papp announced in June that this would be his last production at this theatre. *The Cherry Orchard* was planned to run into the fall of 1977, but in fact it closed a month or so earlier than expected, early in August. The theatre then went dark and essentially remained so for most of the next decade.

A three-play season was attempted in 1980, with little success. After another dark two years, the theatre presented a single offering, a guest production of Peter Brook's *Carmen* from Paris in 1983. It was not until 1986 that Gregory Mosher, from the Goodman Theatre in Chicago, managed to bring life back into the Beaumont, and it has since remained a respectable part of the New York theatre scene, generally considered a step up the cultural ladder from the Broadway houses, but nothing like the national repertory theatre of its original sponsors' dreams.

1978 Squat Theatre's *Andy Warhol's Last Love*

Squat Theatre brought together many of the concerns of the late 1970s. Founded as a collective in Budapest in 1969, they produced nonnarrative highly visual pieces that, though their content was not as specifically po-litical as many similar groups of that time, aroused the anger of the Hun-garian government, and they were forced to go underground and to flee to the West, eventually ending in 1977 in the United States. Although they would have fitted well into the Village theatre scene, the already high rents in that area and the company's desire for a particular kind of space, with a large storefront window, led them to settle at 236 West Twenty-Third Street.

Although Twenty-Third Street had been a center of New York the-atre a century before, such activity had long disappeared and it was in the 1970s quite devoid of theatre ventures, equally distant from Times Square to the north and the Village to the south. It did contain, however, just a few doors from the new space, a center of American culture, the Chelsea Hotel, which has probably sheltered more literary figures, musicians, and visual artists than any other hotel in the city.

I did not attend the first offering of Squat Theatre, *Pig! Child! Fire!*, which they brought with them from Europe, but I was much intrigued by reports of their challenging the traditional separation of the real and the theatrical. In 1976 I had attended a performance by the installation artist Robert Whitman, called *Light Touch*, which made a profound impression on me. The installation/performance took place in a warehouse on Washington Street, near the Hudson River. The audience was seated on temporary bleachers set up in the warehouse, facing a large floor-to-ceiling loading door that had been hung with curtains as if it were a proscenium stage. When the curtains opened, the street outside was revealed, with passing cars and pedestrians magically made to appear theatricalized by this shift in framing. The two worlds merged when a truck backed up to the door and several objects, including an apple and a cement block, were unloaded and picked up with lights inside the warehouse. Such theatrical framings of the real world have since become an important part of experimental performance, but in 1976 I had never seen this device before, and was fascinated by it.

When I heard reports of *Pig! Child! Fire!*, which similarly positioned the audience as observers of the street (through a plate-glass window), to observe exterior actions that mixed the real and the fictional in a much more complex manner than did *Light Touch*, I looked forward eagerly to this group's next offering. This was their first created specifically for their Twenty-Third Street storefront, *Andy Warhol's Last Love*, doubtless inspired at least in part by Warhol and his entourage's strong presence in this neighborhood and at the Chelsea Hotel. Although Warhol was a central figure in the text, that text was a collage of material from pop culture, advertising, literary and film references, and current events. It had something of the freewheeling associations of the Theatre of the Ridiculous, but I really remember seeing nothing like this montage of elements before in the American theatre and not elsewhere until the 1990s when Frank Castorf began creating similar layerings of reference with similar material and use of video in Berlin. Warhol shared the focus of the evening with Ulrike Meinhof, a far less familiar figure to

U.S. audiences but for central Europeans an equally iconic figure of the 1970s. The Red Army Faction, a far-left organization which she founded in 1970, terrorized Germany with bank robberies and bombings until her arrest in 1972. She was found hanged in her jail cell in 1976.

When I arrived at the Squat Theatre for the performance, audience members were gathering outside the famous storefront window, but when the door was opened we were not ushered into the space behind that window but taken to an upstairs waiting room, part of the actual apartment of members of the company. I was at first disappointed that we were apparently not going to share the storefront experience of the company's first production, though what we were offered at this time was an experience equally unusual in the New York theatre of the late 1970s, though common enough a couple of decades later. This was a small intimate production for a limited audience performed in an actual living space—a genre that came to be generally known as living room or apartment theatre. During this decade in Eastern Europe, however, such theatre was already widespread and utilized by dissident authors like Kohout and Havel as a way of staying beneath the radar of state censorship.

The room utilized for this first section of *Last Love* had simple stepped seating along one wall, but was clearly a living space and was presented as such. An actor was stretched out dozing under a blanket when we came in and an actress soon entered to prepare coffee for the two of them on a hot plate, and to turn on a radio, changing stations that seemed to be actual current broadcasting. Not only was the space an almost embarrassingly intimate one, but the actors had nothing "theatrical" about them. On the contrary, they seemed calculatedly awkward and amateurish. After two other actors entered the room, the radio programming shifted into the world of the play, presenting the presumed voice of Meinhof announcing that at the moment of her death she was abducted by aliens, and was now associated with an intergalactic revolution that demanded that the people of Earth make their deaths more public so that they too could be seized at that moment and transported as Meinhof was. As if to begin this process, one of the men shot the woman, and from a window at one end of the room, opening onto a fire escape, a "space alien"—a woman in a silvery gown from which protruded a large erect penis—entered in a pool of light. She cradled the dead figure in her arms to create a tableau and the audience was led out of the room and down the stairs into the main performance area.

Seated on bleachers downstairs and facing the window onto the street, I assumed that the next part of the performance would feature the anticipated theatre/street interaction, but that was not yet the case. The window was covered by a large white curtain, upon which was projected a TV commercial by Crazy Eddie, a then familiar and eccentric promoter of electronic goods, but instead of his spiel we heard an exaggerated reading of a part of the Kafka piece "An Imperial Message," telling of a messenger who carries a critical note through so many obstacles that its meaning becomes hopelessly distorted, if it is ever delivered at all.

As the reading continued, we saw a film of a modern reconstruction of the messenger's journey, with an actor in an Andy Warhol mask riding on horseback through obstacles (including a pie thrown in his face) in contemporary lower Manhattan. When his horse was stolen, he hailed a taxi, which took him to the Chelsea theatre, outside of which he met a woman. The film changed to color as they entered the actual theatre and the presence of the actual audience.

This was the first time I had witnessed this bleeding together of an outside filmic experience and a live appearance onstage, but similar sequences became an important part of American and European avant-garde theatre during the rest of the century. I encountered one of them again in an untypical sequence in the Blue Man Group's *Tubes* in the early 1990s. They briefly abandoned their food- and paint-smeared spectacle to leave the theatre and go on a brief, presumably live videotaped but surely prerecorded Squat-type taxi ride out into nearby Manhattan streets. Much more substantially, Frank Castorf and his video designer Jan Speckenbach during this decade in Berlin made offstage live video views of their actors a major part of their visual aesthetic. This kind of mixture was also anticipated by Squat, which in addition to film clips presented as if they were live video, in fact used a live video camera in a number of sequences, providing different perspectives on the action.

This was seen in the next sequence, inside the Squat theatre, where the woman with "Warhol" identified herself as a witch and began a ritual, removing her cloak to expose her nude, 250-pound body. This body was in turn revealed to an astonished public outside when "Warhol" finally pulled aside the white curtain and opened the performance to the street. Not surprisingly, a crowd quickly assembled, and perhaps equally unsurprisingly, a city official complained about this display to Mayor Koch, who sent representatives to observe the production and who found it a legitimate artistic expression. During the ritual, a video monitor onstage offered the audience a variety of imaginary views, such as a burning Empire State Building, and real ones, such as the Alien and Ulrike Meinhof having tea among the parked cars behind the audience in the street.

After the ceremony, the witch, still nude, sat at a table with "Warhol" for an interview, in which his questions, such as "Do you believe in God?" were recorded and hers improvised. After this sequence, an actress with a face mask resembling Ulrike Meinhof, who had earlier been mingling with the spectators outside, entered from the street, joined the others at the table, and began her own interview of Warhol. At the end of this she read a declaration from the alien committee that abducted her commanding her to shoot Warhol so that he could join her in that alternative universe. She took a gun from her purse, shot the artist, and left with the witch. The Alien from the first scene entered to claim Warhol just as we had seen her claim the body of the dead woman in the first scene.

A final manipulation of the planes of reality and spectatorship followed this last action. To the ball music from Mozart's *Don Giovanni*, a set of Mylar panels that had formed a part of the roof over the acting area were lowered, forming a barrier between the audience and the stage. Thus the audience saw itself reflected in a kind of mirror curtain, like the famous one installed in London's Royal Coburg theatre in 1822. When the panels were raised back into place, the performance space was empty, but the inside audience found themselves reflected in another, and more uncanny, way, by the partially illuminated faces of the spectators who had gathered on the street outside to watch the performance. As a final touch, the live camera and the video monitor also remained onstage, so that the onstage audience had also a miniature image of themselves on the monitor, scaled down from the disappeared Mylar mirror-curtain. Both literally and figuratively, Squat offered its viewers, official and casual, a true hall-of-mirrors experience, in which not only identity but perception itself remained in constant instability and negotiation.

1979 Cornell University's *Rosencrantz and Guildenstern Are Dead*

As the contents of this book doubtless make clear, my primary relationship with the theatre over more than half a century has been primarily that of spectator, historian, and theorist, but these have not by any means been my only relationship, nor can my spectatorship and scholarship be truly understood without realizing that both have been profoundly influenced by my experience in other capacities. I began my career as scene designer for the Cornell University Theatre, and like many academic theatre people, I directed two or three plays a year for many years both at the university and in community and summer theatres. I also acted in many productions, in university theatres, community theatres, and once at the Theater for a New City off-off-Broadway in New York.

Both to represent this more active involvement and to give an example of another important part of my theatre-going experience, I am including for 1979 an account of my last and one of my most ambitious directing projects before leaving Cornell, where I had worked in the theatre program for over twenty years. This was Tom Stoppard's *Rosencrantz and Guildenstern Are Dead*, which appeared in April 1979 as part of a long-planned Hamlet Festival, which included *Hamlet*, directed by Richard Shank, played in repertory with *R and G* in the Cornell major theatre, Pavel Kohout's Hamlet-based *Poor Murderer*, presented by a guest director from Russia, Sergey Ponomarev, in our small, experimental theatre in another building, and a series of films and lectures. I have since seen two other combined repertory productions of the Stoppard and the Shakespeare produced, as ours was, by using the same actors to play the same roles in each play, but neither attempted what we did, which was the exact duplication of the overlapping scenes in the two plays. This is possible but not easy, since it required not only the close cooperation of the two directors, but also the development of the action in those scenes that complements the very different actions in which these scenes are embedded.

This interpenetration of the two plays was reinforced by the ambitious scenic design created by guest designer Victor Becker from the University of Alberta. Central to the design was a round, castle-like structure, the walls twelve feet high, built on a revolving turntable, with two large movable sections that could rotate around it, creating in all around three hundred possible scenic combinations. Creating such a structure would have been something of a challenge even in a German public theatre or in many of the new university theatres being built across the United States in that decade, almost all of which had permanent revolving stages built in, but the Cornell theatre was far from possessing such facilities. It had been built in 1924, when the study of theatre was still just developing in American universities. Cornell was one of the first universities to offer such study. Its first theatre course was offered in 1922, just two years before the theatre was opened. Theatre was still then seen more as an extracurricular activity than an academic one, and its home was thus located in the basement of Willard Straight Hall, the Student Union building. In the 1970s it had a lovely period charm, with handsome art deco murals covering the two long side walls, with characters from Shakespeare on the right and the Greek tragic dramatists on the left. Alexander Drummond, the founder of the Cornell Theatre, watched over its fortunes from a rather garish art nouveau portrait painting of him mounted at the rear of the auditorium.

The stage, however, left much to be desired. There was a simple rigging system but not really enough space to fly full pieces of scenery. The cafeteria was immediately above, not only restricting overhead space, but creating a distinct aural distraction whenever chairs or tables were moved. Worse yet, there was little backstage space and no offstage space left, where the proscenium arch stopped just a few feet from the exterior wall of the building. Under the circumstances, with little space above, behind, or to one side of the stage, a revolving platform, even if temporary, seemed a reasonable, if difficult and expensive, solution to the problem of multiple scenes. In fact when it was working, which it did most of the time, it fitted the overall concept of the paired plays very well, since one could follow actors moving from one room to another and, even better, see, in passing, bits of the other play taking place in rooms that passed by as the table turned. The traditional separation of auditorium and stage was also softened by building a lower forestage out into the front of the auditorium, with steps leading down to it rather after the model of the first proscenium theatres of the Italian Renaissance. Stairs were even built out from the upper level of the castle to a small side balcony over an exit door in the front of the house, rarely incorporated into the stage designs in this theatre. This extension also allowed for the installation of some working traps in the new down-stage areas. Ophelia seemed to be actually buried and her grave filled in (the actress had to crawl out through a tunnel beneath the forestage), and the last disappearance of Rosencrantz and Guildenstern was into two barrels at either side of the stage, from which they had emerged at the beginning of the shipboard scene and which allowed them to make their final exit out of sight into the space under the stage.

An important feature of the production, often utilized by leading university theatres throughout the latter part of the century and still today, was the hiring of several professional actors to perform the leading roles, thus strengthening the production as a whole and providing the student actors who made up the rest of the cast the opportunity to work with these more advanced artists in the field they were studying. Clearly the students appreciated this experience and the professional actors also clearly were energized by the enthusiasm and the energy of their youthful cohorts. Seven professional actors were hired for the two productions, an unusually large number for such a university project. They played Hamlet, Gertrude, Claudius, Polonius, Rosencrantz, Guildenstern, and the Player. Two of these had particular ties to Ithaca. Greg Bostwick (Guildenstern) was an acting teacher at Ithaca College and a familiar figure on local stages. John Hostetter (the Player) had graduated from Cornell with an M.F.A. in acting in 1972 and had since, among other things, toured as King Lear in the National Shakespeare Company.

The remaining professionals were selected from auditions held in New York City. Archie Smith, who played Polonius, and his wife, Kay Doubleday, who played Gertrude, both performed in New York, but were best known as key members for many years of the Denver Theatre Center. Peter Aylward, who played Hamlet, and Jack Hollander, who played Claudius, were both New York actors, but also were both active in films. Warner Shook, a director and actor, later director of the Intiman Theatre in Seattle, played Rosencrantz. Almost fifty student actors made up the remainder of the cast.

The audience that regularly filled the approximately three-hundred-seat theatre was, as was normally the case at Cornell, not primarily students, but rather more weighted toward faculty members and townspeople, especially when the theatre offered a familiar classical author like Shakespeare. The production that they saw was, in terms of general acting style, especially in the *Hamlet*, very much in the traditional

American Shakespearian style, rather formal and articulate, with a touch of traditional British formality on the one hand and of American psychological projection and body work on the other (I remember Hollander in rehearsal seeking to "ground" his body by assuming a pose simultaneously reaching up to heaven and down to the earth). The *R and G*, especially in the cross-talk scenes, reflected the clown-like interchanges of *Waiting for Godot*, with which this play, from the beginning, has been often compared. The only scene of violent physical action was the boarding of Hamlet's ship by the pirates, which, both for contrast and for comic effect, was performed in the most swashbuckling style imaginable, with pirates cartwheeling across the stage and making wild swings out over the audience on ropes.

Thanks in large part to the enormous visual influence of England's Royal Shakespeare Company's minimalist turn during the 1960s and 1970s, in turn influenced by the London visit of the Berliner Ensemble in 1956, the standard approach to Shakespeare in most commercial and academic productions of this period was tending toward an almost empty stage, with only a few platforms and draperies as scenery. The monumental castle of the Cornell production therefore came as something of a surprise to its audience, and emphasized the dark and heavy tone of Elsinore in this project—adding in turn to the menace and inexplicable danger felt by the hapless Rosencrantz and Guildenstern, who find themselves trapped in this forbidding pile of stone.

Director Shank took the war preparations mentioned early in *Hamlet* as a way to help set the dark tone, beginning the play with the sound of cannon fire and offering the dark shapes of the cannon themselves on the ramparts of the castle. His interpretation was not a radical one, but was solid and clear, firmly grounded in the text. *R and G* naturally had a much lighter tone. I remember the actors found Stoppard's suggestion of playing scenes as if they were competitive games most useful. The setting was visually a very heavy one. A crude and massive surface was achieved for the walls of the castle, inside and out, by covering them with squares of carpeting sprayed with layers of latex paint. The overall effect was rough and heavy, the surfaces made up of many layers of material—real wool, fur, and leather—built up over buckram, felt, and wire frames. For *Rosencrantz and Guildenstern*, I developed a compatible but contrasting tone, built upon the vaudevillian cross-talk sequences and the casual and relaxed approach to existential questions of the Leading Player. In keeping with this approach these three characters were dressed in much lighter costumes, united with the rest in color and tone, but not in texture and apparent weight.

The scope and ambition of the Hamlet Festival gained it unusual attention. The mayor of Ithaca, Edward B. Conley, and the governor of New York, Hugh L. Carey, both proclaimed the week of April 9–15 "Hamlet Festival Week," and such attention encouraged the Cornell program to issue invitations to New York reviewers to attend the production, but even in those days, with many more such reviewers than today, a university theatre production rather remote from New York, even one with a number of professional actors and a flurry of political attention, could not really expect to draw the attention of city reviewers, and none in fact came. Like most such productions, the Hamlet Festival had to rely for its official journalistic appraisals upon the local and university press, which were, in fact, unusually enthusiastic.

The Hamlet Festival, though by almost any standards a commendable success, also clearly indicated the inadequacies of Cornell's 1924 theatre space, and during the next two or three years after this event support steadily grew for providing Cornell with the kind of modern theatre facilities enjoyed by most of her sister institutions across the country. Funds were raised and in 1989, just ten years after the Hamlet Festival, a new theatre building opened, designed by the leading architect James Stirling of London. The new auditorium, elegantly suggesting an Italian court theatre and embedded in a building evoking an Italian hill town, is a far cry from the crowded subterranean quarters of Willard Straight Hall, but I still fondly and proudly remember my last production at Cornell for what a dedicated company of actors and designers were able to accomplish even in these challenging quarters.

The 1980s

Roger Rees (right) and unidentified actors in the stage production of *The Life and Adventures of Nicholas Nickleby*. Photo from the Billy Rose Theatre Division, New York Public Library Digital Collections.

1980 Peter Brook's
The Conference of the Birds

As the 1980s began, Peter Brook was unquestionably the most highly regarded director in the English-speaking world, thanks to such major international successes as *Marat/Sade, King Lear*, and *A Midsummer Night's
Dream*. Somewhat ironically, however, he had a decade before turned
aside from the path that had produced these works, the path of a major
innovator within the British theatre. He left Britain in 1970 and for the
next decade devoted himself to research into the bases of theatre. After
three years of touring and experiments in Iran, Africa, California, and New
York, with an international company representing a wide range of training
backgrounds, he established a base at the Bouffes du Nord in Paris. None
of the productions created there during this decade were seen in the United
States until 1980, when four representative works of the new direction
were presented during the spring at Ellen Stewart's La Mama.

Brook's choice of La Mama was a somewhat surprising and significant one. The two names then most associated with the presentation of
major contemporary avant-garde drama were Joe Papp at the Public and
his other venues and Harvey Lichtenstein at the Brooklyn Academy of
Music. Both sought to bring these new Brook works to their theatres,
and BAM would have seemed Brook's likely choice, since it had presented his *Midsummer Night's Dream* in 1970 and hosted a workshop
for Brook's company in 1973 when *The Conference of the Birds* was in
development. Brook, however, went to the far more modest La Mama,
partly no doubt in acknowledgement of Stewart's active involvement in
international projects, but also doubtless because the rougher and more
improvised space at La Mama fitted his current aesthetic much better
than the larger, more elegant, and more traditional spaces Papp and
Lichtenstein could offer.

In any case, La Mama was in 1980 widely regarded as the leading
experimental venue in New York, a position solidified by Brook's
choice. Her theatre was about to celebrate its twentieth year of activity,
during which time it had grown from a tiny coffeehouse performance
space on East Ninth Street to the complex of buildings on East Fourth
Street that it still occupies today. A series of European tours, guest ap-

pearances, encouragement of young American experimental dramatists, and the much-praised productions of Greek classics by Andrei Serban had made it a center of New York experimental theatre. Brook's appearance was unquestionably the high point of this season, but even without him La Mama was a major venue, offering just before Brook's arrival a Serban production of *As You Like It*, and soon after a new work by Joseph Chaikin, the founder of the much-lauded Open Theatre.

In 1974, after three years of touring and research, Brook found a home for his company in an abandoned late nineteenth-century theatre in Paris, the Bouffes du Nord. Far from restoring its crumbling interior to its former glory, he and his designer Chloe Obolensky treated the Bouffes du Nord as another "found space" like the many nontheatrical spaces where they had worked the previous three years. They made only minimal repairs for health and safety, and kept the stripped-down space as the basis for a series of minimalist productions whose physical requirements were as calculatedly spare as the space in which they were created.

Four of the productions so created in the late 1970s were brought together as a unit and first performed as such at the Adelaide Festival in 1980, after which they traveled to La Mama in New York. These four were *The Conference of the Birds*, which the company had been developing in workshops since its 1973 tour to Africa and which reached its final form in 1979 at the Avignon Festival; *Les Ik*, based on the dispossession and suffering of a Ugandan tribe, chronicled by anthropologist Colin Turnbull, premiered in 1975; *Ubu aux Bouffes*, premiered the following year and based on the play by Alfred Jarry; and *L'Os*, premiered in 1979, a short piece based on a story by Birago Diop, a Senegalese author.

The four plays were presented for several weeks in a three-evening repertory (with the short *L'Os* serving as a curtain-raiser for *Ubu*) and then together for a full afternoon and evening. In view of the anticipation of the first new Brook work to be seen in New York in almost a decade, demand was great, and ticket prices were doubled to $10 instead of La Mama's normal $5. Audiences were urged to see the plays in sequence from *L'Os* and *Ubu*, followed by *Les Ik* and *Conference*, which I did, although they could also be seen as separate productions. Together they presented a panorama of human greed and longing for a better order, as well as an effective contrast in dramatic modes—farce/comedy, tragedy, and romantic/epic. *The Conference of the Birds* was universally praised as the richest and most interesting of the three, as well as the most visually and aurally imaginative, but all four productions were striking in their simplicity and minimalism of approach.

In 1974 Ellen Stewart, who had been located at 74A East Fourth Street since 1969, acquired a large building just two doors away. Though now abandoned and derelict, it had a significant theatre history, beginning in 1882 when, as Turn Hall, it presented the first American Yiddish play, Thomashevsky's *The Witch*. A large rectangular space on the second floor became La Mama's third and largest stage, though it still seated only 299. It opened with Serban's trilogy of Greek adaptations.

When I attended *The Conference of the Birds* in 1980 I was already familiar with all three of the La Mama theatres, which had much the same configuration as theatres La Mama has today, although other spaces, especially in the Annex, have been altered. Entering the Annex, one goes up a large staircase to the second floor and to a fairly capacious lobby and bar, far more comfortable than the tiny lobby area in the nearby La Mama, which was filled with thirty people or so, and became almost suffocating when several times that number tried to crowd in on wet or cold evenings.

At the south end of the lobby, double doors lead to the performance space, today usually half filled with temporary bleachers, but for the Brook evenings left essentially open, with audience members seated at one end, along the sides, and along the narrow balconies that ran along three sides of the space. The proscenium stage at the far end was not used, as it often has not been in the open-stage performances La Mama has generally favored. The seats were hard wooden benches without backs, making for a fairly uncomfortable evening. I later found, visiting Brook's theatre in Paris, that he preferred this uncomfortable seating, perhaps because he felt it suited his general minimalist approach (indeed he once claimed that he sought to find the most basic elements for actors, scenery, and audience) or perhaps because it guaranteed no one would doze off during the performance.

When I came to *The Conference of the Birds*, I had attended the two other Brook offerings on previous evenings. As I have noted, all worked with the simplest of means, but in sharply contrasting tones. *L'Os* and *Ubu* were performed on an essentially bare stage, the only set pieces a group of bricks and two large industrial wooden spools normally used for wrapping cables. Both of these, however, were constantly and ingeniously used—the bricks allowed Ubu to build his unstable structures of power, and to be gnawed for nourishment by his impoverished subjects, and the spools served as tables, thrones, and, most memorably, as a juggernaut to be ridden across the rest of the company by the ruthless Ubu.

Les Ik was more primitive, but equally simple. The playing area was strewn with earth, raked into paths and patterns, and instead of bricks, was dotted with occasional rocks. For *Conference*, however, both floor and walls were covered by opulent oriental rugs, and despite the absence of other scenic elements, these by contrast with the other evenings seemed to convert the bare space into a place of magic and luxury. In the following years, Brook continued to employ the oriental carpet so regularly in productions from a wide variety of theatre traditions that it became almost a hallmark of his late twentieth-century style.

The music for all three evenings was provided by Toshi Tsuchitori, who was Brook's composer and musical director from the beginnings of the Paris experiments. For the first two evenings he performed alone, although on a wide range of instruments, while for *Conference*, in keeping with its more elaborate style, he was joined by a flutist and violinist. There were many interesting parallels during the 1980s and 1990s between the work of Brook and another of the most-honored directors of that era, his fellow Parisian, Ariane Mnouchkine. Much has been written on their parallel interests in Oriental subjects and performance techniques, but comparatively little on the striking similarity of their musical accompaniment. In 1979 Mnouchkine was joined by Jean-Jacques Lemêtre, who, like Tsuchitori, became an essential part, both aurally and visually, of subsequent productions. Both produced their accompaniment in full view of the audience, surrounded by an array of instruments, mainly percussive, modern, antique, original, and unconventional, producing a soundscape unique to each production not only in melody but in a full range of acoustic effects.

The Conference of the Birds, in keeping with Brook's interest in non-Western culture, was based on a twelfth-century Persian poem in which the hoopoe, the wisest of birds, leads the birds of the world, each flawed in some way, in a quest to find a king. The quest ends at a lake in which they view their own images. Although Brook's production was very simple scenically, the same could not be said for the visual effects generally. The lighting, which had been an intense, unchanging Brechtian glare for the first two evenings, here became softer, more infused with color, and varied from scene to scene. In addition to the splendor of the carpets themselves, the actors, who had been clothed in simple homespun for the other productions, all wore rich costumes, with distinct Persian overtones, and Brook sought in a variety of Oriental performance traditions other inspirations for visual display. The actors carried and sometimes wore Balinese masks, and many of the birds were formed by hand puppets. In movements clearly suggestive of the Japanese Bunraku puppet theatre, the actors themselves seemed to become the human manipulators of these elaborate bird figures, which, through the graceful arching of the actors' arms under their capacious robes, seemed to operate almost independently of their manipulators and in an astonishing variety of birdlike movements.

Despite Brook's interest in international performance, his company in 1980 was still largely European. The African actors Sotigui Kouyate from Senegal and Bakary Sangaré, both major contributors to the next phase of Brook's work, were not yet in the company, although Malik Bowens, also from Mali, translated and performed in *L'Os*. The major non-European contributions to *Conference* came not from actors, but from the music of the Japanese Tsuchitori and the masks and costume trimmings designed by the Balinese Tapa Sundana. Not in a leading role in *Conference* but a key member of the international company from the beginning was the Noh-trained Japanese actor Yoshi Oida, probably the single actor most closely associated with Brook's later work.

In the program notes to the New York production, Brook announced that with this New York season the "first phase" of his Center's work was completed. Both those who were enthusiastic about the new minimalist focus and those who looked back with greater respect to the more monumental RSC productions of the 1960s looked forward with equal interest to where this major innovator would move next.

1981 The Wooster Group's *Route 1 & 9*

Off-off-Broadway has been centered, from its beginnings, in Greenwich Village, first on the Western side and later moving more to the east. The traditional southern boundary of the village is Houston Street and until the end of the 1960s that street also marked the southern boundary of off-off-Broadway theatre. Then in 1967 Richard Schechner, the NYU professor who had become a leading voice for the new theatre as editor of the *Drama Review*, created a new experimental company, the Performance Group, which purchased a space for the first important theatre in modern times south of Houston, at 33 Wooster Street. Although in fact a former flatware factory, the building has become known as the Performing Garage.

Houston was more of a psychological than an actual barrier. The Performing Garage was in fact much closer to New York University, in the center of Greenwich Village, than many of the established village theatres to its east and west. The mental barrier was still great, however, so much so that Clive Barnes, the *New York Times* reviewer who reviewed (and intensely disliked) the opening productions at the Garage, *Dionysus in 69*, with its nudity and audience involvement, and *Makbeth*, with its almost total disregard of the Shakespearian original, advised his readers that if they attended the Garage they should take a map, as not even New York cabbies would know where Wooster Street was.

Actually by this time many empty former industrial buildings in Soho were being taken over by performing and visual artists, attracted by the low rents and large spaces. By the mid-1970s Wooster Street had become a center of such activity, with the Performing Garage joined by the Anthology Film Archives and the new Ohio Theatre. Another important new venture, the Soho Rep, was also established just two short blocks away, on Mercer Street.

I attended most of the productions at the Performing Garage from 1969 onward, equally fascinated by the boundary-pushing creations of Schechner and by the fascinating autobiographical explorations of Spalding Gray, beginning with the 1975 *Sakonnet Point*. Although the subject matter of these Gray texts, directed by Elizabeth LeCompte, was much different from the normally classic-based works of Schechner, both appeared as offerings of the Performance Group and, given their common interest in spatial and structural experimentation, were, I assumed, based on a common group orientation. By the end of the decade, however, it was clear that this was not the case. Schechner withdrew in 1980 and the Performance Group faded away, while the actors around Gray and LeCompte constituted themselves as a new organization, distinct from the aesthetics and the approach of the earlier Performance Group. Their new organization, the Wooster Group, now became the primary residents of the Performing Garage, which remains their home still. During the coming years they became the best known of the experimental New York theatre groups, nationally and internationally.

Although the Wooster Group retroactively claimed the early Gray works as their own, the first production they offered under their new name was *Route 1 & 9*, in the fall of 1981. Not only did they now reclaim those previous works as Wooster Group productions *avant la lettre*, they also now offered them as elements in a larger, ongoing project. In 1978 the three Gray pieces so far created were presented as a trilogy entitled *Three Places in Rhode Island*. *Point Judith*, presented in 1980, was subtitled "an epilogue," and its three sections, all in the unconventional, highly self-conscious style of the group, moved away from an individual coming-of-age exploration to considering the family and the community. *Route 1 & 9*, the following year, was subtitled "The Last Act," suggesting that these five works be considered as a unit, a perspective confirmed by the presentation of all five works in repertory in the spring of 1982.

Route 1 & 9 broadened the field of the series still further. If *Point Judith* moved from the individual to the family and community, *Route 1 & 9* claimed the entire human experience from birth until death, drawing heavily upon the American drama most famously devoted to this concern, Thornton Wilder's *Our Town*. The reworking of material from the traditional (especially American) repertoire had already become a part of the Wooster Group aesthetic. Selections from T. S. Eliot's *The Cocktail Party* had been woven into *Nayatt School* and from O'Neill's *Long Day's Journey into Night* into *Point Judith*. The use of such recycled cultural material was one of the Group's strategies to explore the American psyche, and it was one of several features that connected them with other artists and groups to which the term "postmodern" was beginning to be widely applied.

More recent productions at the Performing Garage have been confined to the large lower area, an empty rectangular space, used in various configurations, but in the 1970s and 1980s, partly as a result of Schechner's interest in utilizing alternative spaces, the upstairs was frequently incorporated into productions. I first saw this use in Schechner's 1969 *Makbeth*, where the audience first worked their way through an upstairs maze depicting Macbeth's history before descending to the rebuilt space below where the main action occurred. This use of an alternative space as prologue area, forcing the audience to change locations, was a popular device during the 1970s and 1980s, when interest in unconventional spatial relationships was strong in the experimental theatre. I have already noted its use by the Squat Theatre, and the Wooster Group used it again for *Route 1 & 9*.

The action thus began upstairs, where the audience witnessed a typical Wooster Group offering, mixing live and mediatized performance, reality and mimesis: actor Ron Vawter on a video monitor, re-creating, complete with gestures and intonation, a dry 1950s educational film explicating *Our Town*.

Following the video, which the audience read as a rather gentle satire, we descended to the ground floor theatre and a very different experience. The audience members were seated on bleachers stretched along one of the long side walls of the open rectangular space. As soon as they were seated, the lights went out and in the darkness the voices of two men discussed plans to build a "skeletal house" "out in Jersey." When the lights went up, the two men were revealed as white actors in extreme blackface (Ron Vawter and Willem Dafoe) and wearing glasses that kept them blind while the audience could see. Nevertheless they consulted blueprints and began their construction project on one side of the stage, in the comic style of early silent films, installing walls upside down, running into each other trying to carry out their projects, and so on.

During this sequence, two women, also in blackface (Kate Valk and Peyton Smith) appeared and placed a series of live telephone calls, broadcast over loudspeakers, mostly to restaurants in far-off Harlem, asking for food to be delivered to the theatre for a party. In an amusing but obviously unconscious echo of Clive Barnes's complaint, the restaurants would invariably refuse to deliver to such a remote, virtually unknown location. Finally one of the phone calls reached the two men in their mostly constructed skeletal house, and they were invited to come to the party and to bring drinks.

The two men removed their glasses and changed character, now entering as party guests and changing the dynamic of the scene almost completely. The most notorious sequence of the evening followed. The actors, still in blackface, presented scenes based on crude and racist sexual and scatological routines of a black vaudeville performer of the 1960s, Pigmeat Markham. The sequence was both shocking and, in its outrageousness, strangely liberating and theatrical, creating a very ambivalent reaction in me as a white theatre-goer. I had somewhat the same reaction to the outrageous racist routines created to call attention to these same ingrained stereotypes by Branden Jacobs-Jenkins in his disturbing 2010 comedy *Neighbors*.

After the excessive party scene the production moved to a sharply contrasting mood and approach. The four actors partially wiped off their heavy makeup and sat quietly in four chairs. Above them four television monitors, which had been suspended near the ceiling, were lowered to a position just above head-height, facing the audience. On them actual excerpts from Wilder's play were performed in a quiet and traditional style while the audience and live actors watched, as if all were ghosts in Wilder's cemetery. At the end of this sequence, the motionless actors suddenly leaped to their feet and entered a savage dance, making horrible grimaces toward the audience, false fangs in their mouths. So the elegiac tranquility of the Wilder conclusion was replaced by a savagery echoing that of the earlier blackface.

This was not yet the end of the production, however. Like many Wooster Group creations, *Route 1 & 9* was composed of a series of elements, with overlapping images and themes, but in sharply different styles and use of media. The final section after the cemetery consisted of two videotapes, played at the same time. On the four monitors the same sequence appeared, a contemporary colored "road film" like that in Squat Theatre's *Andy Warhol*, showing director Elizabeth LeCompte and actor Ron Vawter driving from the vicinity of the Performing Garage out onto the New Jersey Turnpike to the exit to Routes 1 and 9. On the way they picked up two "hitchhikers"—Willem Dafoe and Libby Howes—who continued the journey with them. Simultaneously, a hitherto unused ancient black-and-white video monitor was rolled out of the skeletal house and projected an apparent pornographic film—a series of sexual scenes enacted by the "hitchhikers" and directed (on camera) by Vawter.

Interestingly enough, the porn film, though specific and graphic, aroused little protest. By this time nudity and simulated sex had become a common feature of the New York experimental scene, not least at the Performing Garage, which had been launched just over a decade before with Richard Schechner's celebration of sexual excess, *Dionysus in 69*. The crude racism of the blackface routines was something else, however. Most importantly, of course, it put a spotlight on the still largely unresolved racial tensions in the United States, and moreover did so in the theatrical vocabulary of minstrel show and burlesque blackface, the tradition in which theatre had historically most openly engaged these tensions. The fact that the routines came from popular entertainment forms that the high-culture supporters of authors like Wilder held in near-contempt added to the shock, as did much of the Wooster Group's frequent blending of high and low forms of expression that were traditionally carefully held apart.

The controversy surrounding the blackface routines attracted much attention in the New York theatre during the following year, especially when the New York State Council on the Arts, a major source of funding for the group, made a substantial cut in the group's subsidy in protest against these sequences. Despite protests from many leading artists and critics and an official appeal by the Group itself, the Council stood by its decision.

This setback did nothing to deter the company, however, which continued its work as one of the most innovative and iconoclastic of American theatres in the years to come. It continued experiments with mixing material from across the cultural spectrum, and although it did not again present any racial material as charged as the Pigmeat Markham routines, the use of blackface to call attention to racial stereotyping reappeared in a number of later productions. The free adaptation of earlier texts continued too, and resulted in the Wooster Group's other most famous controversy, when in 1984 they were forced to close their production of *L.S.D.* after Arthur Miller protested their use in it of material from *The Crucible*. Controversies such as these, however, only added to the company's reputation as a challenger of the establishment, like the Living Theatre before it, whose preeminence in the world of American avant-garde theatre it essentially inherited.

1982 The RSC's *The Life and Adventures of Nicholas Nickleby*

The full-page advertisements began to appear in New York newspapers in July 1981, and their arrangement and content were revealing and memorable. After the words in large block capitals, THE LIFE & ADVENTURES OF, came, in even larger capitals, NICHOLAS NICKLEBY. Then, still in bold lettering, only slightly smaller, the striking subhead: **The Ticket is One Hundred Dollars.** The paragraph that followed, containing such assertions as "Every civilized family—man, woman, and child—should book tickets now," began "You are about to spend more money for a theatre ticket than you ever thought possible." Certainly the jump in ticket prices was shocking; even major musicals that season, such as *My Fair Lady*, with Rex Harrison, charged around $35 for their most expensive seats. The Royal Shakespeare Company production was first announced for the Winter Garden, one of the larger New York musical venues, with over 1,500 seats, but in fact the show opened in the much smaller Plymouth, with 975 seats, a theatre that normally offered more intimate regular dramas, its most recent major hit having been Peter Shaffer's *Equus* in 1974. This choice virtually guaranteed that the much-publicized production would sell out for its limited run of only fourteen weeks, and thus in fact tickets sold through brokers went at two or three times the printed price and on the black market even higher. Anticipating this response, I obtained tickets soon after the production was announced, although I saw it near the end of the run, in the opening days of 1982. Now teaching at Indiana University, I had to concentrate my New York visits during academic holidays.

News stories about the production gave endless information about the expenses incurred by the Royal Shakespeare Company, and looking back upon the marketing of the production, one of the things that strikes me is that it was the first time I can remember the costs and ticket prices becoming central to the advertising and image of the play. With the Broadway production of *Nicholas Nickleby*, the New York theatre world may be seen to have entered what many social commentators and economists now call the Second Gilded Age, when, with the coming to power of Margaret Thatcher in 1979 and Ronald Reagan in 1981, England and the United States entered that era of capitalistic excess that heavily favored banks, corporations, and the wealthy while worsening the conditions of those at the bottom of society. In its own way, ironically, *Nicholas Nickleby* became the first highly visible example in the theatre of the new age of conspicuous cultural consumption.

I say ironically because the ostentation and greed of the rich and the suppression and suffering of the poor were of course social conditions all too familiar to Dickens, and *Nicholas Nickleby*, like most of his works, has a strong element of criticism of this sort of social inequality. Indeed this aspect of the work clearly particularly interested the directors Trevor Nunn and John Caird and adaptor David Edgar. While the strongly political flavor of much U.S. experimental theatre of the late 1960s and early 1970s had distinctly faded by the early 1980s, leading playwrights and companies in England still retained their distinctly leftist political orientation, established with the Angry Young Men a quarter century before, and both the RSC and David Edgar clearly shared this commitment.

Thus this production ironically worked in two directions—within the establishment and through its producing apparatus, it strongly reflected the growing centrality of wealth and privilege, while its selection of subject matter and even its selection of imagery placed it in direct opposition to this orientation. Nowhere is this more clear than in the logo of the production, a black-and-white poster-style illustration of the ruggedly handsome Roger Rees, who played the title role, directly confronting the viewer with an intense gaze, his frock coat whipping in the wind and his fist raised in the salute that was at this time widely associated in the international public mind with political resistance.

In a few scenes Edgar and the directors stressed this direction more than Dickens had, but clearly their overall concern was with trying to offer as complete as possible a staging of this huge narrative, and even more important, to create a memorable theatre experience. It was generally felt that they impressively achieved both of these goals (although some reviewers, while enthusiastic, suggested some characters and episodes could easily have been removed). Probably most viewers, like myself, became so caught up in the brilliant acting and the stunning stage pictures, the reveling in theatricality, that they gave almost no thought to the political implications of the piece until the final scene, one of the production's most powerful.

The overwhelming effect of the eight and one-half hours of performance were an experience much closer to the spirit of Barrault's *Rabelais* than to Mnouchkine's *1789*, but a strong emphasis on theatricality infused all three productions. The audience entered the Plymouth Theatre to discover an exposed but clearly nonrealistic setting—hanging loops of rope, ladders, ramps, platforms, and catwalks filling the stage, decorated with odd bits of Victorian cast-iron decoration and extending over balconies and boxes halfway out into the house. To a theatre historian it somewhat suggested a Meyerholdian constructivist gymnasium for the display of actors, and that is in fact how it was used. The actors, like the scenery, moved into the audience space, greeting the incoming public and welcoming them to the event. Since forty-two actors were used to play the more than two hundred roles in the performance, the cast was large enough to personally greet a substantial portion of the audience.

The production utilized an innovative and highly effective technique for presenting the novel. Many scenes were presented in traditional dramatic fashion, but most mixed this with narrative passages, and some scenes were almost entirely narrated. These narrations, however, were broken up among company members, often speaking in character, and mixed with illustrative or symbolic movement (in a sequence describing in detail the display of costly foods and objects observed by the poor through Christmas shop windows, the cast, delivering the description, also portrayed the disenfranchised poor as they regarded these inaccessible treasures through the windows).

There were occasional properties and bits of furniture, but most of the scenic environment was created by the words and actions of the company. One particularly striking example was the onstage construction of the Yorkshire stagecoach, rapidly built up on one of several small wagons onstage out of a collection of boxes and baskets by the actors, who then all clambered onto this construction, a jumble of arms and legs, and rolled triumphantly away, appearing remarkably like an actual stagecoach, amid the cheers of the audience.

Probably the theatrical high point of the production was the performance of a happily ending *Romeo and Juliet*, performed by the enthusiastic, if very modestly talented, traveling Crummles Company, which Nicholas and his companion Smike have joined. The production, which took up much of the latter half of part 1, was a triumph of theatrical parody, carried out by actors totally in command of the tradition they were spoofing. The production, and part 1, ended with the entire company, surmounted by the figure of Britannia, joining in a spectacular tableau and patriotic song.

Like most of the audience, I left the first part so exhilarated by this final sequence that I rather regretted not being able to immediately return to my seat for the next four-hour installment, but I had to fill up the break, as did most, with a light dinner in a nearby restaurant (almost every restaurant in the area offered special *Nicholas Nickleby* interval meals). We returned from this break eager to see how the production could move forward from the spectacular ending of the first part. It did so most ingeniously. The entire company gathered on stage and the auditorium erupted in applause and laughter when one of their number stepped forward to deliver the opening line, "The story so far."

In fact, however, the company then did give us, over the next five to ten minutes, a marvelously entertaining recap of the first four hours of action, using their by now familiar style of mixed in-character narration and brief dramatic scenes. The ending was as imaginative, moving, and theatrically effective as any scene in this monumental production. The entire stage was filled with several levels of brightly illuminated little rooms, festooned for Christmas. As traditional Christmas music filled the auditorium, and snow fell softly on the stage, Roger Rees stepped forward in a downstage spot and looked toward a corner of the proscenium, where was discovered a small, huddled, ragged figure, apparently one of the abused urchins from Dotheboys Hall, where Nicholas began his adventures. Rees picked up the urchin, carried him downstage center in his arms, and there raised his fist toward the audience in the gesture pose that everyone knew both from news stories of the past decade and the logo of this production.

1983 Mabou Mines' *Cold Harbor*

Richard Schechner, often the main critical spokesman for the American avant-garde theatre during the 1960s and 1970s, naturally caused a considerable stir when in 1981 he announced in a two-part essay in *Performing Arts Journal* the death of this avant-garde. Few historians of the American theatre would concur with Schechner's assessment today, but it is worth noting that the two groups that he mainly cited as examples of the cul-de-sac into which the contemporary theatre had gone were the Wooster Group and Mabou Mines, the two groups that would surely be cited by most historians today as evidence of the continuing vitality of the American avant-garde during the 1980s and after.

Putting aside Schechner's natural distrust of the Wooster Group, which after all had split away from his own Performance Group in order to do a different sort of work, his appraisal does point out changes in the American experimental theatre at this time, which Schechner attributes to postmodernism, a reliance upon a more diffuse creative process, upon more personal material, and upon a less focused gathering of and presentation of other material. The avant-garde of the 1960s had broken away from the author, and new work was breaking with the director, with no clear part of the dynamic left to make the work meaningful and emotionally significant to the public.

Although the Mabou Mines shared with the Wooster Group (and indeed with many earlier groups during the 1960s) a concern with creating works in a truly collaborative manner, most typically with each participant bringing material, some verbal, some physical, to be assembled into a kind of performance collage, as in the early *animations* with which the group began, the Mabou Mines were from the beginning far less tightly connected than any other important experimental group in the city. Although the Wooster Group creations were basically collective ones, Elizabeth LeCompte served in a directorial capacity, doing the final shaping and editing. Mabou Mines productions also had directors and designers, but these posts would move around from member to member, and most served over time in a wide range of capacities—actor, director, designer, puppeteer, and so on. In the early productions, programs, if there were any, did not provide information on who had served as director, actors, designer, or author (in the case of new pieces), and although certain members did tend to specialize in one of these functions, most served from time to time in a variety of positions. Moreover the Mabou Mines was never really stable as a group, though it had a number of central members. Any of its members, alone or working with other members, could and did create productions under the Mabou Mines name.

Cold Harbor, which I saw at the Public Theater in the spring of 1983, was an excellent example of this. The names from the beginning most closely associated with the group were those of the original members: Ruth Maleczech, Lee Breuer, JoAnne Akalaitis, Philip Glass, and David Warrilow. Encouraged first by Ellen Stewart at La Mama, then by Joe Papp at the Public, these five artists and their associates had by 1983 become a noticeable presence off-Broadway, primarily as a result of their abstract but highly visual *animations*, all created by Breuer, and their imaginative staging of a number of hitherto unstaged prose works by Beckett, mostly directed by Akalaitis and featuring Warrilow as the leading or sole performer. Maleczech had acted in both and had also begun to direct works on her own. Glass provided the music for many of these productions, though after *Einstein on the Beach* in 1976, he was much better known in the theatre world for his collaborations with Robert Wilson.

The only one of these at that time relatively familiar names who was involved with *Cold Harbor* was Philip Glass, who provided the music, and indeed I would very likely not have attended the production had it not been advertised as a Mabou Mines offering. In fact, this was a fortunate choice, since I found it one of the most engaging and moving productions that the group had yet produced, an opinion that was widely shared by the press and the public. It was presented at the Public Theater, which had by this time become essentially the home theatre of the group. Joseph Papp, after seeing some of their first productions, had offered them the old prop room of the theatre as a rehearsal space, and they had presented much of their work since 1976 at the Public. The single stage with which Papp opened this building in 1967 had now expanded to five, and *Cold Harbor* was presented in one of the newest and smallest, the LuEsther Hall, created in 1973 in the former south reading room on the third floor of the building. Although the space has been arranged in different configurations, it has normally been a block of bleachers, seating about 140, facing the playing space, as it was on this occasion. The stage design was by Linda Hartinian, the visual artist who designed many of the early Mabou Mines productions. It, like the play itself, departed sharply from most of the group's previous work. The stage was essentially bare, but the elements within it were quite realistic. At the beginning the dominant element was a large glass case, partially broken, within which was displayed the seated figure of Ulysses Grant, in fact a living actor, Bill Raymond, the cocreator of the production. As the darkness around him lightened and the figure of Grant remained immobile, we saw that the area contained a jumble of material through which two young men were sorting, preparing some kind of museum exhibition of Grant's life.

As the two curators carried on their work, displaying material ranging from documents and photographs to charred bones from the battlefield and even a tear-stained pillow that might have been Grant's, the seated figure became more and more bored and agitated, not least because this laborious reconstruction of his life and career apparently bore no resemblance to his own experience and opinions. After crossing his legs, fidgeting nervously, and trying to calm himself with some long pulls at a pocket flask, he finally stumbled out of his glass case, took control of the stage, and began his own version of his life story, a rambling monologue that made up the bulk of the evening.

Before long I recognized Raymond as an actor I had in fact seen in a number of previous Mabou Mines productions, although this was not easy, since he was one of those actors who are able to easily shift into other personae, altering posture, facial configuration, and vocal quality to a remarkable degree. Indeed, even within this virtuoso performance, Raymond portrayed not only Grant, but a variety of other key men in Grant's life such as Robert E. Lee and Jefferson Davis, creating in each case an apparently totally new character for even a brief passage. He did not present Grant's wife, however, who was portrayed by a small doll (thanks in large part to Lee Breuer, Mabou Mines has from the beginning had a strong interest in puppet figures) and an offstage female voice, who spent much of her time complaining of the passing of the prewar society where everyone, especially the slaves, knew their place. Not surprisingly, this miniscule figure, like most of the production, served primarily as a foil for the fascinating creation of Raymond, who played Grant as a rough, defensive, intemperate, self-justifying bear of a man, with whom we could not help sympathizing, in respect to the clear vulnerability beneath all the bluster. The play was aptly named for Grant's greatest defeat in the Civil War, with tremendous loss of life, and although in fact Grant famously devoted only two sentences of his autobiography to this crushing event, Raymond returned to it again and again, obsessively insisting that this, like Grant's many other shortcomings, personal and political, was not his own fault. At best, whatever these shortcomings, he saw himself as superior to his more refined but now defeated adversaries, Lee and Davis. He reveled, for example, in the fact that the site of his tomb is known to everyone, while that of the tomb of Jefferson Davis is known only to a comparative few.

Although in its subject matter and its strong and unified narrative line, *Cold Harbor* marked a new direction for Mabou Mines, it continued, in many fundamental ways, features that had characterized their work from the beginning, and which, interestingly enough, they shared to an important extent with the Wooster Group, whose artistic formation was taking place at almost exactly the same time. One of these, as I have mentioned, was a strong interest in collage—the combination not only of different linguistic and textual material, but even more important, of material from the visual arts—painting, film, cinema, and of course found objects. The use of found material, both visual and textual, was central to both groups, as was the experimentation with this material in various forms and combinations as an essential part of the development of each production.

The odd collection of Grant memorabilia the curators are sorting through is clearly related to this process, but the production as a whole was a calculatedly eclectic one. Civil War photographs and film clips punctuated the action, somewhat in the manner of a Living Newspaper of the 1930s. In addition, on a small stage at the rear of the set six actors created a series of tableaux vivants, a highly popular form both in the theatre and in private homes during Grant's lifetime. These were both reflective of the historical events being narrated by Raymond and also included abstract representations of qualities such as "Suffering" or "Justice," the kind of themes that were in fact often found in the historical phenomena they were re-creating.

One feature that separated this work both from early Mabou Mines productions and from those of the Wooster Group, however, was the actual subject matter of the work and the manner in which it was found and utilized. Despite the variety of material presented—the photographs, the tableaux vivants, the charred bones and tear-stained pillowcases—the actual text of the play utilized extensive quotations from two sources, the autobiographies of Grant and of his wife, Julia Dent Grant. *Cold Harbor*'s use of material of this sort thus anticipated the vogue of so-called verbatim theatre in the United States and England during the following decade, but its approach to such material was much more self-reflective, using this material not only to build a theatrical picture of Grant and his surrounding culture, but equally important, in the actions and debates of the two curators, to emphasize how the "facts" of history are subject to manipulation by the succeeding curatorial interventions. Such reflexivity was often lacking in the verbatim dramas of the 1990s, and stimulated criticism of their assumed "objectivity." I cannot recall another production that confronted this editorialization of history so directly as *Cold Harbor* until Jackie Sibblies Drury's 2012 *We Are Proud to Present a Presentation . . .* , created in the wake of turn-of-the-century verbatim drama.

Within the trajectory of the Mabou Mines, however, *Cold Harbor*, despite its success, remained something of an isolated experiment. The work continued to be extremely varied, following the interests of individual members. Raymond's own next Mabou Mines project, in 1985, was directing an adaptation by Linda Hartinian, the designer of *Cold Harbor*, of *Flow My Tears, the Policeman Said*, the dystopian science fiction novel by Philip K. Dick. Other company productions continued the presentation of Beckett works and added several by the German naturalist Franz Xaver Kroetz, while other experiments went in different directions entirely, such as Ruth Maleczech's innovative one-woman video/live performance *Hajj*, which opened almost simultaneously with *Cold Harbor*. Lee Breuer, who wrote the text for *Hajj*, became the first member of the company to gain major critical attention with his *The Gospel at Colonus*, premiered in the BAM Next Wave Festival this same year. Amid all of the performance directions being explored by Mabou Mines members in the early 1980s, the type of historical exploration represented by *Cold Harbor* was not repeated, even though it prefigured an important part of the experimental theatre of the following decade.

1984 Dustin Hoffman in *Death of a Salesman*

The great triumvirate of playwrights Williams, Miller, and O'Neill received more regular major revivals in the late twentieth century than anyone else, each averaging four to five Broadway revivals per decade. Given the actor-oriented emphasis of the American theatre, almost all of these were presented as showcases for major actors of the period, often not theatre stars, but stars of film or television. The 1984 revival of Miller's central work, *Death of a Salesman*, starring Dustin Hoffman, represented a clear example of this dynamic. Hoffman was at this time one of the best-known and most-admired American actors, but his reputation was built almost entirely upon his film work.

In fact Hoffman had begun his career with a few off-Broadway appearances in the late 1960s, and indeed I saw him in 1967 as an amusing, quirky cockney in Henry Livings's play *Eh?* at the Circle in the Square, but even though this role won him several awards, it was not until Hoffman's triumph in the film *The Graduate* the following year that I, along with most of the film and theatre-going public, recognized him as a major new talent. During the next several years he firmly established himself as one of the leading Hollywood actors, excellent in roles as the new rather offbeat film protagonists that characterized many of the major films of this period. From these years came, among others, *Midnight Cowboy* (1969), *Lenny* (1974), *Kramer vs. Kramer* (1979), and the 1982 comedy *Tootsie*, in which he created a memorable drag role.

During these triumphant years his early stage work was virtually forgotten, and the announcement that he would be returning to the theatre to play one of the central roles in the American repertoire, Willy Loman in *Death of a Salesman*, created a tremendous stir. Of course far less attention was given to the rest of the cast, or to the director Michael Rudman, although he had created a well-received revival of Miller's play at the National Theatre in London five years before. The most pre-show publicity about cast, aside from that concerning Hoffman, concerned the role of Willy's older brother, Ben. A striking indication of the privileging of name recognition over talent or experience was manifested by the announcement that G. Gordon Liddy was being considered for the part. Liddy had never appeared on the stage, but was in the early 1980s a major cultural figure. Convicted for his participation in the Watergate scandal under Nixon, he served a prison term, after which he published an autobiography and took to the lecture circuit, becoming the most popular speaker on U.S. college campuses in 1982.

Happily, this possibility did not work out, and after the production opened the cast member most noticed, after Hoffmann, was John Malkovich, who played Willy's son Biff. Although Malkovich, like Hoffman, did not much resemble the by-now iconic figures of the original production, each put his or her own stamp on these figures, and redefined them in the theatrical consciousness. Malkovich had had only a single previous New York appearance, but it was a highly significant one. In 1982 he appeared as one of the leads in a touring production of the Steppenwolf Theatre Company in Chicago, of which he was a key member, at the Cherry Lane Theatre. The play was Sam Shepard's *True West*, which gained Malkovich a number of important awards. It was also the first Steppenwolf production to come to New York, although in subsequent years that company would be one of the most important regional theatres to send actors and productions to New York, and these would bring a rough new vitality to the stages of that city.

This production of *Death of a Salesman* opened at the Broadhurst

Theatre, in the middle of Forty-Fourth Street between Broadway and Eighth Avenues. Today it is near the center of the Broadway theatre district, but in 1984, it and its fellow theatres along Forty-Fourth Street marked the southern boundary of this district. Forty-Third Street served as a kind of buffer between the theatre district and the most notorious section of Forty-Second Street, then considered, as I have noted, one of the worst streets in America for drugs, sex, and street crime. It would have been almost unthinkable to walk into the theatre district from that direction, close as it was, and on our New York visits at that time my wife and I used to stay in various hotels in the more respectable north. For some years we favored the rather rundown but charmingly Victorian Great Northern Hotel, once home to Isadora Duncan and William Saroyan, and a favorite for bargain-conscious young Cornell faculty members. After it was torn down in 1980 to make way for the luxurious Parker Meridien hotel, we shifted to the Hotel Empire, near Lincoln Center, which in those days was still an economical choice, though a bit longer walk down to the theatre district. On Forty-Fourth Street, the Broadhurst stood between two large musical houses, the Shubert on its right, where at that time *Chorus Line* was in its eighth year, and the Majestic on its left, where *42nd Street* was in its third year. Across the street were two theatres, the St. James, offering *My One and Only*, with Tommy Tune and Twiggy, and the recently renamed Helen Hayes, Broadway's smallest house, where Harvey Fierstein's *Torch Song Trilogy* was then in its third year. In this neighborhood a classic revival, even of an American classic, was clearly something of an anomaly. Nevertheless the combination of Miller, Malkovich, and Hoffmann proved most attractive, and this *Death of a Salesman* was the major hit of the season.

Any actor undertaking a revival must deal with the ghosts of his predecessors in the role, especially if one or two of them have left particularly strong memories. This was certainly the case with the memory of Lee J. Cobb, who created Willy Loman in 1949, whose rear image carrying two display suitcases is one of the most familiar icons in the American theatre and whose 1966 TV film version kept alive the memory of his performance for new generations. In fact, Dustin Hoffman was physically much closer to Arthur Miller's original view of the character than was the rather bulky Cobb (Miller famously changed the "shrimp" epithet thrown at Willy to "walrus" for Cobb, and Hoffman restored the original). I had not seen the original stage production, but like most theatre fans I had seen the TV film, and found Hoffman's Willy totally different and highly effective. He was a small nervous figure, always twitching and full of tics, taking off and putting on his jacket, polishing his glasses, drumming on the table. One could still see the energy and drive of the young hustler in him, but now tinged with exhaustion and a hint of losing control. Unlike Cobb, Hoffman was immaculately dressed, in a dashing, if somewhat outdated three-piece suit with elegant matching tie and handkerchief. Even his thin, wispy silver hair (reportedly Hoffman shaved his head and then pasted on these thinning strands to get this effect) was carefully composed. The effect, however, was not that of an impressively decked-out man of the world, but rather of someone desperately trying to project that image, but unable to hide that desperation.

Although the British-American actress Kate Reid shared top billing with Hoffman and Malkovich, it was the latter two and their relationship that totally dominated the production. Arthur Kennedy, who created the role of Biff, first achieved major recognition in this part, for which he received a Tony, but he had left a far less specific concept of how the role should be played than had Cobb. In any case, I think my reaction to Malkovich's interpretation was less colored by a mental comparison with Kennedy, or with some abstract image of the fading former high school sports star than by a comparison to his previous award-winning New York appearance in *True West*. So effective had Malkovich been as the scruffy, drunken, toaster-smashing renegade in that play that I could hardly imagine him in anything delicate and sensitive. Malkovich's Biff therefore was a real revelation of his versatility. His voice was soft and tentative, his gestures often large but vague and undirected—he was the picture of insecurity and self-doubt. This made him an excellent foil for the unthinking exuberance of his younger brother Happy, played by Stephen Lang, who still did not realize, as Biff clearly did, the hollowness and pointlessness of the Loman dream.

The emotional center of this production was clearly in the relationship between Willy and Biff, and Hoffman and Malkovich developed a chemistry between them that was almost overpowering. I particularly remember the moment when Hoffman wrapped his arms around his son and Malkovich, at first hesitating and resisting, at last succumbed to the pressure and returned the embrace. Almost like long-separated lovers they swayed back and forth for an extended period without speaking. I found tears rising to my eyes, and was not surprised to see that not

a few of my fellow audience members had brought out their handker-
chiefs as well.

It is a measure of the effectiveness of that relationship that I remember other members of the cast much less clearly, especially since my
memory has been overlaid by other revivals of the play since that time,
headed of course by another, unrelated Hoffman, Philip Seymour Hoffman, in 2012. This is especially true of the third leading role of the play,
that of Linda, Willy's protective wife. Linda Emond, who played the role
in 2012, brought such energy and passion to it that she has quite eclipsed
my memory of Kate Reid, whom I remember, perhaps unfairly, as much
more deferential, much more the traditional supportive wife. Of the
rest of the cast the only one who sticks in my memory was David Hud-
dleston, one of the great character actors of his generation, who presented a jolly, rotund, easy-going Charlie, Willy's successful neighbor,
who appeared as the very antithesis of Hoffman's small, nervous, and
preoccupied Willy.

Director Mike Nichols received much critical praise in 2012 for the
highly unusual choice to present his revival in a scrupulous re-creation
of the original setting by Jo Mielziner, as iconic an image in the history
of American scene design as the rear-view silhouette of Lee J. Cobb
among images of dramatic characters. In 1984, Michael Rudman had no
interest in such theatrical nostalgia, as his choice of Dustin Hoffman, a
completely different physical type for Willy, clearly showed. The scenery that Ben Edwards designed for this production had some similarities
to the Mielziner setting, but to my mind offered even greater fluidity.
Again a group of rooms were presented, with rather dowdy furnishings,
and inset areas for the various nonhome scenes, but there was less attempt to actually construct a kind of model house, and the shabby living area of the Lomans is, as Miller suggested, overshadowed by huge,
indifferent apartment houses, but Mielziner left these rather dim and
suggested, while those of Edwards were more encompassing, detailed,
and threatening.

The actual reconstruction of a period setting was a delight to me as
a student of theatre history, but also a confirmation of why this practice
has been so little utilized in the modern theatre. Our tradition and our
expectations are that each new generation of actors, and indeed each
new distinctive talent, will provide us with a fresh view of a character
like Willy Loman, and however important the legacy of the originating
artist, in this case Lee J. Cobb, no one would wish to be deprived of the

insights on this memorable little man provided by talents like Dustin Hoffman and Philip Seymour Hoffman.

1985 Thomas Langhoff's
The Merchant of Venice

Although my main interest in foreign theatre during the 1960s and 1970s was in that of London and Paris, I did make a quick trip to Berlin in 1968 to visit the Berliner Ensemble, where I found the *Coriolanus* a somewhat disappointing, museum-like piece, despite the presence of the great actress Helene Weigel. Then, during the 1980s, I became increasingly interested in Germany, where the new generation of directors, headed by Peter Stein, Claus Peymann, and Peter Zadek, was bringing about a revolution in that theatre. In 1984 I visited several cities in the Ruhr Valley such as Bochum and Wuppertal, which seemed the center of this new energy, and a year later, during a sabbatical leave, I spent my final weeks in Berlin.

My sabbatical in the spring of 1985 reflected my changing interests in the European theatre. I spent the first two months in London, the second two in Paris (then the center of my research), and the final month in Berlin. In all three cities I saw remarkable theatre: in London, *The Mysteries* at the National Theatre and Lyubimov's *The Possessed* on tour, and in Paris Ingmar Bergman's *King Lear*, Daniel Mesguich's *Romeo and Juliet*, Patrice Chéreau's *Quartett*, and a dress rehearsal at his own theatre of Peter Brook's projected *Mahabharata*. Despite this heavy competition, I found the variety and depth of theatre available in Berlin even more impressive, and it has since become my favorite theatre city.

When I first visited Berlin in 1968, it was already a divided city, the Western part an enclave within the Soviet-dominated German Democratic Republic, and separated from the GDR by a razed area and a substantial concrete wall totally surrounding it. When I returned in 1985 this wall had been made even higher and stronger, and I still remember seeing this formidable barrier, stretching on for miles, which was clearly visible from the airplane as we flew over it and into Berlin to attend the annual theatre festival (*Theatertreffen*) in May of that year.

When I visited in 1968, the western part of the city, centered on the main shopping boulevard, the Kurfürstendamm, was far more lively and commercially active than the still clearly depressed East, but the division of the city had left most of the city's major historical theatres in the East. The much more prosperous West, aside from a few boulevard-style houses, offered only two major venues, both rather pale imitations of the leading theatres in the East. These were the Schiller Theater, opened in 1951 to compete with the East's classic Deutsches Theater, and the Theater der Freien Volksbühne, opened by Erwin Piscator in 1963 to rival the long-established Volksbühne in the East.

The situation in the West was distinctly improved when I returned in 1985. At the beginning of this decade the city had converted a large film theatre on the Ku-damm into a major venue to house the company of Peter Stein, then clearly the leading West German director. On this trip I saw at the Schaubühne two memorable productions: Stein's *The Hairy Ape* and Luc Bondy's elegant interpretation of Marivaux's *The Triumph of Love*, which was also featured in that year's *Theatertreffen*. The rest of the offerings were held in the Freie Volksbühne and the nearby Theater am Kürfurstendamm, which has since become devoted to light entertainment, comedies, and musicals. Despite this impressive fare, I also wanted to see some offerings in the East. Having visited the Berliner Ensemble during the previous trip, this time I went to the nearby Deutsches Theater, which since the days of Reinhardt had been generally regarded as Berlin's leading theatre. It was now directed by one of the most honored theatre artists in the East, Thomas Langhoff. Particularly attractive to me was Langhoff's *Merchant of Venice*, which had premiered at this theatre only two months before.

Travel from West to East Berlin had become much more regularized in the two decades since my previous visit, but it was still a difficult and tension-filled process, even for foreign tourists, and much more for the Berliners themselves. There were only a few official and rigidly controlled gateways through the Wall. The most famous was Checkpoint Charlie, but the most important was at the Friedrichstrasse Railway Station, which I used on both trips since it was very close to both the Berliner Ensemble and the Deutsches Theater.

Nothing in Berlin more reflected the bizarre and complex division of the city than the Friedrichstrasse Station. Long the most important local and international station in the city, it continued in significant measure to fill that role after the division, even though it was not in fact located on the border, but entirely within East Berlin, and thus in significant measure an enclave of its own. Visitors from the West could arrive by train and be deposited in neutral areas. Foreign visitors then went through a warren of stairways and halls to emerge into a large waiting room, where they were assigned a number and stood for varying lengths of time trying to hear their number (and also the number of their examination booth) announced in German over a very inferior loudspeaker system. At one end of the room was a wall of numbered doors, each giving access to a small corridor where each arriving visitor was examined and cleared for passage. All were also required to exchange twenty-five West German marks for the same number of East German marks. This was essentially a gift to the East German economy, since officially the exchange rate was ten eastern marks for one western, but in fact eastern marks were essentially valueless in the West. Nor were they that easy to spend in the East, since one immediately discovered upon leaving a station a totally different world, with almost deserted and dimly lit streets, with scarcely a hint of the holiday decorations across the Wall, and with almost nothing of the crowds of little shops one normally finds clustered around a station.

In the East, one emerged into a large open plaza, the main feature of which was a large glass-walled enclosure to the left. This was the famous "Palace of Tears," where German citizens, East and West, passed through, with few from the East permitted to pass, hence the unhappy name. Just behind the Palace of Tears, today a museum devoted to the division of the city and to the importance of this location, flows the river Spree, and on the opposite bank one could see the distinctive tower of the Berliner Ensemble. It was quite overshadowed, however, by an enormous boxy structure to its right, the Friedrichstadt-Palast, one of the legendary performance spaces in the city. Originally built as a huge public market, it was converted into a circus, and then, most famously, into a modernist fairy interior, the Grosses Schauspielhaus, where Max Reinhardt created some of his most ambitious spectacles. Later it featured operettas, musical spectacles, and political gatherings through the 1970s. When I passed it on my way to the Berliner Ensemble in 1969 it was hosting a major East German political event, and I was reluctant to try to get in. Later I regretted that decision, since when I returned in

1986 it was in the process of demolition and surrounded by high wooden fences. Thus I missed an opportunity to see its unique interior.

I walked around the site on my way to the nearby Deutsches Theater, but could only catch glimpses of the huge, now partly destroyed structure through cracks in the wooden walls surrounding it. I circled the entire area, taking up most of a city block, but aside from gaining some idea of its size, I was disappointed to catch little more than an occasional glimpse into the massive ruin. Upon its site today stands a huge new luxury hotel that opened in the summer of 2014, and which, rather strikingly, offers a huge architectural block that overshadows the Berliner Ensemble very much in the way the old Friedrichstadt-Palast used to do.

Just a little more than a block beyond the ruins of the Palast was the courtyard in front of the formal neoclassic facade of the Deutsches Theater, actually two adjoining facades, because early in the twentieth century Reinhardt built an adjoining theatre, the Kammerspiele, to the left of the main theatre. The lobby of the Deutsches Theater, with its pillars and chandeliers, was much more elegant than the rather spartan lobby of the Berliner Ensemble, but within the auditorium this situation was reversed. Instead of the lavish baroque interior of the Ensemble, the Deutsches Theater offered an elegant but simple interior, with modest pilasters and sconces on its balconies instead of the elaborate trimmings of the Ensemble.

Before taking my seat, however, I went to the more elegant space of the upstairs lobby, where I could get a modest wurst and bread for supper. Today the route between the Friedrichstrasse Station and the Deutsches Theater is lined, especially at the station end, with restaurants, but such eating places were few and not very attractive in the East Berlin of 1985. The food was not much better in the theatre, but at least the surroundings were much more attractive. In any case, it was all very inexpensive. Even after purchasing my ticket and supper, I still had most of the twenty-five marks I had been required to purchase at the border.

The interior of the Deutsches followed a standard European model—a horseshoe auditorium with boxes on the sides and galleries at the rear, a shape not unlike the Berliner Ensemble, but without the exuberant baroque decor, much more in line with the modified neoclassic taste at the end of the nineteenth century. The dominant color was a deep rich red, with white, cream, and occasional gold accents.

That same deep red was carried through into the *Merchant of Venice* sets, which did not seek to differentiate scenically between bustling, urban Venice and idyllic, pastoral Belmont. A single neutral unit setting, vaguely suggestive of Shakespeare's arrangements at the Globe, served for both.

This merging of Venice and Belmont reflected Langhoff's approach to the play, which saw it not as a battle between two opposed cultures, but rather as a struggle among equally determined and ruthless parties for superiority, especially economic superiority. It was not immediately easy to distinguish Shylock from his fellow merchants, who were Christian. All had something of the look of Brechtian depictions of capitalist overlords—heavy and rich fur coats, gloves, and cigars—although their style, somewhat mannered and rhetorical, had little of the Brechtian directness and edge. Shylock, played by the great actor Fred Düren, who in fact converted to Judaism a few years later, was no revengeful monster, but a richly textured human being who operated according to the same laws of survival of the fittest as did Antonio and the rest, neither more nor less. If there were a villain in the piece, it was probably Lorenzo, whose cocky exultation at his own rise and Shylock's fall was deeply distasteful. He and the rest left Jessica forlorn and abandoned alone on stage at the end. In short, the production seemed to me a highly successful reading of the work as a condemnation of the excesses of capitalism, a reading that seemed highly appropriate for the leading German theatre in socialist East Berlin.

In those days, most German productions, especially of classics like Schiller and Shakespeare, often ran four or five hours, or even longer, and although I was fascinated by this *Merchant*, I began to worry, as midnight approached, what difficulties I might encounter at the border. All went well, however. The large crowds at the Friedrichstrasse station earlier had dwindled to a few late theatre-goers like myself, and the bored guards waved us through rather perfunctorily, although they were careful to collect what remained of our forced purchase of DDR currency. We walked out into the sharply contrasted bright lights of the West with the distinct impression of emerging into quite a different country, which it indeed was.

1986 The Market Theatre's *Asinamali!*

In the summer of 1985 the Vivian Beaumont and Mitzi Newhouse theatres at Lincoln Center stood empty and almost forgotten, not having produced a single play in over four years. The former New York mayor John Lindsay asked Gregory Mosher, the successful young leader of the Goodman Theatre in Chicago, to take over the enterprise, and Mosher, if he did not fulfill the visions of their founders, succeeded for the first time in making these theatres a viable and ongoing enterprise. He announced his first full season for 1986–87, included a sampling of American works from the 1920s and 1930s, some new plays, and most notably, a strong representation of African theatre, with Wole Soyinka's *Death and the King's Horseman* and a monthlong festival of South African plays opening the Mitzi Newhouse in September and October. The festival was to be called "Woza Africa!" and opened with a new South African work, *Asinamali!*

Mosher's choice was an inspired one. South African theatre was not unknown to New York theatre-goers, although that knowledge was primarily based on the works of a single politically engaged white writer, Athol Fugard. Fugard had appeared on the New York theatre scene more than two decades before this, with his powerful *The Blood Knot*, and had been recognized as a major contemporary figure during the 1980s, with two revivals of *The Blood Knot*, at the Roundabout in 1980 and on Broadway at the John Golden Theatre in 1985 and also with a Broadway production of *Master Harold . . . and the Boys* at the Lyceum in 1982.

The visibility and success of these plays clearly contributed to the growing awareness of the problem of apartheid in South Africa, and although Fugard was a unique voice, the New York theatre showed a growing interest in dramatic work from that nation during the early 1980s, as Fugard was gaining in public attention. In 1983 I saw a small but well-received storytelling theatre piece, *The Long Journey of Poppie Nongena*, at St. Clement's Church by South African author Elsa Joubert. It had received its premiere in South Africa, but was presented in New York by American actors of South African descent. The following year I saw at the Lucille Lortel Theatre in Greenwich Village the Obie Award–winning *Woza Albert!*, from which Mosher obviously derived the title of his festival two years later and which had many elements in common with *Asinamali!*—including, obviously, the exclamation mark in its name. This punctuation has of course long been popular in the enthusiastic world of the American musical comedy, going back at least to Gershwin's *Oh, Kay!* in 1926, but if these two South African productions were drawing upon a previous theatrical source, it was more likely *Can't Pay! Won't Pay!*, the internationally best-known work of the great political satirist Dario Fo, written in 1974, and first translated into English the following year. *Asinamali!* is in fact almost a literal translation of Fo's title into Zulu, meaning, "We have no money," and is a similar protest against inhuman economic conditions.

Woza is another Zulu expression, this one meaning, "Rise up!" another political rallying cry. In *Woza Albert!*, two black actors played a wide variety of roles, some rather similar to those in *Asinamali!*, although the subject matter of *Woza Albert!* was more fanciful, dealing with the results of the Second Coming of Christ to South Africa. Both productions made liberal use of mime, singing and dance, and storytelling, and importantly, both were products of Johannesburg's Market Theatre, a center for the antiapartheid struggle during the 1970s and 1980s. A close tie between the artistic approach of the two works was assured not only by their development within the same artistic crucible, but by the overlapping presence of Mbongeni Ngema, who collaborated on the earlier piece and who both wrote and directed *Asinamali!*. The success of these two works brought the Market Theatre to international attention, and its repertoire provided Mosher with the basis of his "Woza Africa!" festival.

Rarely in American theatre history has a production in a major theatre so closely reflected upon current events as did the opening of *Asinamali!* at Lincoln Center in the fall of 1986. South Africa and its segregationist policies had become an increasingly significant international concern for almost two decades and a major policy question raised by the Congressional Black Caucus in the United States ever since its establishment in 1971. These concerns resulted at last in the Comprehensive Anti-Apartheid Act of 1986, calling for sanctions and the release of all political prisoners, including, most famously, Nelson Mandela. The passing of this act encouraged similar actions in Europe and Japan, and was clearly instrumental in bringing the apartheid system to an end. The bill passed Congress on September 10 and was vetoed by President Reagan on September 26. Congress overrode the veto on October 2,

1986, the twentieth century's first override of a presidential veto on foreign policy.

Remarkably, *Asinamali!*, the opening production of Mosher's South African Festival and a powerful theatrical denunciation of apartheid, opened on September 10, the very day that Congress passed this decisive legislation. The festival coincided almost precisely with these major legislative events, ending with the mixed racial production *Born in the R.S.A.* on October 5, just three days after Reagan's veto was overridden. It was virtually impossible for audiences of the festival not to be aware of its relationship to these rapidly unfolding international events. The nearest parallel I can think of was audiences attending *Fun Home*, the first Broadway musical with a lesbian protagonist, as the Supreme Court was debating the issue of same-sex marriage in June 2014. (The day the affirmative ruling was handed down, a spontaneous party took place after the production of this play—as it did in many of the theatres in New York.) On a more personal level, *Asinamali!* was one of the first productions of the new season, the first season that I experienced as a resident of New York City. I had moved to Brooklyn that summer to take up a position at the Graduate Center of the City University of New York and henceforward needed no longer confine my theatre-going to academic vacations, but could make it a yearlong activity, which I have done ever since.

Actually this was not *Asinamali!*'s first appearance in New York; it had been presented in April 1986 at the New Heritage Theatre near West 126th Street in Harlem, its first showing outside of South Africa, but that production was scarcely noticed by downtown theatre-goers. The situation was very different when it was given as the first offering of a theatre festival at the newly reopened Lincoln Center, especially at a time when South African race relations were prominent in the news.

Although I could not anticipate that Mosher would finally restore stability to the long-ailing Lincoln Center, I was very pleased to return to the Mitzi Newhouse, the smaller downstairs space there that had been dark for most of the previous decade. The last play I had seen there was David Rabe's *Streamers* in 1976, one of the last successes of the Papp administration. *Asinamali!* was extremely well suited to this intimate and open space. Its setting consisted of only five chairs for the performers, who in fact rarely sat, but were in almost constant motion for the seventy minutes or so of the production.

The cast was composed of five black men, similar in size and shape, all bald and all wearing identical khaki prison uniforms. They represented five men who meet in a single prison cell and represent a spectrum of the victims of the South African regime, having in common only their skin color. Only one is an actual lawbreaker, a pickpocket. Others are a political activist, a farmer, a migrant laborer, and a man actually caught in a security raid. As they entertain each other with the stories of their trials, both their physical movements and their verbal texts moved seamlessly from individual contributions to group movement, from spontaneous songs to choral recitations and a wide range of vocal effects. Despite the fact that there were distinct narrative and even short dramatic scenes, the impression was more that of a "choreo-poem" like *for colored girls* than a conventional dramatic action.

Despite the openness of the stage space, the continued close physical proximity of the actors and the restricted lighting rarely let us forget that they were confined in a very tiny space, and indeed one with only a limited view of the external world. Particularly moving was the repeated act of standing on tiptoe on one of the chairs to catch a glimpse outside through a peephole apparently located high up in the unseen wall of the cell. In fact one of the few sequences that I felt ineffective in this production was the only one that seriously broke this claustrophobic concentration. It was initiated when one of the actors shouted out that there was an informer in the audience. The entire cast then left the stage and circulated through the audience, angrily seeking this betrayer of their cause. It was easy to imagine how powerful this scene must have been in the racially mixed audience of the Market Theatre, which was always under close police surveillance and where audiences doubtless frequently did contain real informers. In the comfortable and solidly liberal confines of the Mitzi Newhouse theatre, however, the sequence conjured up not very positive memories of the audience invasions of the Living Theatre after their return from Europe, when such intrusions had become for most theatre-goers a somewhat embarrassing and dated device.

So long as the actors remained within their imaginary cell and their recounted stories, though, their effect was very strong. A wide range of dramatic styles were suggested—absurdist comedy, debasing embarrassment, horrific personal and social conditions, and a wide range of reactions to a deeply dysfunctional society, determined not to recognize this dysfunction. A program provided important background information and explanations of many unfamiliar words, but although the general situation of the prisoners was clear, the unfamiliar accents, the musical nature of much of the delivery, and the continual mixing of language made this much more a visual than a verbal text. Each of the actors told something of the events leading to his incarceration, and in one typical sequence, a courtroom was evoked, in which the judge spoke Afrikaans, which the court interpreter translated into muddled and heavily accented English, while the defendant, who could understand little of either language, had to make do with fragments of Zulu muttered to him by a court orderly. The program also informed us of the meaning and origin of the play's title, which had become the rallying cry of a South African rent strike in 1983.

The glowing reviews and audience enthusiasm for *Asinamali!* as a part of the Lincoln Center Festival encouraged backers to support it for a move to Broadway, the first play from South Africa to be offered there. The theatre was one of the most intimate on Broadway, however. It was the Jack Lawrence Theatre, with only 499 seats, located on the very fringe of the theatre district, at 359 West Forty-Eighth Street. Despite the small size, the play had only a short run, in May 1987, and was in fact the last production offered in that space. This disappointment was more than compensated for, however, by the success of Mbongeni Ngema's next creation, *Sarafina!*, dealing with the Soweto antiapartheid riots of 1976. After its premiere at the Market Theatre in 1987, it opened early in 1988 at the Cort Theatre, a larger and more centrally located Broadway house, where it ran almost two years, garnering a large number of awards.

1987 John Krizanc's *Tamara*

In the spring of 1987 the New York newspapers announced an innovative production from Canada based on events in the life of Italian playwright Gabriele D'Annunzio. I had been working during that decade on D'Annunzio and the Italian theatre of his time and so this subject had a particular interest for me. In fact although I did enjoy the depiction of the colorful dramatist and his circle, the innovative staging of the production is what made a lasting impression on me. Neither in its original form in Toronto in 1981, nor in its first revival in Los Angeles in 1984 (where it ran for nine years) had *Tamara* been performed in a conventional theatre, but in spaces with multiple elegant rooms already decorated in the general style of D'Annunzio's period. As the play progressed, audiences were required to follow actors from room to room to watch the evolving action.

In the almost three decades since that production, performances with mobile audiences have become an important part of the international experimental theatre, but at that time, this was an almost unheard-of phenomenon. The environmental theatre of Richard Schechner in New York and the early theatrical experiments of Jerzy Grotowski in the 1960s consciously overlapped audience and actor spaces but rarely moved audiences into multiple spaces. Squat Theatre, La Mama, and some other experimental groups during the 1970s who were fortunate enough to possess multiple performance spaces sometimes used more than one in a production, but I had never encountered a production where a mobile audience in multiple locations was central to the concept. The closest example I had yet seen of this approach was *Fefu and Her Friends*, by one of America's most innovative theatre artists, Maria Irene Fornés, at the American Place Theatre in 1978. After an initial scene in a living room, the audience was divided into four groups and visited three other locations, a kitchen, a bedroom, and a garden, in different order, with the actors playing the same scenes four times for the different groups. *Tamara* moved this device to the center of the production, affecting every part of the experience.

Ticket prices for *Tamara* were the highest I had yet seen in New York. Although the matinees charged only $85, weekend evening performances were $135, surpassing even the famously high-priced *Nicholas Nickleby*, with less than half the running time. *The Phantom of the Opera*, then one of the most expensive Broadway shows, had a top ticket price of $50, although BAM, which was at this time hosting Peter Brook's *Mahabharata* from Paris, was charging up to $96 a seat, almost up to the magic $100 mark. An important part of the justification for the high *Tamara* prices was that the evening, unlike *Phantom* or even the lengthy *Mahabharata*, included a catered buffet dinner and free champagne. The dinner was catered by Le Cirque, a restaurant opened in 1974, replacing the Four Seasons as the preferred dining spot for those New Yorkers whose possession of and display of wealth in the 1980s placed them within what cultural historian Kevin Phillips and others labeled the "Second Gilded Age." Whatever their artistic or gustatory achievements, this pairing of a restaurant like Le Cirque with a theatre production charging more than $100 a ticket seemed an ideal combination. It is striking that when the vogue for "immersive" theatre hit London and New York in the first decade of the next century, the strongly commercial and consumerist orientation of *Tamara* was repeated by such productions along with the innovative staging style. Very high prices, often including meals, the audience numbers limited, creating a sense of exclusivity, and a strong pressure to return for repeated viewings were all characteristic of the new post-2000 "immersive" productions, as they had been of *Tamara*.

Not to be omitted from this concatenation of conspicuous consumption was the venue itself. Probably no public space in New York could have been better suited to stand in for the palatial Vittoriale where D'Annunzio lived after 1921 than was the Park Avenue Armory. In addition to its massive drill hall and other spaces, the Armory possesses an unparalleled suite of rooms, opened in 1880 for the comfort and relaxation of members of the Seventh Avenue Regiment, which was largely drawn from the social elite of New York. These rooms were designed and decorated by some of the leading architects and decorators of the period, headed by Louis Tiffany and Stanford White, employing a wealth of marble, carved woodwork, and stained glass. In short, one of the great interiors of New York's first Gilded Age was made available in *Tamara* (for a suitable fee) to participants in the second.

When I arrived at the Armory in December 1987 for the production, I had only been inside the building once or twice and, like most visitors, had almost no concept of the interior spaces that would be used for *Tamara*. For a number of years the Armory had hosted a major antiques show in its huge drill hall, one of the city's largest indoor spaces. Although I had attended this show, I had little memory of the building itself, aside from the fact that it was a huge, fortress-like brick structure occupying an entire city block near Hunter College. To enter, one walked up a stone front staircase, through large double doors into a large lobby and hallway and moved directly forward, between two side staircases through another set of doors into the huge drill hall, broken up into many small individual display booths for the show. Although side halls to the lavish interior rooms ran to the left and right just inside the lobby entrance, they were not open for display during the antiques show.

With *Tamara*, the use of space was totally different. The massive drill hall was not used and the audience assembled in the lobby-like space between the two sweeping staircases, where we were provided with the rules of the performance. These were given to us by an imposing and distinctly threatening actor who addressed us from a high position on the stairs and played the Italian police officer who was in charge of maintaining security in the villa where the action occurred. The presumed year was 1927, and the setting the villa where D'Annunzio had been placed under an unofficial house arrest by Mussolini. The Tamara of the title was the scandalous painter of the era, Tamara Lempicka, who comes to the villa to create a portrait of the famous poet and womanizer.

Finzi, the police officer, gave the audience of approximately one hundred strict instructions. Instead of a program we were issued a passport and were divided into smaller groups, each of which was required after the opening instructions to follow a member of the cast. We were not allowed to move about on our own, although if the cast member we were following was involved in a scene with others, which obviously happened frequently, we could then follow someone else when they left that scene. We were informed that if we were discovered on our own or could not produce a passport when requested, that we would be expelled from the building.

I would have preferred to follow D'Annunzio, but I was assigned to one of the maids. Actually this turned out well, since during the first sequence my group was alone with the maid and she in fact treated us as house guests, giving us useful information (at least from her point of view) about many of the other characters. In fact this was the only time during the evening that I was acknowledged by an actor. Normally the audience simply grouped themselves around the actors wherever they were doing a scene and were totally ignored by the actors, even when they had to be pushed aside for an entrance or exit. After a couple of scenes, the maid encountered D'Annunzio, giving me the opportunity to follow him instead. This took me into more elegant rooms and generally more formal settings, but on the whole D'Annunzio seemed to have little interest in anything other than drugs and romantically pursuing most of the women in the house, and even before the intermission I had come to realize that the machinations and intrigues among the servants were probably more lively than those among the aristocrats. Indeed I was reminded of the enormously popular TV series *Upstairs, Downstairs*, which I had followed avidly a decade before and which similarly followed the interwoven and complex intrigues of the various social classes within a large, aristocratic home of this type.

During the intermission, the audience gathered around the elegant buffet, and almost the entire conversation concerned the exchange of information. Everyone had only a piece of the story and was curious to see how it fitted elsewhere. What was that upstairs shot? Or that apparent fight on the stairs? What had happened in a previous scene to make a particular character act in a certain way? And most important, what were the various intrigues, political and romantic, that seemed to involve in some way almost every character? Like most couples in the audience, my wife and I had followed different characters in the first act, but that still left eight other characters interacting with these and others while we were not present. My wife had followed one of the upper-class women in the first part and decided to switch to Finzi, the dark and mysterious police official, after the intermission. I changed to Mario, the chauffeur, who seemed to have a hand in almost everyone's plot and who indeed kept me and his other followers very busy rushing from room to room and up and down the stairs for most of the second act. At one point, Mario left D'Annunzio's bedroom (the aristocrats slept on the second floor, while the kitchen and servants' quarters were in the basement), and practically ran down three flights of stairs to his own room at the far end of the building, made a furiously quick costume change (my wife had seen him in the nude earlier) and rushed off again to a scene in the kitchen. The action took place in thirteen major rooms, but stairs, hallways, and various nooks and crannies were utilized as well, perhaps doubling the number of possible locations. In large scenes, with most of the cast present, actors and audience would almost totally fill a room, but I also remember a scene where D'Annunzio secretly telephoned a contact in the government in a small vestibule where I was one of only two audience members present. Following the production, most of the audience remained in the theatre for another half-hour or so, drinking complimentary coffee and exchanging further information on different plot and character elements they had experienced. Not a few of them promised to come back to see the work again from other perspectives.

In the twenty-first century, a production like *Tamara* would doubtless be described as "immersive," and it in fact anticipated many of the features of that genre, artistically, socially, and economically, but that term was still unknown in the early 1980s. Most reviewers who needed a generic classification called it a "promenade production," a term that had come to prominence in England during the previous decade, especially in reference to the informal seating arrangements in many of the offerings at the small experimental theatre, the Cottesloe. *Entertaining Strangers* and the more famous *Mysteries* were leading examples of such productions. In fact, so-called promenade productions in the National Theatre and elsewhere at this time were content to encourage audiences to stroll about within a large but confined area. The sort of multiple space and necessarily fragmented and partial experience that resulted, as seen in *Tamara*, was still a rarity, although during the next two decades it became a major part of the experimental theatre in both Europe and America. Most of the key elements in productions of this sort—the more or less active participation of the audience, the fragmented and multiple perspectives, the denial of closure, could also be clearly seen as related to the project of postmodernism, a major feature of intellectual and cultural life of the late twentieth century.

As for the Park Avenue Armory, *Tamara* was the first of a steadily expanding number of offerings of major avant-garde theatrical productions, so that in the new century the Armory became one of the favored New York locations for such work.

1988 David Edgar's *Entertaining Strangers*

This one essay differs from all the rest in this collection, which were written in the second decade of the twenty-first century. This is another autobiographical memory, but was created only a few months after the performance. In 1988 I coauthored a beginning theatre history text with Yvonne Shafer called *The Play's the Thing*, which included seven fictional "eyewitness" accounts of historical productions and one actual eyewitness account written by myself of a performance seen that year. The original account is too long to include here, but I have extracted the following condensation:

In January 1988 my wife and I traveled to Paris to see *L'Indiade*, the new production by Ariane Mnouchkine, and then to London to see a new play by David Edgar, *Entertaining Strangers*. Although *Entertaining Strangers* was a new and unfamiliar play, there were several reasons for selecting it. Two of my favorite actors were appearing in the play's leading roles—Judi Dench and Tim Pigott-Smith. The author, David Edgar, also interested me, especially for his marvelous stage adaptation of *Nicholas Nickleby*, one of the most memorable theatre events of the decade. Finally, the ads noted that Peter Hall, the leading director of the National Theatre, was presenting the play as a "promenade production" in the experimental Cottesloe Theatre, a very interesting theatrical space, especially for a production of this kind. In promenade productions, a few reserved seats are available, as are a larger number of unreserved seats, but at least half of the audience is accommodated in the large central acting area, seated or standing, while action occurs among and around them.

Rather surprisingly, neither of London's two major state-supported theatres, the National and the Barbican, is located conveniently near a stop on London's generally accessible subway system. The nearest stop for the National is at Waterloo Station, but I prefer to leave the subway at the Embankment Station across the river and cross the Hungerford footbridge to the South Bank. The walk across the river is very attractive except in the most unpleasant weather, and at the far side one can follow the esplanade along the river past other parts of the South Bank complex to the theatre.

At the first turning of the stairway leading up to the bridge, we found an elderly beggar with a piece of cardboard laid out before him to receive coins. His presence reminded me that in previous years, the area adjoining the Embankment Station to the west, under a railway arch, was a major place of shelter for homeless men. This year some construction project had filled all this space with walls and scaffolding and I wondered what had become of these victims of society. In London as in New York, a visit to the theatre today often brings one past examples of society's failure, and the contrast between the glitter and wealth frequently on display within the theatre's walls and what may be seen just outside has often made me uneasy.

The evening of January 26 was a typical January evening in London, overcast and a bit damp, with temperatures about fifteen degrees above freezing. Winters in London seem damp but quite mild to a visitor from New York. On the bridge a beautiful panorama stretched out to the east, with the South Bank complex to our right and other monuments illuminated ahead of us and reflected in the Thames. Crossing the bridge, we came at last to the huge concrete structure of the National Theatre. The Cottesloe is located to the rear of the building, but we postponed that final approach to have our supper instead at one of the buffets in the much more spacious lobbies of the main theatres, the Lyttleton and Olivier. There is a more interesting selection of dishes there, and, moreover, one has the pleasure of hearing live chamber music while dining. The group that evening was a piano trio.

After dining, we left the main lobby to go outside and around the building to the back corner and the much more modest entrance to the Cottesloe. We checked our coats and umbrellas, which can be a considerable nuisance during a promenade production. Near the cloakroom, signs provided a special warning: "Promenaders: During the action of the play, metal bridges pass through the promenade area. Please move out of their path when asked to do so."

The two lobby doors gave access to the south end of the theatre. From each door a corridor ran northward, with a wall on one side and the other side open to the central playing space. Partway along each corridor, an open stairway led to a second and third level, each with a single row of seats on three sides of the space. The north section had no seats and was used only by the actors. The open central area, perhaps twenty feet east to west and forty north to south, was for this production almost entirely occupied by a platform covered with imitation grass. At the north and south ends playing areas had been constructed several feet above the grassy promenade, with pieces of furniture on each. Although we could not tell this at the beginning, a section about three feet wide and running the full width at the front of these platforms was separate, and could be moved electronically the length of the hall to join the front of the platform at the opposite end. These were the metal bridges mentioned in the lobby signs.

My wife decided to sit at the south end of the upper level, but I joined the promenaders sitting on the grass. There were perhaps a hundred people sitting in this area or standing around the edges when the performance began, with approximately the same number seated above in the galleries. Not surprisingly, the promenaders were in general young and more casually dressed. Many appeared to be students. Two sitting next to me at the opening were reading Shakespeare's *King Lear*. The play began with five musicians coming to the center of the area and playing traditional folk songs. Actors followed and circulated among the spectators, introducing themselves. A traditional British mummers' play began the evening, depicting a life-and-death battle between St. George and the dragon, a battle depicted on the program cover.

More conventional scenes followed, played on the two opposing platforms. Tim Pigott-Smith played Henry Moule, the combative new vicar of St. George's Church in a nineteenth-century Dorchester village, and Judi Dench played Sarah Eldridge, the proprietress of the local brewery, named, appropriately, the Green Dragon. The north platform generally represented the Eldridge home, while the south platform would most commonly represent the vicarage. The promenade between was a generally neutral location, but often represented a street or outdoor site. During the earlier promenade production of *The Mysteries*, a medieval religious cycle, the promenade audience sat only for certain scenes, and moved about a good deal during the play. In *Entertaining Strangers* we sat for most of the play, although as we had been warned at the beginning we were occasionally asked to move, especially to make way for the moving bridges, surely the most spectacular element of the production. Though the focus of the play was on the spiritual concerns of Moule and the capitalistic interests of Eldridge, it attempted also to present a historical panorama of the nineteenth-century community, often in a spectacular fashion.

For the coming of the age of steam, for example, the front of a steam locomotive was mounted on the center of the south bridge and it moved slowly northward, only a few feet above the heads of the seated promenade audience. With the noise, the clouds of steam, and the spotlights directed at us from the galleries above and behind the locomotive, we indeed almost felt as if we were being swallowed up by this new age. A variation of this effect ended the first act, showing a celebration of the Battle of Balaclava in Crimea in 1854. Victory flyers were showered on the heads of the promenade audience as Turkish, French, and Russian cavalry officers, straddling the shoulders of horses whose heads projected from the bridge, moved slowly from north to south over the heads of the promenade audience. When they reached a welcoming crowd at the south, however, a monstrous puppet horse emerged from beneath the platform and pushed its way north directly through the audience, its body the slats of a beer keg, its legs shocks of grain, its head a horse's skull. On it sat Moule, who had come to warn the revelers of the arrival of a new stranger, the cholera.

The effects of the cholera epidemic on the village were a dominant concern of the second act. We now witnessed a procession of strange figures clothed in straw, their faces covered with black featureless masks. Some of these figures remained among us in the audience for the next several scenes, and they were gradually joined by others, similarly dressed, some with skull masks and carrying scythes. When Sarah Eldridge's husband, Charles, died, his passing was represented by his slow descent down a stairway revealed by the opening of a trapdoor in the floor of the promenade area. This door, emphasized by a cloth tunnel, was then open continually. A procession of townspeople of all ages filed into it as a narrator called out their names and ages. Spotlighted in the four corners of the upper balcony appeared masked white figures, the angels of the apocalypse, each shouting out the description of one of the four horsemen. Shouting and singing mounted to a climax as a bridge bearing a huge steaming copper cauldron, attended by three mysterious figures shrouded in white, rolled over the promenade audience and the crouching, half-hysterical Moule. This was the visual and aural climax of the cholera sequence. In the final scene, set eighteen years later, Sarah and Moule have a final confrontation in the churchyard, at the grave of Moule's son. Among the pleasure in seeing these two fine actors creating these rich parts this evening was the experience of seeing how convincingly they aged, in voice, movement, and physical appearance. The last scene was played among us in the promenade with the tombstone at the center, and the actors only a few feet from us, and the conviction and emotion of their performance was extremely powerful at this close range. As they talked quietly together, a light "snow"— tiny flecks of paper—began to fall on them and on us from above, and we seemed truly to have entered their world. As they left the churchyard, a final mummer figure appeared on the south platform, the triumphant King George, conqueror of death and the dragon, waving a huge St. George flag. Bells rang in all corners of the theatre, and the hymn "O Holy City" broke out. An actress appeared on the platform to the north to sing a traditional wassail song, the final gift to strangers coming to be entertained. The song was then taken up by actors in all parts of the theatre to end the performance.

After lengthy curtain calls, the musicians, who took their bow last, struck up the song again to accompany the departure of the audience. As so we departed, most to take buses, subway, or private cars home, some to remain in the main lobbies of the National Theatre for a postshow supper or cup of coffee, and some pausing for a few final minutes to enjoy the warmth of the wassail song and the spirit of the Cottesloe world for a bit longer before their departure into the cool, damp, January night.

The full version of this description, about four times the length of this condensation, can be found on pages 582–595 of *The Play's the Thing: An Introduction to Theatre* by Marvin Carlson and Yvonne Shafer (New York: Longman, 1990).

1989 Yuri Lyubimov's *Three Sisters*

In 1989 I visited Moscow as one of a committee charged with assessing Moscow as a host city for an international theatre conference. It was a time of tremendous international excitement, of which the proposed conference was only one very minor part. During the previous year, the Soviet Union had ended its long war in Afghanistan and Reagan and Gorbachev had met several times. Clearly the Cold War, which had dominated world politics for more than forty years, was drawing at last toward an end. Among the productions I saw during a week in the Soviet capital, the one that left the most lasting impression was also closely tied to the evolving new international situation.

Yuri Lyubimov was widely considered the greatest Russian director of the late twentieth century, but he ran afoul of the Soviet authorities. While he was on tour in Western Europe in 1984, his protector, Yuri Andropov, general secretary of the Communist Party, died, and soon after he was removed from directorship of his theatre, the Taganka, then expelled from the Party and his citizenship revoked. Theatrically speaking, this loss for Russia was a distinct gain for the West. I was fortunate enough to see Lyubimov's *Crime and Punishment* in London in 1983, a brilliant minimalist interpretation that had been closed in Moscow and was one of the productions that led to his exile. As a part of the thaw of 1988, however, he was invited to return to the Taganka, the theatre he had founded, and he went back to work at once, even though his full citizenship was not restored until 1991.

When I visited Moscow in 1989, Lyubimov was in the middle of his first season back in the Taganka, and by far the most prominent theatre figure in the city. I was able to visit this theatre to see a revival of his *Three Sisters*, created there in 1981 and one of his most outstanding productions. In 1981 Lyubimov had already created enemies who resented his unfavorable references to contemporary Soviet life, but his theatre was still the most popular in Moscow. A new stage was opened this year to accommodate the growing number of spectators, and it opened with *Three Sisters*. It was the first theatre constructed for a particular director since that of Meyerhold in 1920, but Lyubimov's departure left the project half completed, and the result was a rather awkward blend of the old nineteenth-century building and a new configuration of three rather modest performance spaces. The largest of these was a new 773-seat space where *Three Sisters* was presented.

During the Soviet era, visitors to Moscow could not make their own travel arrangements, but provided a projected itinerary to an official government tourist authority that arranged for transportation and hotels within the Soviet Union. The favored hotel in Moscow for Western visitors was the art deco, aging, but still elegant Metropole, where I was assigned for this visit and where I had been assigned for my first visit to the city fifteen years earlier. The hotel had become a little more worn, but with the same cavernous public areas, the same elderly woman, the *dezhurnaya*, guarding each floor at the elevator entrance, the same endless corridors with full-size nude statuary and of course portraits of Lenin and Stalin. Upon my first visit I had been astonished to find that an international hotel in a capital city would from time to time run out of toilet paper, coffee, or even electricity. By my second visit I was no longer surprised, except by the determination of the U.S. government to see this economically dysfunctional society as such an existential threat.

For most tourist purposes, the Metropole location was ideal, very close to Red Square, the Bolshoi, and the Moscow Art Theatre. The Taganka was in a more remote neighborhood, but this was no disadvantage, since like most of the city, it was easily accessible by the subway, whose ornate stations, every one in a different architectural style, are one of the wonders of the city. From the Taganka subway stop it was a short walk up a busy commercial street to the functional red-and-white facade of the theatre, which occupied most of a city block. During Lyubimov's absence, a new lobby had been opened, though which I passed to reach the theatre. The stage space had also been enlarged, but for this production it was framed down to its 1981 size by large metallic panels, like interior stage walls, dimly painted with what appeared to be fading icons, suggesting perhaps the interior of one of the abandoned and deserted churches that could then be found throughout the city. In the middle of this stage area was a small, slightly raised wooden platform with two lines of simple bentwood chairs facing it with their backs to the audience. The arrangement suggested a small theatre on the stage itself and it was several times used in that way.

There were downstage subsidiary acting areas to the right and left of this central space. On the left were three beds like those in a military barracks, one made up, one bare, and one piled with stones. This space was particularly associated with the military men. On the right was a small more realistic setting with three covered chairs and a piano, clearly the main space for the sisters and Andrei. Running down the wall to the right, actually to the right of the audience, was a kind of runway, backed by four mirrored panels, each about three feet wide and perhaps twelve feet tall. These reflected the audience and whatever actor moved out onto the runway. Masha used this area the most frequently and often observed herself in the mirrors, treating this space as a kind of boudoir.

As the houselights dimmed (although they came on and off during the performance), faint military music was heard offstage, surely the band which adds a poignant undercurrent to the final scene, as the soldiers leave and the winter closes in. As the music played, the mirror wall slowly opened, revealing that it was composed of a series of revolving panels, and exposing a line of band members against a dark background. As they continued playing, the dark wall behind them similarly slowly opened to reveal the world outside—a dark courtyard, a jumble of buildings and dead trees, and in the distance the dark shapes of some undistinguished urban structures, possibly apartment houses. Suddenly the realization struck us that here in reality was the dream city of the play, the longed-for and never attained Moscow, in fact a jumble of dark, cold, forbidding structures. The reality of that dark and grim city inevitably came to mind frequently in the performance that followed, through the often-repeated "To Moscow!" of the characters, through the motif of the military music, which ran through much of the production; and through the wall of mirrors itself, since Masha in particular and occasionally others from time to time would rush against it, like trapped birds seeking an escape through a closed window. The movement would have been a powerful one in any case, but it was made vastly more so by our knowledge of the darkness beyond those glittering surfaces.

Lyubimov retained the general shape of the action, and the actors moment to moment played with great psychological subtlety and conviction, but the overall impression still was of a highly formal, almost antirealistic presentation. Two features especially reinforced this. One was the theatrical use of the small inner stage. The set speeches so common in Chekhov were often delivered quite theatrically here, with soldiers and others serving as an audience on the bentwood chairs. When the soldiers photographed the family in the first act they then turned and similarly photographed the real audience. Andrei's long speech in the last act about the depressing conformity of the townspeople was delivered on this platform utilizing clear mannerisms of Lenin and thus becoming a condemnation of the surrounding society itself. At such moments one could easily see why only a few years earlier this production and others like it were banned.

The other common and distinctly nonrealistic device was the constant reuse and recombination of visual material, creating an extremely dense web of cross-references. An excellent example of this strategy occurred near the beginning of the production. A whole sequence was added depicting the duel that in Chekhov occurs near the end and offstage. Tusenbach and Solyony, who had been seated in the onstage "audience," rose up, moved to opposite sides of the stage, and began to dress for the duel, Ferapont standing beside Tusenbach with a lighted candle and the military band softly playing beneath. Then Tusenbach and Solyony, in parallel movements, turned, went upstage, and mounted up onto the inner stage. When Solyony gave his line about putting a bullet in Tusenbach's forehead, he fired a pantomime gun directly at the audience. Tusenbach, facing front at the other side of the stage, pantomimed the impact of the shot. He fell back against the rear wall of the small inner stage, spread his arms, and threw his head back against the wall. He then moved a step to his left and repeated this action four times, bringing him to the rear door of the inner stage. He then exited backward through this door, falling against the metallic rear wall of the actual stage with a hollow crash. Ferapont, who remained on the floor level of Tusenbach's side of the stage during all this, then blew out the candle.

This entire sequence was never repeated, not even at the end of the play when the duel actually occurred, but its various elements—the candle, the dressing, the pantomime shot, the fourfold impact, the hollow crash—having been powerfully established at the very beginning, were repeated here and there throughout the evening to emphasize or to comment ironically on various moments. Striking images of this sort pervaded the evening, and once established, often served as visual leitmotifs. Andrei first appeared pushing Bobick's pram long before his marriage, and later, when Natasha tried to convince him to turn Irina's room over to the infant, she wound wool from the pram around her husband until he became so entangled that he could not move. Later this visual entanglement of Andrei was repeated by Ferapont, who brought onstage a heavy rope, which he tied across the stage, trapping Andrei and the others within it. At first I saw this rope only as a striking image of the entrapment of Andrei, and by extension, of the sisters, but then I realized it was drawn from a specific textual reference, the rope stretched across Moscow that Ferapont mentioned later in his supposed wandering comments to Andrei.

The mirror wall never let the audience forget that they were an audience, as well as being in a certain sense onstage themselves. They represented the ghostly future of which Chekhov's characters dream, and that dream, always imbued with irony, was made far darker by Lyubimov. Chekhov called for the play to end with the military music playing, but after the final line the theatre was here plunged into silence and darkness. As the houselights came faintly on, the mirrors opened once again, but now there was no music, no life, only an empty hole opening out onto a dark cityscape. The full impact of the sisters' false hopes was inescapable, and surely other audience members thought, as I did, of Vershinin's seemly casual but devastating line from early in the play: "You won't even notice Moscow when you live there. We don't have happiness. It doesn't exist. We only long for it."

The 1990s

Angels in America, 1993. Photo by Joan Marcus. Used with permission.

1990 Reza Abdoh's
Father Was a Peculiar Man

One of the major features of the Western theatre throughout the twentieth century was the continuing importance of a tradition that defined itself largely in opposition to the established theatre, a tradition variously called the avant-garde, experimental, or alternative stage. By its nature such activity was extremely varied, but during the first half of the century, it was largely concerned with developing alternatives to the essentially realistic and illusionistic mainstream drama inherited from the previous century. During the later twentieth century, two other types of experimentation steadily grew in importance, and were in many cases interrelated. One was the production of theatre in spaces outside of traditional theatres, as we have seen in *Tamara*, and the other was a shift in the role of the audience member from passive observer to a figure in some manner actively involved in the production, as in a promenade production like *Entertaining Strangers*.

The variety of such experimentation was great, and every decade or so a different term was favored for it by the media and many theatregoers, although among these terms there was always much slippage and overlap. During the 1960s and 1970s "environmental" and "participatory" theatre was favored. During the next decade, especially in England, there was a vogue for "processional" or "promenade" theatre, terms that were then overtaken, both in England and in the United States, by "site-specific" theatre, a much-disputed but very widely employed term in the last two decades of the century.

A number of companies in London and New York were devoted exclusively to this type of theatre, the first and most important one in New York being En Garde Arts, founded in 1985 by Anne Hamburger and operating until 1999. During its decade and a half it garnered many major awards, commissioned plays by most of the leading experimental dramatists in the city, and took New York audiences to a stunning variety of performance locations, many in parts of the city none of them had ever experienced before. I first became aware of this company in 1989, when strong reviews of their work led me to a group of four plays, *At the Chelsea*, intimate dramas performed in actual rooms of that historic hotel and featuring some of its many famous inhabitants, and later to *Plays in the Park*, another set of short works performed in different locations in Central Park. Their theatricalization of unconventional spaces fascinated me, and I missed almost none of their subsequent productions. At the time the media often casually defined site-specific theatre as theatre utilizing nontheatre spaces, which was generally true, but one of the most interesting En Garde projects was its next one, *Crowbar*, in 1990, created by Mac Wellman and utilizing the lobby, stage, auditorium, and balconies of the abandoned Victory Theatre on Forty-Second Street. This was the first time the Victory had presented legitimate theatre in more than sixty years. For a time a burlesque house and then a house for pornographic films but now empty, in 1990 the Victory Theatre was one of seven theatres the City of New York restored during the next decade, in an effort to revitalize this long-disreputable neighborhood.

Crowbar was performed in February and March. By June, En Garde Arts had prepared another production, by far the most ambitious in its fifteen-year history. A cast of sixty actors and musicians took to the streets, rooftops, windows, doorways, and some interior spaces of a four-square-block area in the New York meatpacking district to the west of Greenwich Village. In this rather grim area, then unfamiliar even to most New Yorkers, ominous carcass hooks hung from tracks outside brooding warehouses and irregular cobbled streets, and low-lying buildings and rare street illumination gave the impression of the dark corner of some late nineteenth-century European metropolis. In was, in short, an almost ideal locale for an adaptation of Dostoevsky's *The Brothers Karamazov*, here called *Father Was a Peculiar Man*. The director was Iranian-born Reza Abdoh, a rising star of the Los Angeles experimental scene, presenting his first production in New York.

The audience began to gather approximately an hour before the performance at the corner of Little West Twelfth Street and Ninth Avenue. Eventually the "box office"—Ms. Hamburger's white car—arrived with tickets, limited to 150. About nine the performance began, with most of the cast running, dancing, and singing all over the large square formed here by the convergence of several streets. Some actors were dressed in nineteenth-century Russian costume, others in American clothes of the 1950s, still others in the motley garb of the present Village upon whose outskirts we were gathered. There were odder elements too—two ladies gossiping under hair dryers, two men pushing a wheeled open coffin down a street, a Russian monk offering cryptic religious advice and toiletries to audience members, a man chasing a woman with a chainsaw.

After some minutes of this scattered activity, the audience was guided into a large circle around a small house with a picket fence set up on AstroTurf in the middle of the street. Although scattered activity continued elsewhere in the area—fencers, a woman singing suspended from a roof, a man being whipped tied to a bed, a running video screen, a violent fight in a darkened doorway—the majority of spectators and audience remained grouped around the house. Even there, however, focus was scattered, with several actors addressing the audience from different sides of the house. Some of these presented direct passages or phrases from Dostoevsky; others offered scraps of song or doggerel verse. This "scene" ended with a campground song about Zacharias climbing his tree, members of the company moving out to contact individual audience members and to illustrate each line of the song in mime. Then actors, musicians, and a few players acting as guides led everyone off to the next station, on another street.

Almost all of the play's eight sections (plus prologue and epilogue) shared this same general shape—a more or less guided procession to a new location, defined by a number of theatrical set pieces, this location serving as a central gathering spot for a variety of images, events, and speeches (but with tangential activity spreading away in various directions, and sometimes flowing in and out of the central location) and the sequence terminated by a larger "production number," involving most of the company in song and dance. The songs and dances were varied in period and style, but most were popular and familiar. Despite this general structural similarity, each scene had its own distinct ambiance, and three were for me particularly memorable. Section 2, "The Banquet," literally took place around (and on top of) a huge banquet table extending down the middle of a street for almost half a block, with grotesque chandeliers hanging above it, and in the center a huge Poe-like pendulum constantly swinging. Audience and actors sat around this table, as in the famous Grotowski setting for *Dr. Faustus*, as seductions, births, deaths, carnival acts, and beauty queen pageants vied for attention amid the banquet furnishings on the table.

Section 7, "The Execution," crowded the audience onto a set of rough bleachers set up across a narrow street facing a curtain suspended from the overhead supporting girders of the West Side Highway and literally closing off the street from one side to the other. The scene began in front of this curtain, but it presently opened, revealing the street running for a block or more away and terminated by a far warehouse. The entire visa was thus "theatricalized" by the curtain frame, by lighting, and by its being filled with actors alone or in small groups carrying on a variety of activities, many of them having to do with death or the preparation for death.

Section 8, "Ivan's Nightmare," was the only part of the performance held indoors, and since the space utilized here was a relatively confined one, tickets were collected only for this section. The rest of the sections could, and did, allow passersby without tickets to participate, if they wished, in the event. This section was set in a series of interconnecting rooms on the upper floor of an abandoned packinghouse. A narrow, twisting stairway, cluttered with debris, led up into a hallway that gave access to several small cubicles and three large rooms with low ceilings. At first the audience was allowed to wander freely through these dimly lit environments, past living tableaux of prisoners in cells or in confessionals, scenes of degradation and torture and scenes of religious and physical ecstasy. In one room banks of white material and white swags of material hanging from the ceiling suggested a winter environment; in another room darker hues, contorted nude bodies, and chiaroscuro lighting, with red accents, suggested an inferno, or perhaps a room for modern torture. The real-life associations of these rooms with the business of butchery reinforced their effect. After the audience had an opportunity to circulate through these rooms, a sequence of phantasmagoric scenes was offered in two of them. The nudity, the grim and claustrophobic quarters, and the necessarily close intermingling of actors and audience members gave the events in this section a quite different feeling than those outdoors, even though many themes were here repeated. There was much less of the carnivalesque and much more of the threatening and the transgressive.

Although the epilogue, which followed this powerful section, included such strong images as a mock crucifixion, its return to the open air effected a kind of release, and the death procession following the crucifixion gradually evolved into a kind of celebratory street dance, with cheering for the Karamazov family and the marching band swinging into a rousing rendition of "Dream a Little Dream of Me." Back at the evening's starting point, actors and musicians danced and marched off in a kind of reverse recapitulation of their original gathering, to the cheers of the audience.

Although the evening offered a series of specific focused scenes, there was a constant feeling that tangential performance was always taking place throughout the area. From time to time actors stationed in upper windows or fire escapes portrayed "residents" who commented loudly, sometimes positively and sometimes negatively (for example, dumping trash onto the activities below). Often it was difficult to determine the difference between actors, audience members, and casual passersby, and actors made up to resemble iconic figures of the 1950s and 1960s mingled with the crowds to add to the confusion. Marilyn Monroe and Richard Nixon made appearances, and the assassination of John F. Kennedy was reenacted at one point on the outskirts of the main action in chilling and yet vaguely cartoonish detail, complete with a red Eldorado convertible making its way down the street among the audience.

A wide range of references from the experimental theatre of the previous quarter-century was suggested by this remarkable production—the audience arrangements of the early Grotowski, the spatial manipulations of Ronconi's *Orlando Furioso*, the absorption of the city texture of Squat, the environmental experimentation of Schechner and his Performance Group—but despite all these echoes Abdoh was clearly striking out visually and spatially in new directions of his own. He presented only three further productions in New York before his untimely death at the age of thirty-two in 1995. The thousands of people lost to the AIDS epidemic of the late twentieth century included a devastatingly large number of victims from the theatre world, and some indication of that loss can be seen in the passing, at the heights of brilliant and innovative careers, of Reza Abdoh and Charles Ludlam.

1991 Split Britches' *Belle Reprieve*

As with much of the experimental work I saw in New York from the 1960s onward, I was introduced to the WOW (Women's One World) Café by the *Drama Review*, which in the spring of 1985 presented a special issue on East Village performance. By the time this article appeared, WOW had already lost its lease on the theatre it had occupied on East Eleventh Street since its founding in 1981 and was preparing for its move to East Fourth Street, where it has remained ever since. It purchased the property from the City of New York as a permanent home in 2000.

Peggy Shaw and Lois Weaver were two of the founders and guiding spirits of WOW. The first of their shows that I saw was *Upwardly Mobile Home* in the spring of 1984, a highly theatrical presentation of life among a group of people left homeless in the affluent 1980s. The other two productions I remember from the WOW Café of the late 1980s were both from 1988. One was an all-female production of Sheridan's *School for Scandal* that was, like many WOW productions, a strange blend of quite sophisticated performance and the most outrageous amateurism. The other was *Paradykes Lost*, written by Lisa Kron, who was more than a quarter-century later to make history as the author of the book and lyrics of *Fun Home*, the first musical on Broadway with a lesbian protagonist. As its title suggests, *Paradykes Lost* struck me as a lesbian development of many of the same strategies used for the gay community at Ludlam's theatre. Here too were wildly exaggerated costumes, characters, and plot situations, a bombardment of references to high and low culture, and a reveling in sexuality, especially heteronormative sexuality.

Attending a production at WOW Café was a distinctly different experience for me than going to theatre anywhere else. First, although its performances were regularly reported in the *Times* and the *Village Voice*, the theatre itself was almost totally unmarked, its entrance a simple door on the north side of Fourth Street, then becoming something of a theatre hub with the Duo just across the street and La Mama only a bit to the east. When one found the door, there would normally be two or three papers posted inside the glass telling of current and upcoming productions—no marquee, no flag (common to off-off-Broadway theatres in those years), not even a distinguishing external name. Opening hours would be posted, but were usually only casually followed.

Once the door opened, audience members climbed unadorned stairs to the rough fourth-floor performance space. Five-dollar tickets were sold at a desk that filled most of the landing at the top of the stairs, and then one entered the actual theatre space—a large room with simple black curtains surrounding the acting area, and a set of bleachers containing about fifty folding chairs for the audience. The atmosphere was much more that of a club than a theatre, since almost all of the audience members seemed to know each other, and mixed and chatted freely both before and after the show. One might wonder how I fitted in, often the only male in the house. The answer is that I of course did not, particularly, although I never felt the uneasiness or even disapproval that I occasionally (though not often) encountered in almost entirely black theatres. I felt rather like a large but presumed friendly dog that had wandered in off the street and was not exactly welcomed, but certainly not seen as a problem so long as he behaved himself. Obviously I did not understand, and did not expect to understand, many of the in-jokes central to productions in such a group, but as in the Theatre of the Ridiculous, I found plenty of theatrical material to encourage me to return. Certain artists and groups I first encountered at WOW interested me sufficiently to follow their careers elsewhere, particularly the Five Lesbian Brothers, headed by Lisa Kron, and Split Britches, primarily composed of the actresses Lois Weaver and Peggy Shaw and the author and performer Deb Margolin.

Although they remained most closely associated with WOW, I also saw Split Britches' works at this time at the Women's Interart Center on West Fifty-Second Street and, most memorably, at the Club at La Mama, which I first visited to see the Split Britches / Bloolips *Belle Reprieve* in 1991. I had been attending productions at La Mama since director Ellen Stewart opened her Fourth Street theatre in 1969, and had seen many shows in the two theatres in that building and next door in the annex she opened in the 1970s, but I had not yet been on the third floor of her main building, long a rehearsal space but converted into a small cabaret, the Club, during the 1980s. It had much more the feeling of a cabaret than a regular theatre, with a simple stage built between the exposed brick walls of the building and the audience space basically filled with round café tables and bentwood chairs. At the rear was a small bar. In this intimate space I saw the next several productions of Split Britches (including *Lesbians Who Kill*, in which the normally demure Weaver moved out among the small audience to deliver her song *Boogie Man* in so threatening and direct a manner that she really made me uneasy).

Although Weaver and Shaw worked with a number of other performers over the years, no collaboration seemed to me more effective than their work on this show with the English group Bloolips.

Before meeting Weaver, Shaw had worked with British drag artist Bette Bourne in a New York–based gay cabaret troupe, the Hot Peaches. Since then both had found partners and created queer companies, Split Britches in New York and Bloolips in London, headed by Bourne and his partner Precious Pearl (Paul Shaw). Neither of these two groups had so far worked with members of the other gender, queer or straight. Their collaboration on *Belle Reprieve*, this variation of Tennessee Williams's *Streetcar Named Desire*, thus provided an opportunity to theatrically play with sexual identities to a degree far beyond the previous work of either company or their predecessors. The major reference of the production was rather to the iconic Vivien Leigh / Marlon Brando film from 1961 than to the stage text, and many moments and gestures came directly from the film, even though the actual text of this production was much more commentary and elaboration than quotation. Peggy Shaw presented a Brando type of hypermasculinity as Stanley, identified in the program as a "butch lesbian." Stanley's partner, Stella, was played by Weaver, identified as "a woman disguised as a woman." Bourne brought the traditions of drag performance to the role of Blanche, as was made clear by the bald description "a woman in a dress," while Paul Shaw, who played Mitch as outrageously fey, was described as "a fairy disguised as a man."

Although Williams's characters and character relationships were constantly mined for comic and gender potential (including, of course, the development of homoerotic relationships between Stanley and Mitch and Blanche and Stella), and specific images and themes from the play were utilized, this was not strictly speaking a parody of the play, since it made no attempt to reproduce, even in parody, Williams's overall action, or indeed any coherent action. It was closer in style to a kind of musical revue, with themes drawn from or suggested by the play and the film. Occasionally a line or two from Williams appeared in distorted form (Blanche's opening line was the memorable "I have always depended on the strangeness of strangers"). Stella's "That's not funny, Stanley," when he slaps her thigh during the poker game, was extended into a lengthy interchange between the two on what was funny and what was not, beginning with a verbal argument, escalating to Stella ripping off Stanley's shirt (incidentally exposing the curve of a breast beneath), and ending with the classic "funny" action, Stanley pushing a cream pie into Stella's face. There were also scenes that were not precisely parodies, but clearly inspired by scenes in *Streetcar*. Stanley's pillaging of Blanche's suitcase was carried out both literally and metaphorically during the first act, and the climax of the production and one of its most memorable sequences drew its inspiration from the notorious rape scene in the original. Late in the second act, the production briefly threatened to actually move into the world of Williams. Mitch, alone on stage, reminisced about a beautiful young man he once saw and, taking out a ukulele, began a sentimental but moving rendition of the Gershwins' "The Man I Love."

This mood was abruptly shattered by the entrance of the other three cast members dressed as tap-dancing Chinese lanterns, clearly a reference to Blanche's love of lanterns to hide a harsh reality. Their routine began impressively but soon fell apart as they slammed into each other and into Mitch. Blanche emerged from the ruins of her costume in a harsh light complaining: "What are we doing? I can't stand it!" And "I want to be in a real play, with real scenery, with a beginning, middle, and end!" echoing not so much Williams as the frustrated maid, Sabina, in *The Skin of Our Teeth*. In vain the more honest Stella reminded her that they all had agreed that realism did not work for them. When Blanche insisted, Stella and Mitch left and Stanley began to move into the tonality and situation leading up to the rape scene in Williams. They began consciously playing Brando and Leigh, in fact agreeing to do so. Actual lines from Williams began to appear. Almost too late, Blanche tried to stop the dynamic, asking, "Do we have to play this scene?" to which Stanley responded that she was the one who wanted realism. In desperation Blanche dropped Vivien Leigh, pleading in her Bette Bourne persona, "I don't want to get raped and go crazy. I just wanted to wear a nice frock, and look at all the shit they've given me."

Clearly, as Stella had warned her, this is the price of playing realism, or at least the gendered realism of the traditional American theatre. Happily Stella and Mitch returned at the last moment to restore the production to the tone of the musical variety show. After a song challenging the audience and each other to figure out the identity secrets of the various characters, all joined in a rousing finale expressing the true love they all shared, the love of the theatre and of the singing, dancing, and role playing that it offered, a preferable alternative to their actual lives.

Never before had Split Britches so directly dealt with the articulation in the theatre and in the culture of gender roles, and never before so fully manifested the challenging of them that would, often in other works with similar projects, come to be described in the coming decade as "queering." Other themes were never absent from the individual and collective work of Weaver and Shaw, however. The negotiation of emotional relationships, especially their own, has always been a central concern, and they have continued, together and apart, to consider other aspects of the human experience, dealing searchingly in more recent years with themes of illness, aging, memory, and loss. I have long felt a close emotional tie to these artists of my own generation, and am proud that one of Weaver's works, *On the Scent*, a coproduction with the imaginative young Split Britches–style London company called Curious (Helen Paris and Leslie Hill), was given its American premiere in my own apartment in New York in August 2003.

1992 Anna Deavere Smith's *Fires in the Mirror*

The year 1991 marked the end of an era at the Public Theater, and indeed in New York theatre as a whole. In May Joseph Papp, who had been a major force, often the leading force in that theatre scene for the past forty years, resigned for health reasons the directorship of the Public, which he had founded. He named JoAnne Akalaitis, one of the leading figures of Mabou Mines, as his successor. Of course he left a number of projects in process, and the last one to bear his name as producer appeared in the spring of 1992, and provided yet another example of his support of some of the most important and original work in the city. This was *Fires in the Mirror* by Anna Deavere Smith, and it immediately established her as a major figure in the New York experimental scene.

The inspiration for Smith's piece was a series of events in recent New York City history, the repercussions of which were still in the headlines when the play opened in the Public's Shiva Theater May 1, 1992. Less than a year before, in late August 1991, New York had suffered one of the most serious race riots in its history. A car in a three-car Jewish motorcade in the mixed neighborhood of Crown Heights in Central Brooklyn jumped the curb and hit two black Guyanese children, one of whom died. The driver of the car was beaten by bystanders and removed from the scene by a private ambulance while the children were still being removed from the wreckage. Many in the black community saw this as ethnic bias, and tensions between the black and Jewish communities erupted in three days of rioting, during which a gang of blacks killed a Jewish exchange student from Australia. Repercussions of these events were long-lasting, in Brooklyn and throughout the city.

The contemporary and controversial nature of the subject matter and the brilliance of Smith's concept and execution made this one of the most talked-about offerings of the season, and so I went to the Public knowing more or less what to expect—the presentation of the Crown Heights events from a variety of different perspectives, all played by a single actress.

The one-person performance was clearly growing in popularity in the New York theatre at this time. What had begun in small off-off-Broadway houses and cabarets, especially those concerned with feminist and gay issues, had moved in the mid-1980s to Broadway with the work of Lily Tomlin, to Lincoln Center with that of Spalding Gray. It entered mainstream public discourse in 1990 when four solo performance artists—Karen Finley, Holly Hughes, John Fleck, and Tim Miller—were denied funding by the National Endowment for the Arts. As the "NEA Four," they became highly visible symbols of the threat that the conservative establishment felt was posed to the nation by artists dealing with matters of sex and gender. During the run of *Fires in the Mirror* their appeal was making its way through the courts. Normally one-person shows at this time were either essentially autobiographical, like that of Gray or the NEA Four, or else were collections of short character studies, like those of Tomlin. Smith's creation was something else altogether.

The show was performed in the small Shiva Theater, a rectangular space directly behind the main lobby at the Public and seating fewer than one hundred, normally on bleachers along the long side closest to the lobby. When the audience entered, the stage, surrounded by dark curtains, was empty except for a table and chair, and I was at once reminded of the setting for a Spalding Gray monologue. Indeed one characteristic of many of the solo performances of this time was that they were presented with almost no properties, and with only minimal if any adjustments of costume. In presentations like this one, where in the course of the evening the performer would embody a variety of personae, an important part of demonstrating the skill of the performer was that he or she could create the impression of these different identities almost entirely by the adjustment of voice and body. This was certainly true of Smith, whose mimetic range and ability clearly surpassed that of many of her fellow solo performers. Her costume throughout was simple and minimal, a white shirt, dark pants, and her feet bare. Now and again, but not frequently, she would add a simple accessory such as a yarmulke, a bowler, an African knitted cap. For the most part, like Gray, she sat at the desk in the chair, although she did not, as he often did, refer to a preexisting text. Her text was the hours of tape-recorded interviews she had meticulously assembled and culled during the previous year, and then committed to memory in every detail—each inflection, each pause, each stammer. She became a channel for those voices, operating like a medium speaking in the authentic voice of the departed.

Previous solo performers who presented multiple characters normally offered only a handful of such characters, but Smith, seeking to present a panorama of an entire society, cast her net much more widely, offering twenty-nine vignettes, men and women, black and white, laymen and police, people from many walks of life and highly diverse economic, political, and cultural backgrounds. Her presentations of these characters differed from conventional multicharacter solo performance in that they were created from the actual words of real people, not the imagination of the artist. In this way the material in *Fires in the Mirror* reminded me rather more of the oral histories gathered by Studs Terkel in his book *Working*, which had in the 1970s been converted into a Broadway musical that was far indeed from the sort of simulation of the original voices Smith offered.

In fact, it seemed to me that despite a surface similarity to many solo performers who were at that time beginning to offer multivoiced work, Smith was doing something quite different, something that had not really had a serious vogue in the United States since the Federal Theatre Project of the 1930s, an attempt to put on the stage a direct and honest transcript of real contemporary historical material. During the 1960s there was an important vogue of document-based theatre in Germany, and although Broadway productions were mounted during that decade from each of the three German leaders of the movement, Peter Weiss (*The Investigation*), Heiner Kipphardt (*In the Matter of J. Robert Oppenheimer*), and Rolf Hochhuth (*The Deputy*), and although the portrait of Pope Pius XII in the latter created a considerable controversy, these works did not really inspire much imitation by U.S. authors. I can only recall a single American documentary drama of that era, Martin Duberman's *In White America*, a 1963 collection of letters, memoirs, and other material on America's racist history.

In short, although Smith's production had aspects in common with a number of contemporary and historical performances, it really offered something new, a kind of blend between documentary theatre and the solo performance of multiple characters. The twenty-nine monologues Smith presented during the evening were based on interviews with twenty-six persons, each titled with its subject's name and a short quotation from the monologue, which called attention to some aspect of it. Since many of the people presented were already somewhat known to the audience members, and others were known to be involved in some important way with the overall subject, programs were constantly being consulted, to a greater extent than I can ever remember in the theatre. As each new character appeared, almost the entire audience consulted their program not only to get the identification, but also to get the key phrase, which clearly guided their reception of the monologue as a whole. Smith's grouping of the monologues provided another, more overarching guide. The first group concerned personal identity, the second issues of race, ethnicity, religion, and physical appearance, the third various issues connected directly to the Crown Heights events.

There was also an ingenious and sophisticated arrangement of material within the various sections, so that the darker and heavier pieces would be set off with lighter ones, a strong statement on one side of the controversy balanced (but never in a simple or mechanical manner) with one from the other side. Sometimes connections were made that helped to enrich the experience of the piece and the insight into the different personalities even when these did not directly relate to the Crown Heights events. One lovely example was an unguarded but typical riff by the Reverend Al Sharpton on his hairstyle, a tribute, he confesses, to the singer James Brown, which was followed by a discussion from a Hasidic graphic artist on her misgivings about wearing a special ritual wig. Some characters expressed outrage, some deep sorrow; some clearly wished to use the events to advance their personal agenda or to reinforce personal prejudices, but while the audience was naturally more sympathetic to some than to others, Smith's commitment to embodying the articulation of their opinions gave the impression that we could to some extent understand the thinking and the positions taken by even the most difficult among them.

Not all of the characters were willing to be identified; four remained anonymous, although their profession, area of residence, gender, ethnicity, and approximate age were provided. The remaining identified interviewees represented a broad spectrum, but only about half of them were residents of or had direct ties to Crown Heights. The rest were informed and concerned outsiders, some of them well known to the public, others with less general recognition but representing important points of view. The most public figures, such as the Reverend Sharpton, who was accorded two monologues, were so well known on television that Smith's exact rendering of their voices and mannerisms gave a further authority to her re-creations of less familiar figures. Other familiar figures included California scholar and activist Angela Davis, and two then highly controversial New Yorkers, CUNY professor Leonard Jeffries and activist Sonny Carson. Two other important African Americans with special ties to the Public Theater were also included: Ntozake Shange, the author of *for colored girls*, and George C. Wolfe, at that time the director-producer of the New York Shakespeare Festival. Less than a year after the presentation of Smith's play, Wolfe was appointed to replace JoAnne Akalaitis, whose tenure as the successor to Joseph Papp was brief and tumultuous, lasting less than two years. Wolfe, on the other hand, would have a generally quite successful eleven-year directorship of the Public, during which he continued the strong interest in multiethnic theatre that Papp had begun. His association with this production thus anticipated an important orientation of this major theatre during the next decade.

Smith followed up her enormous success *Fires in the Mirror* with a similar and equally well-received presentation, *Twilight: Los Angeles, 1992*, dealing with an even more destructive series of racially motivated riots on the other coast. Her later work has continued to present documentary material on specific topics, such as the American presidency, illness and death, and religion. She remains most associated in the public mind with these two interview dramas, however, and although no other performer has taken up that approach with equal success, these two works may be seen as initiating a new interest in verbatim material in the American theatre which brought the documentary theatre in this country to an even greater prominence than it had enjoyed in Germany during the 1960s.

Of that development I will say more later.

1993 Tony Kushner's *Angels in America* (Part One: *Millennium Approaches*)

The work of Tony Kushner first came to my attention with a production of his play *A Bright Room Called Day* at the Public Theater early in 1991, in the final year of Joe Papp's administration. Papp had made the Public one of the leading theatres in New York for new and controversial work, and *Bright Room* was no exception. Set in a Berlin apartment in two time periods, the 1930s and in 1990, the play shows, in the earlier period, a group of friends watching helplessly the rise of Hitler and in the later one an expatriate American who has fled the America of Ronald Reagan, gripped in the rise of a new style of reactionary politics with uncomfortable parallels to those of early fascist Germany. I found the work rather scattered but exciting and full of elements all too uncommon in most serious American plays of that era (or since) such as Living Newspaper–style projected headlines on overhead screens, a half-successful séance briefly uniting the two worlds, and a guest appearance, in a short reenactment of material from *Faust*, of an immaculately clad Devil in clouds of billowing smoke.

Clearly this was a dramatist with a strong political bent and a strikingly unconventional use of visual and theatrical material, and I looked forward to his future work. The promise of *Bright Room* was more than fulfilled by the epic two-part *Angels in America*, which arrived in New York with an almost unprecedented outpouring of critical anticipation, increased by the circuitous route the play took to New York. Developed at the Mark Taper Forum in Los Angeles, it premiered at the Eureka Theatre in San Francisco in 1991, where its enthusiastic reception attracted the attention of Richard Eyre, the artistic director of the National Theatre in London. Eyre booked the play for the intimate Cottesloe and engaged one of London's most honored and innovative directors, Declan Donnellan, to stage it.

The London production was a sensation, and as an American play with a resounding success in London, it became the most sought-after property on Broadway that season. An unprecedented struggle among New York's theatrical power brokers was the result. The play was at first announced as the centerpiece of that season at the Public Theater, which as the producer of *A Bright Room Called Day* was the obvious choice, especially since no major Broadway house was likely to have the slightest interest in a seven-hour nonmusical drama on gay themes. All that changed, however, with the play's triumph in London. Suddenly it was seen as a highly valuable product, and a heated struggle resulted between Broadway's two leading producing organizations, the older and more powerful Shuberts, who controlled seventeen of the forty Broadway theatres, and a much smaller but determined young challenger, the Jujamcyn group, who controlled five. JoAnne Akalaitis, struggling with her first year as director of the Public, reportedly urged Kushner to keep the play downtown, but eventually had to settle for the Public being a coproducer. The Shuberts offered Kushner one of its most desirable venues, the Booth Theatre on West Forty-Fifth Street, even though that would mean expensive relocation of the successful show then running there, *Someone Who'll Watch over Me*. Jujamcyn offered its own most attractive house, the recently restored Walter Kerr, slightly larger than the Booth, but still one of Broadway's most intimate houses, seating just under a thousand.

Eventually Kushner selected the Walter Kerr, but the struggle had distinctly added to the public interest in the production. Nor was it the only controversy that preceded the New York opening. The selection of a director proved almost as difficult. Declan Donnellan was considered, but was not available, and eventually George C. Wolfe was selected, his star rapidly rising through the success of the musical *Jelly's Last Jam*, which he both wrote and directed. Wolfe was eager to do the play, but he had to back out of a commitment to the Hartford Stage for a show just going into rehearsals, causing still more conflicts and ill feelings. Nonetheless, Wolfe's decision proved a wise one. His direction of *Millennium Approaches* earned him a Tony Award and assured his invitation to replace JoAnne Akalaitis, whose brief directorship of the Public ended on May 15, less than two weeks after the triumphant Broadway opening of the Kushner play.

With all of these developments, on top of the reports from California and London, I cannot remember a Broadway opening more eagerly anticipated than that of *Millennium Approaches*, but in fact the excitement was increased further by the announcement in mid-April, two weeks before the opening, that the play had won the Pulitzer Prize and then a delay of almost a week as various technical problems delayed the late April opening until May 9. I already had tickets for May 1, for what was supposed to be the first Saturday night of the run, but that night became one of the final dress rehearsals. All of the technical difficulties had apparently been resolved, however, and I saw nothing to indicate any problems with any of the production's sometimes very challenging scenic effects. Indeed the settings, designed by Robin Wagner, who had also worked with Wolfe on *Jelly's Last Jam*, were on the whole suggestive rather than overwhelming, often simply fragments of a location, but their mechanics clearly called for great precision as they slid in and out as smoothly as the scenes, fantasies, and dreams of the characters flowed seamlessly into one another.

Eight actors performed the twenty roles in the production, and the audience was confronted at the outset by a surprising choice in casting and doubling. Actress Kathleen Chalfant launched the evening by presenting an extended funeral monologue in the character of an aging rabbi. The monologue introduced many of the central themes of the play, but it also suggested the play's wide range of tonality, from the deeply serious to the almost farcically comic, and, in this almost Brechtian appearance of a middle-aged woman as an aging man, an ambiguity Chalfant did not disguise, alerted us to the unconventionality and theatricality of the work we were about to witness.

The complex action and multiple levels of the text were brilliantly set forth by the cast, almost all of whom were actors I had not been familiar with before, but who from this production onward would encourage me, by their very participation, to attend plays that might not otherwise have interested me. Among these certainly was Chalfant, whose major role was as Hannah, the straightlaced Mormon mother of Joe Pitt, a gay man in denial of his proclivities, but equally impressive was her heartwarming presentation of historical figure Ethel Rosenberg, presented as a central victim of the repressive 1950s political system that creates the ominous destructive force operating in the play. In addition to enjoying her many moving subsequent creations, I admired Chalfant in the new century for her strong engagement in political action, especially in her work with Theaters Against the War, founded in 2002 in protest of the invasion of Iraq and in many of whose rallies and actions I participated.

Ethel Rosenberg, portrayed by Chalfant, is seen in this play as the victim and nemesis of the darkest character in the play, the complex Roy Cohn. Cohn, a villain of almost Shakespearian dimensions, was marvelously portrayed by Ron Leibman in what many considered the production's outstanding performance. Cohn, a ruthless and cold-blooded conservative of the McCarthy era, died of AIDS but denied his homosexuality, insisting (as he does in the play) that although he slept with men, he was not a homosexual because his sexual partners were weaklings whom he held in contempt. Kushner was not the only dramatist at the height of the AIDS epidemic to see the theatrical potential of the deep, even tragic irony of Cohn's career and protestations. A much less publicized but brilliant solo performance was offered in New York at this same time by Ron Vawter of the Wooster Group, who offered a contrasting presentation of two gay public figures, *Roy Cohn/Jack Smith*, pairing the gay-denying politician with the flamboyantly open gay performance artist of the same era.

A third much-praised performer of the production was Stephen Spinella, who played Prior Walter, a young man dying of AIDS as the play opens and who at the end of Part One is the unlikely choice of divine powers to become the prophet of some still undisclosed divine message. Prior was at that time unhappily typical. In 1993 AIDS was the leading cause of death for American gay men between the ages of thirty-three and forty-five and no effective antiviral treatment had yet been discovered. The appearance of the disease was, in effect, a death sentence. One of the most shocking moments of the production came early in the evening when Spinella revealed his almost naked body. The ugly lesions were forbidding, but his body was so thin and vulnerable that he seemed already at the door of death. The visions of this dying figure alternated and on one occasion even combined with those of Harper, the Valium-popping wife of Joe Pitt, allowing Kushner through these visions to extend his drama across great reaches of space and time, as when Harper hallucinated about traveling to Antarctica, and when two delightfully cartoonish ancestors appeared in Prior's bedroom to help prepare him for his coming mission. One of these ancestors was a medieval farmer, the other a seventeenth-century Londoner, both named Prior and both victims of former plagues. Their appearance added another level of theatricality to this already richly textured production.

The most memorable scene, and the one to which the Prior plotline in particular had been building through the evening, was the final one. While Prior lay in troubled sleep in his apartment, the audience was alerted to the fact that the long-awaited moment of revelation was approaching. The more or less dim and realistic lighting in the room gave way to an incandescent play of colors across Prior's body. Cracks appeared in the ceiling above him and larger and larger pieces of plaster began to fall. Then Spinella gave perhaps the most famous line in the play, "*Very* Steven Spielberg," eliciting a roar of laughter from the audience, delighting in this acknowledgment of the production's self-conscious theatricality. At that time Spielberg was probably the best-known film director in the country, particularly associated during the previous decades with blockbuster adventure spectacles like *E.T.* and the Indiana Jones series, featuring dazzling special effects.

As great chunks of the ceiling fell away and light from above poured in, a huge flamboyant angel (the actress Ellen McLaughlin) descended on visible wires, a dazzling otherworldly but familiar figure with unfurled wings, flowing robes, her upturned face illuminated and framed by white ringlets. Over the prone body of the stunned Prior she pronounced the oracular phrase: "Greetings, Prophet; The Great Work begins; The Messenger has arrived." It was one of the most stunning endings I had seen in the New York theatre, and the audience leapt to its feet in lengthy applause (a much less common occurrence than it has become since). In terms of sheer unexpected theatrical spectacle on Broadway, I can compare the angel's appearance only to the famous, and equally iconic, sweeping of the giant chandelier out over the audience at the opening of *The Phantom of the Opera*.

So overwhelming was the effect that only afterward did I begin to wonder what the words meant. Who was the Messenger? And even more important, what was the Great Work? These major unanswered questions and the sheer energy and theatrical imagination of the evening left me with much the same feeling I had after the first part of the almost equally lengthy *Nicholas Nickleby*, with a profound desire to plunge as quickly as possible into the next three to four hours of the play. With *Nicholas Nickleby*, however, this desire was fulfilled later that same day, while with *Millennium Approaches* my fellow audience members and I had to wait until the fall, when at last we had the pleasure of experiencing the working out of the complex strands of *Millennium Approaches* in the equally impressive second part, *Perestroika*.

1994 Tadashi Suzuki's *The Tale of Lear*

During the 1980s and 1990s I found my theatrical interests becoming more and more international, not because, I regret to say, the New York theatre was becoming more international, but because elsewhere in the world there was an increasing amount of touring of particular productions, headed by leading international directors like Peter Brook, Giorgio Strehler, Peter Stein, and Tadeusz Kantor. Even leading American international directors like Robert Wilson and Peter Sellars were in fact more likely to be seen abroad than in New York, where soaring production costs discouraged producers from importing anything but proven hits from London, long the lodestar of more highbrow American theatre.

This explains why I saw the first major Shakespearian work of the leading Japanese experimental director Tadashi Suzuki, not in New York, but at the Barbican Centre in London, as part of their first festival of international Shakespeare in 1994, a kind of festival that would be inconceivable in New York then or since. At the same festival I was introduced to the dazzling work of Karen Beier, from Germany, about whom I will write later, and to productions from the Habima Theatre in Israel and the State Theatre of Georgia. None of these ever appeared in New York, not even a *Merchant of Venice* by Peter Sellars from the Goodman Theatre in Chicago. By 1994 Suzuki was well established internationally, having been touring the world with his company for more than twenty years, but, typically, he had appeared only twice in New York, for brief runs at small theatres. His version of the *Bacchae* had been offered at La Mama in 1982 and again as part of the Lincoln Center festival in 1994.

The Tale of Lear marked a new phase in Suzuki's work, his first non-collage development of a single play. It was first performed in Japanese at Suzuki's theatre center in Japan in 1984. Then, in a striking example of the growing internationalism of theatre, Suzuki reconceived the work in English, using twelve male actors from four regional theatres in the United States: the Milwaukee Repertory, StageWest, the Arena Stage, and the Berkeley Repertory. The actors prepared the production in Japan and then toured it to these four participating theatres in 1988.

By 1994, when I attended this production at the London Barbican, that arts center had been open for somewhat over a decade. I first visited it during my 1984–85 sabbatical in London, and during that time the theatres I most often attended were the Barbican, which had been created as a London home for the prestigious Royal Shakespeare Company, and the National, which had opened its monumental home on the other side of the Thames a decade before. Many of Britain's best actors moved back and forth between these two theatres, and if neither offered the kind of bold directorial vision of a Peter Brook, a Tadashi Suzuki, or leading contemporary directors on the continent, both presented intelligent and often highly effective British and international classics that were rightly the envy of many U.S. theatre-goers. Not surprisingly the RSC offered more Shakespeare, but I also recall a wonderful *Mother Courage* there in 1984 starring the always remarkable Judi Dench. It was not therefore surprising that it should be the RSC that decided in 1994 to offer for the first time in England an international festival devoted to Shakespeare.

In keeping with this desire to present Shakespeare as viewed in other theatrical cultures, the production that I saw at the Barbican in 1994 was not the American version, but the original Japanese version with its original cast. The space was not ideal. Almost no one has ever had much good to say about the Barbican Centre. The largest arts complex in Europe when it was built, it also included a major housing development and was located (like New York's Lincoln Center) much to the north of the city's theatre center, in an unfrequented area the city wished to develop. Unlike Lincoln Center, however, the Barbican was not conveniently served by the subway system, and its huge labyrinthine structure made it from the beginning a trial for visitors to negotiate. Still today one must carefully follow paths marked through the corridors over considerable distances to find one's way.

Once the performance area is attained, there is a spacious, multi-level lobby, giving access to a concert hall, an eleven-hundred-seat main stage, and a small downstage space, the Pit. *The Tale of Lear*, like the Beier and Sellars productions, was presented in the large theatre, which did not suit it well. Since the production was in Japanese, supertitles were projected on the proscenium, but this was so far above the action that it was impossible to both read the titles and follow the sometimes rapidly evolving visual configurations on the stage below. On the other hand, the radical cutting of the text and the abstraction of the action made it almost impossible to know where we were in the story without constant reference to the supertitles. For audience members in the rows closest to the stage, this double vision was almost impossible. For those sitting further back, as I was, reading the supertitles was less difficult, but the very large stage area flattened out the beautifully composed stage pictures. The smaller downstage theatre, the Pit, where the Georgian and Israeli productions were given, would have suited the intimate staging much better, but it contains only two hundred seats, and doubtless the producers felt that the greater reputation of Suzuki would justify moving this production to the larger upstairs space. Certainly the audience the night I attended would have overwhelmed the Pit, but they only took up something more than half of the much larger main auditorium, with, I think, considerable loss to the total experience.

The stage for *The Tale of Lear*, indeed the visual design of the entire production, was very minimalist, essentially a huge black box, shot through with shafts of light, occasionally directly down from above, but most often directly from the sides, so that actors often appeared in sharp silhouette. Perhaps in part due to the difficulty of looking directly into this dazzling cross-lighting, the actors rarely if ever seemed to be looking directly at each other, but played primarily frontally. The opening sequence established the referential world of the production. The audience was plunged into darkness out of which after a moment came a burst of cackling laughter from the stage. A small pool of light revealed two figures sitting in the center of the stage, facing out. Both were men but one was dressed in an all-white modern nurse's dress and cap. The other was huddled in a wheelchair, wrapped in a heavily brocaded darkly colored brown-and-green kimono. The program provided a bit of context including a note by the director: "The world is a hospital and all men and women are inmates of that hospital." The laugh had come from the nurse, who was reading the story of Lear to her huddled patient. From time to time some passage would stir his own memories, and the interweaving of her reading and his somewhat feverish recollections made up the evening's text, a much-abbreviated *King Lear*, lasting about an hour and a half. The general order of the action was intact, but primarily as a series of striking Kabuki-inflected images. Obviously the text was heavily cut, and many scenes and not a few characters, most notably Kent, also disappeared. Very little of the Fool's lines were left, and these were primarily delivered by the nurse, who remained on stage, reading the text and often laughing over it in a kind of demented way for most of the evening, although often in some upstage corner. Lines such as "Let him smell his way to Dover," cruel enough to begin with, became even more so when they generated that leitmotif of cackling laughter.

Many elements of the production were drawn from the classic Japanese theatre, most obviously the costumes and the movements. Except for the nurse, all the other characters wore heavy brocaded floor-length kimono-style robes, largely in earth colors with gold trim, although Gloucester, whose similarities to Lear were constantly emphasized, had a striking touch of red. The lines of the costumes of the female characters were somewhat softened by sashes, but there was clearly no attempt to suggest that these roles were played by women. Indeed contrary to the traditions of the classic theatres of Japan, where men also played female roles, the two evil sisters were both bearded. Although each actor had a somewhat different rhythm of movement, the overall impression was one of a very formal choreography. The floor-length kimonos never allowed feet to appear when the actors were standing, although Lear very shockingly extended a full, naked leg from his wheelchair at one point, and the small gliding steps that all the actors except Lear and the nurse used made them seem simply to float across the floor, often in a striking sideways motion. When they stopped, it was almost always abruptly and in a frozen pose, like a Kabuki *mie*, giving the impression of the production moving in a stately manner from one tableau to another.

Once Lear and the nurse had established the scene, Lear summoned his court to divide the kingdom. This was done by dark screen-like doors parting upstage behind him and revealing the rest of the cast standing in a semicircle illuminated only by downlight. The effect, like many in the production, was of a ritualized moment, with the cast serving as much as an abstract chorus as they did individuals.

Many of the entrances and exits were managed by the use of these sliding screens, which meant that as a rule actors did not move on- and offstage, but they were revealed or concealed by the panels, adding to the formal flow of the scenes.

Props, like scenery, were minimal—a few samurai swords, never in fact unsheathed, a clearly blank scroll that Edmund displayed to his father as Edgar's letter, a fan, behind which Regan and Edmund exchanged a discreet kiss, and most strikingly, a modern hospital laundry cart into which Lear climbed in order to be rolled to Dover by the obliging nurse. In a gesture that to me at least clearly suggested a visual echo of Don

Quixote, he put on a hospital bedpan instead of flowers to represent his lost crown.

Despite the inappropriate space of the venue, the strength of this production, at least for Western audiences, was clearly in the visual rather than the aural. A great familiarity with Japanese performance traditions was not necessary to be impressed by the beauty of the costumes, the grace of the actors' movements, the flowing elegance of the stage compositions. Western appreciation of these was doubtless closer to that of Brecht for Mei Lanfang or Artaud for the Balinese dancers than that of the Japanese public for whom the piece was created, but it was deeply felt all the same. Aurally the work was less successful. The powerful delivery of the lines seemed often strident and excessive, the vocal rhythms less accessible to Western ears than the physical ones were to Western eyes. Moreover, Suzuki's choice of musical accompaniment, used frequently during the production, was almost entirely from familiar works of the classic Western repertoire, such as Handel's *Largo* from *Xerxes* or Tchaikovsky's *Danse Espagnole*, whose familiarity within a Western context made them seem almost always incongruous and inappropriate, doubtless an effect very different from their reception by a Japanese audience.

Although I found the production, despite its flaws, moving and memorable, the British press was almost unanimous in its disapproval of the liberties taken by all of these non-British directors with a national treasure. Over the years, this attitude has softened, and today, the British theatrical establishment on the whole boasts of Shakespeare's "universality." The most obvious recent example was the Globe to Globe Festival in 2012, where the reconstructed Globe Theatre hosted thirty-seven different productions of Shakespeare in thirty-seven different languages. Many of these companies have returned subsequently to this theatre, and if British productions of Shakespeare have not been greatly affected by the alternative production traditions, whose main attraction seems to be their exoticism, their very presence in London provides a welcome performance variety to the theatre of that city.

1995 Karen Beier's
A Midsummer Night's Dream

During the 1990s, as my interest in the contemporary German-speaking theatre grew, I began to visit either Germany or Austria for theatre-going at least once a year. Usually I went to the major capitals—Berlin, Munich, or Vienna—but during Christmas vacation in 1995–96 I went to a number of cities in and around the Ruhr Valley in west Germany, which had been a center of German theatre and dance innovation for several decades. Over a period of a week I attended theatres in five different cities, not a difficult feat, since train travel was frequent and rapid. Mulheim, Düsseldorf, Bochum, Essen, and Wuppertal plus a dozen or so other important theatre centers were all only thirty to forty minutes apart by train.

Significantly, the two productions I most enjoyed provided further evidence of the growing internationalization of the theatre, of which I was becoming more and more aware. In Mulheim I saw a fascinating staging of Brecht's *In the Jungle of Cities*, created by house director Roberto Ciulli (himself from Italy), in which German-speaking members of the company played Garga and his followers, while Shlink and his followers were drawn from the large immigrant Turkish population of Mulheim and spoke their lines in that language. Not only did this give Brecht's conflict a very current and local dimension, but it anticipated the immigrant, especially Turkish, theatre that would become an important part of the German theatre scene in the new century.

Even more ambitious, theatrically and linguistically, was Karen Beier's *A Midsummer Night's Dream*, one of the best productions of this challenging work I have ever seen. I had first experienced Beier's work with her highly unconventional *Romeo and Juliet* in the international Shakespeare Festival in London, itself a manifestation of this new internationalism. Beier was at that time the director of the state theatre in Düsseldorf, and the opportunity to see more of her work was one of the attractions of the Ruhr area for me. Beier was at that time considered one of the outstanding interpreters of Shakespeare in Germany, no small matter in a country that rivals England in the centrality of that author to its repertoire. This particular production had, however, a special background and attraction.

A major event in modern European theatre history was the founding of the Union of European Theatres in 1990 by Giorgio Strehler, head of the Piccolo Teatro in Milan, and Jack Lang, the French minister of culture. In the face of increasing globalization and of rising international economic pressures, the Union was created to gather leading European theatres into a mutual support system, involving organization of international workshops and festivals, sharing of artists, and exchange of productions. One of the first major projects of the new organization was a workshop headed by Beier that brought together a group of fourteen actors from nine countries with no common language to develop a "European Shakespeare" production. The project was similar in its internationalism to Peter Brook's ongoing project in Paris, but Beier's project was for a single production and was restricted to Europe (with the exception of Israel, from the beginning a member of the Theatre Union).

I saw this production in the larger of the two theatres in the Düsseldorfer Schauspielhaus, one of the most distinctive theatres in Germany. Every German city of any size has at least one major state or municipal theatre, and it is almost always a monumental structure near the city center. The Düsseldorfer Schauspielhaus is no exception, but it makes a particularly strong statement as one of the country's leading examples of organic architecture, a huge white building composed of flowing lines and surfaces, as if in constant motion. Inside, spaces are similarly fluid, with a large central area surrounding a pylon with rays extending out over the entire lobby. The main theatre, which seats about one thousand, continues the organic feeling. Although the relationship between stage and audience is a conventional one, there are no balconies or boxes, and, as with the exterior walls, no clear traditional dividing lines between room units. The walls flow without a break into the ceiling and wrap around the rear of the auditorium in a gentle curve. It seemed an excellent modernist enclosure for this very modernist production.

Beier followed Peter Brook and others in using the same actress to play Hippolyta and Titania and the same actor to play Theseus and Oberon. The former was a striking black Swedish/British actress, Josette Bushell-Mingo, whom I had seen in earlier productions at the Royal Shakespeare. She provided the production's memorable opening image. A high backlight in the darkness outlined her nude body, holding a huge golden bow. Slowly she turned and seemed to fire an arrow directly into the audience. There was a strobe flash, then total darkness.

When the light came back up, Hippolyta was seen in a very different condition, as Theseus's nude captive, with Theseus in a dress coat and boots strutting about and giving orders in Italian (he being an actor from Strehler's Piccolo Teatro in Milan). At his orders, Hippolyta was dressed in the "court costume," a dress suit and shirt, too large for her, a bowler hat, and a metallic briefcase. Exact copies of this costume were worn by all the court members, who moved in militaristic formation and used the briefcases as drums to accompany their entrances and exits.

The physical stage for the production was a very simple one, essentially a bare platform with narrow runways giving access to it from the sides and rear. This put full visual emphasis upon the acting, costumes, and lighting. One of the show's most stunning sequences was the first transition from the court to the woods. Philostrate from the court was left alone on stage in a cool accent light. The rest of the bowler-hatted court marched in to surround him, all covered in a dim blue downlight and quietly drumming on their metal briefcases. As they drummed, they began a very low wordless chant of circus-type music, reminiscent of Fellini. To this accompaniment, Philostrate removed his boots and put on high silver shoes, took off his fedora hat and fluffed up his hair, and removed his long dark frock coat to reveal tight black knee breeches and a white feminine breast, changing before our eyes from the stiff court official to the lithe, androgynous Puck. When he had completed this transformation, the others, continuing the circus music but at an ever-increasing volume and tempo, followed his example, removing hats, boots, and frock coats to reveal the colorful and grotesquely exaggerated costumes and properties of clowns—false noses, a red parasol, huge bow ties, while cymbals, drums, and horns mysteriously appeared to support their music. It was an astonishing transformation scene, the essence of theatre magic.

The natural confusion and struggles with communication in a cast speaking nine different languages fitted very well with the confusion, cross-purposes, and misunderstandings of the play itself. Lysander (from Israel) recognized almost at once that Hermia (from England) could not understand him, and began ingeniously acting out his lines, which she enthusiastically translated into English for him. When Lysander and Demetrius (from Hungary) fought, their conflict took on a chilling contemporary metatheatricalism as they exchanged half-muttered taunts of "Gypsy" and "fucking Jew."

Nowhere was the linguistic mélange more effectively utilized than in the scenes with the rude mechanicals. Their arguments during rehearsal about the production took on hilarious new overtones since each wished to perform the piece in his or her own national style. Peter Quince, converted into an Italian diva, Petra Squenz, wished to run things (as did her countryman, playing Theseus) in the manner of an Italian impresario. Flute, the only actual German in the company, suggested playing Thisbe with his sweater pulled over his head to create what he called an "alienation effect." Snug (from France) danced about the stage in a quasi-ballet, insisting upon "delicatesse." Schnauz (a small bouncy clown from Bulgaria) suggested a variety of mime, commedia, and circus turns. Starveling (from the Moscow Art Theatre) cited Stanislavsky and presented a highly emotional speech downstage directly at the audience of which I could understand only the concluding words, a tearful "V Moskva, V Moskva." She was pushed aside by Bottom (from Poland), who insisted instead upon a Grotowskian approach and offered a hilarious parody of such techniques, ending with a kind of seizure leaving him flat on his back. In fact when the play was presented at court, all these styles, in addition to a few others, crept in, so that Philostrate reasonably added to his catalog of the production's ills that it was a hopeless mélange of presentation. It concluded with a wild and extended melodramatic stage death by Bottom, complete with Grand Guignol blood effects that drenched him, the stage, and most of the court. When at last he lay still in a pool of stage blood and the real audience, by now almost helpless with laughter, could imagine virtually nothing else he could do, he leaped up to finish off with a recap of his Grotowskian seizure.

When at last the play was complete and the court departed, the onstage curtain rose again to reveal Puck and the company now costumed as a clown band. The band followed him slowly downstage in a part dance, part processional, whispering among themselves in a babble of languages. Then, as Puck presented his final address to the audience, different cast members repeated phrases from it in their own language. The effect was almost symphonic, and like so much of this ambitious production, profoundly moving and celebrative. The shouting and applauding audience recalled them again and again to express their excitement and enthusiasm.

Beier returned to multilinguistic production, and to Shakespeare, in her 1997 *The Tempest*, subtitled, "A European Shakespeare," which was even more elaborately heteroglossic than her *Midsummer Night's Dream*, since individual characters often spoke in a variety of languages within a single speech. Clearly the humor here came not from conflicting cultural expectations but from the dynamics of trying to forge some kind of cross-European consciousness. The opening sequence, newly created for this production, showed Alonso and his party, all with a distinct mafioso edge, addressing an international congress of tomato producers and championing a new unified European trading bloc. All confirm their commitment to this cause by speaking in polyglot English, German, and Italian, with occasional bits of yet other languages tossed in.

Although Beier has not continued such linguistic mixing, she has remained a leading director, and although she has presented important productions of works from the classic Greek theatre to current drama, her experiments with Shakespeare continue to be among Germany's most innovative. The most recent was a *King Lear*, presented in 2009 while she was director of the Cologne Theatre. The play was reduced to ten roles, all played by six women, headed by Barbara Nüsse, one of the queens of the German stage, as Lear. The same three actresses who played the rival daughters divided among themselves the role of the Fool, and two of them played the sons of Gloucester as well. The physical worlds of good and evil were brought closer together by reversing the sympathetic appeal of the characters, so that the actress who played Cordelia also played the villainous Edward, while the one playing Goneril also portrayed the sympathetic Edgar. This unconventional approach opened up striking new perspectives on the play, its tonalities and its character relationships, just as the much-honored gender-bending 1990 Mabou Mines production of the play did in the United States, with Ruth Maleczech as Lear. Directors in Germany, as in most of the larger theatres in the United States, are predominantly male, but in that generally male profession, Beier continues to hold a secure place.

1996 Caryl Churchill's *The Skriker*

During the 1980s Caryl Churchill emerged as one of the most gifted, innovative, and culturally engaged new dramatists of the British stage, and her New York productions during that decade were almost entirely presented by Joe Papp at the Public Theater, where almost every season during this decade featured a Churchill production. This series was broken at the end of the decade with Papp's retirement and death, and it was not until 1996, in the third year of George C. Wolfe's administration, that Wolfe presented the first and only Churchill play of that ten-year directorship. It was nevertheless a bold and important choice, since *The Skriker* is generally considered not only among the most ambitious efforts of this unconventional dramatist, but also the most challenging in terms of production demands.

Being a regular Public Theater subscriber, I had seen all of the Churchill offerings there and had admired their range of experimentation, their quirky humor, and their serious if unconventional engagement with such contemporary concerns as gender issues and the monetary practices of late capitalism. Given the wide range of Churchill's previous work, I did not go to *The Skriker* with any particular expectations, other than that the piece would be intellectually challenging and theatrically rich and innovative. These expectations were certainly fulfilled, but even so, like almost all the audiences for this work, I was surprised by the demands it placed on the willingness of its spectators to enter into and engage with its unfamiliar and challenging world. For many Public Theater members, accustomed to artistically and intellectually stimulating work, but not to anything so far outside of normal theatrical practice, this production was simply unacceptable, and I had never seen so many patrons leaving the Newman Theater during the first twenty minutes of the presentation. It was almost twenty years later, in 2013, before I witnessed a similar exodus at the Public, when Richard Foreman presented his *Old-Fashioned Prostitutes* there. It contained few elements that were different from what Foreman had for several decades been presenting in his own theatre some seven blocks away, but the reaction indicated how different audiences can be even within the small world of the downtown theatre.

The program for *The Skriker* already gave something of a hint of what was to come. Out of the sixteen listed roles, only two had conventional names: Lily and Josie. Some of the rest suggested an expressionist or symbolist drama: Man with Bucket, Lost Girl, Dead Child, Passerby. Most, however, seemed to come from the world of children's literature, various fairies, a Hag, a Kelpie, Johnny Squarefoot, and most ominously, RawHeadAndBloodyBones. Clearly what we were about to see would be far from the world of realism, or even from the theatricalized reality of

Cloud Nine or *Serious Money*. Even with this warning, the opening of the production was both disorienting and overwhelming. A bedraggled and apparently half-mad old woman emerged from a trap in the stage in the midst of a sentence composed of repetitions, parts of phrases, broken-off thoughts, and echoes of popular clichés and nursery rhymes—a torrent of words lasting several minutes. Although images flitted past, one bled into another, leaving only a general impression of a darkly menacing, fragmented world, haunted by the darker side of the folk and fairy-tale tradition. I probably found this verbal onslaught less overwhelming than some spectators did because I almost immediately could give it a frame of reference. During college I was for a time immensely attracted to James Joyce's *Finnegans Wake*, and although Churchill's flood of language differed in several important ways from Joyce's, I felt a certain familiarity with it—the unbroken flow of thought, the morphing of words into others, the references to other narratives, often made more complex by puns, the starting *in medias res*, even the absence of a narrative, replaced by the building up and combination of images and phrases. Rather than being overwhelmed or irritated by this opening, I felt something of a pleasure of recognition and a desire to see where it was heading. After this rather overwhelming introduction a somewhat more conventional story was suggested, although its central characters, two indigent young women named Lily and Josie, were continually surrounded by the dream or nightmare world of the Skriker and her grotesque companions. Lily was pregnant and the action began with her visiting Josie, shut up in a mental hospital after killing her child. The mysterious Skriker's cryptic interactions with these troubled young women composed the action of the drama. The demanding role of the Skriker was admirably filled by Jayne Atkinson, a British actress who won a Drama Desk Award for this role.

The production was directed by Mark Wing-Davey, a British director who had first gained major attention in New York in 1991 for his award-winning direction of Caryl Churchill's *Mad Forest*, her first work presented in New York for a decade that was not produced by the Public, but by the New York Theater Workshop, which would henceforth share her New York openings with the Public. *Mad Forest*, a fantasy on the Romanian revolution of 1989, did not employ the same sort of linguistic strategies as did *The Skriker*, but it was similarly set in an instable world where historical figures, average people, vampires, and archangels were casually mixed together. Unquestionably his major success with this work inspired his invitation from the Public to create the new work there.

Much more than in *Mad Forest*, which tended to juxtapose elements from different levels of existence, Wing-Davey in *The Skriker* created a visual and aural world that like the title character was a "shape-shifter." There were interior and exterior scenes, but individual elements might suggest both. A basically realistic sofa suddenly sprouted a face. The mirror behind a rather shabby bar reflected a distorted version of the bar, with a dwarf bartender and another distorting mirror behind that one. Odd elements from other scenes or other levels of existence would drift in and out of the bar or a grim London street, while puffy pinkish clouds would drift in and out of both interiors and exteriors.

The characters were more bizarre still. Men on the street dressed in seemingly normal dark business suits would, as they passed, reveal the backs of lobsters or huge cockroaches. Another man, seemingly in normal dress, would casually display a cloven hoof. The Skriker, in her own underworld kingdom, appeared as a queen in full eighteenth-century court regalia, with hoop skirt and elegant wig, but surrounding her were other figures whose appearance was neither internally consistent nor in harmony with hers. One had a short tutu, a neck ruff, a black T-shirt, and rough brown knee-length boots. Another combined a tall man with a boy on his shoulders into a single centaur-like creature. Most of the figures had odd growths or antennae; one sprouted large white wings. Only the two young women appeared in more or less normal costume and appearance throughout the play, in worn jeans, pullovers, and rough jackets. In a few sequences, the Skriker, as a shape-shifter, would be performed by other actors. The most striking of these was Philip Seymour Hoffman, in his debut performance in New York as the demonic RawHeadAndBloodyBones. For a scene with Josie late in the play Hoffman became the Skriker, appearing neither in his demonic form nor as any of the various elderly or youthful figures already depicted by Jayne Atkinson, but as a more or less normal and slightly corpulent businessman in white shirt, tie, dark trousers, and occasionally even a jacket and vest. Despite this, his aura of quiet menace and even suggestions of a barely controlled madness that might erupt at any moment was if anything intensified by this normal outward appearance. I later heard that Wing-Davey, like Peter Brook preparing for *Marat/Sade*, had asked his actors to study people with mental disturbances for inspiration. In Wing-Davey's case this included viewings of *Titicut Follies*, the notorious American documentary film showing inmates of an asylum for the criminally insane.

Although the entire production took place in a kind of surrealistic dreamworld, a key sequence late in the play was set in the underworld home of the Skriker which at first seemed, in its rococo excess, totally opposed to the drab bars and streets above, but after a dazzling first image, which looked almost like an elegant court ball, the same aesthetic as the overworld was revealed—odd and repulsive elements crept out of the corners or were unexpectedly revealed. The food on the elegant banquet tables was seen as mostly composed of twigs and refuse, and so on.

The experience of watching *The Skriker* was a most unusual one. On the level of simple theatrical experience, it was a dazzling visual production, and the actors, especially Atkinson, were extremely impressive. Still, the oblique language and flood of contradictory information and imagery demanded from the viewer, in a way most productions do not, an active ongoing attempt to pierce through the games and puzzles to discover hidden meanings that would clarify some or all of this unusually challenging piece of theatre. Clearly the world presented was a dark and threatening one in which fearsome figures from British folk literature, only faintly remembered today in nursery rhymes and tales, had for some reason reappeared in the contemporary world to add to the suffering of two young women already marginalized by that world. But one naturally was led to ask what had set them loose and what message if any did they bring to us and to the humans in the play who stand in for us?

In 1996, when I saw the play, and considering such questions, I felt that the eruption of these dark underground forces primarily had to do with the increasingly destructive effects human activity was having on the natural world. For most people I know the publication of Rachel Carson's *Silent Spring* in 1962 was a wake-up call to the destructive effects human activity was having on the environment. As the years passed, chemical poisoning of all sorts grew both in quantity and visibility of effects, adding further environmental concerns to those Carson pointed out. During the 1980s a series of major oil spills focused concern on that ecological threat—a threat not just to certain regions or ecosystems but to the entire planet. This subject entered more general public consciousness in the late 1980s with a recognition of the growing damage to the earth's protective ozone layer. Concern for the ozone layer had already entered the mainstream of serious American drama in

Kushner's *Angels in America*, where the threat to the ozone layer appears as a major metaphor in both parts of the play. It plays a much less central role in *The Skriker*, but "ozone" is such a striking word and bore such symbolic weight at that time that even amid the verbal salad of the Skriker it jumped out late in the play. When Josie, now in the Skriker's underground realm, asked to return to her home, the Skriker sought to dissuade her with the line "Up in the smokey hokey pokey? up in the world wind? up in the war zone ozone zany grey?" which seemed to me a clear reference to an increasingly polluted and threatened world.

This orientation in the work seemed to me confirmed by the ending, when Josie does return to her world, only to find, like other folk protagonists who have visited fairy realms or, in more contemporary terms, like Einsteinian travelers returning from stellar voyages, that generations have passed and the distant great-grandchild whom she encounters can only bellow at her in rage as a representative of the "distant past master class" whose heritage is a deathly world of dust.

Since that time, as the connections between environmental damage in general, climate change, and the global economic order created by late capitalism have become increasingly clear, leading commentators on this play, such as Elin Diamond, have read the work in this broader perspective, seeing the emergence of the Skriker as a result of a general crisis in an entire global cultural system of which the environmental crisis is only a part, albeit a particularly disturbing one. Although I was far from recognizing that much broader range of implications when I saw the play in 1996, our growing awareness of interconnectedness of the natural disturbances represented by the dark fairies of the play and the social disturbances manifested in its two troubled human protagonists now bring me to see the play not only as one of its author's most challenging, but also one of the most prescient.

1997 Julie Taymor's *The Lion King*

A new chapter opened in Broadway theatre history with the presentation of Disney's *The Lion King* at the reopened New Amsterdam Theatre on Forty-Second Street in 1997. Not only did this solidify the increasing presence of the Disney corporation on Broadway, a development that elicited sharply mixed reactions in the theatre world, but even more important, this became a kind of keystone in changing the most crime-ridden block in the city back to the entertainment center it had been in the opening decades of the century.

Of course, like any New York theatre-goer I was acutely aware of these developments, but what spurred me to attend the New Amsterdam while its first show was still in previews, at the end of October 1997, was not the much-publicized renovation, nor even the show itself, based on one of the most popular recent Disney films, but the director, Julie Taymor, whom I at that time considered one of the most exciting and innovative theatre artists in the city.

Up until the 1990s, I had paid little attention to puppet theatre, except for the Bread and Puppet theatre, reflecting the common bias that it was primarily a children's entertainment, but the work of Taymor, herself a former member of Bread and Puppet, opened my eyes to a whole new world of possibilities for that art. I became better and better acquainted with her work during this decade, as it appeared at a variety of off-Broadway venues, but the two works that led me to view *The Lion King* with such anticipation were two productions I saw in 1996: the Latin American myth / fairy tale *Juan Darien*, which I saw at St. Clement's Church, and Carlo Gozzi's *The Green Bird*, which I saw at the New Victory.

Although the New Amsterdam was considered the theatre that was key to the revitalization of Forty-Second Street, the New Victory was in fact the first of the street's historic theatres to reopen after decades of neglect or conversion into X-rated film houses. Various schemes for the reclaiming of the street had been advanced for years, but serious change did not come until the early 1990s, when the Urban Development Corporation, which during the previous decade had condemned and appropriated the majority of properties in the neighborhood, marked out seven theatres on the street for restoration and when Mayor Giuliani, by insisting on tougher enforcement of quality-of-life legislation, forced out most of the remaining sex businesses in the area.

Forty-Second Street had a very strange feeling when I attended *The Green Bird*, one of the first offerings of the newly reopened New Victory, in the spring of 1996. The theatre itself, with a beautiful partly restored and partly rebuilt interior, was one of the city's most attractive, and the restored monumental staircase in front made a powerful statement. The theatre seemed very much a part of the busy world of Times Square just a few steps to the east, but the long block to the west, leading to the Port Authority, seemed sterile and desolate, with most of its businesses and theatres locked and vacant, and only a few small stores still operating. The major activity was across the street, where scaffolding surrounded the New Amsterdam, still being prepared for reopening.

Although I was eager to see Taymor's new venture, many in the theatre community had misgivings. How would this unconventional experimental artist who had achieved such remarkable success with limited means work productively with a monster concern and the commercial orientation of the Disney enterprises? Such questions quite dominated more mundane but often-expressed concerns, such as how Taymor could represent a stampede of thousands of wildebeests on stage.

In fact Taymor triumphed equally on both fronts. Her *Lion King* was an unqualified success both commercially and artistically and established her with the general public in a position of prominence that she already enjoyed among off- and off-off-Broadway audiences. It proved one of Disney's most successful theatre ventures and became the cornerstone not only of that organization's presence in New York, but of the renewal of the Times Square theatre district.

The renewal was clearly in process when, not willing to wait for the official opening in November, I attended an October 1997 preview. This whole end of the block was now lively, with the New Victory already open across the street and the new Ford Center (a few doors west of it, created by combining the old Lyric and Apollo Theatres) already selling tickets for its official opening in December with *Ragtime.* Disney had also acquired the property next to the New Amsterdam on the east and was converting it into a major retail outlet for Disney products, to be connected to the theatre.

Simply entering the New Amsterdam was a stunning experience. I had been impressed by the elegance of the restored New Victory, but the New Amsterdam far surpassed it in its art nouveau splendor, every detail of which had been lovingly restored not only in the lavish auditorium, but in the elegant multilevel public spaces—lobbies, bars, smoking rooms—not only more lavishly appointed, but more spacious than those of almost any other Times Square theatre. Everywhere were glowing bas-reliefs, floral bouquets, overflowing bowls of fruit, peacocks, smiling girls' faces festooned with wreaths, flowers and lighted bulbs, rows of elaborate and heavy baroque chandeliers, allegorical figures in glowing pastels celebrating such concepts as "Progress," in the midst of erupting terra-cotta gardens. Before the show, during the intermission, and afterward I wandered through this art nouveau fairyland that offered some new and dazzling visual treat around every corner or turn of the stairs. The interior was similarly lavish, and again a riot of pastel colors, art nouveau vegetation, sweeping curves, and monumental allegorical frescos. Two sweeping balconies terminated in a charming set of little rounded boxes that carried on into the elegantly appointed proscenium arch.

Even expecting to be stunned and dazzled by the visual power and imagination of Julie Taymor, I have to admit that the first ten minutes of *The Lion King* were among the most overwhelming I have ever experienced in the theatre. The opening number, the "Circle of Life," was introduced by the solitary figure of the Shaman Rafiki, in a sense the narrative center of the production. Rafiki's costume, an elaborate construction of fabric, feathers, beads, bracelets, and hairpieces, suggested the heavily textured costume of a character in an African ritual drama, while his elaborate, multicolored facial masks suggested the face painting of kathakali or Chinese opera. As he sang the opening lines, an enormous sun of orange rippling fabric rose behind him, and the first figures summoned forth passed in silhouette in front of it, two remarkable "giraffes" created by actors on six-foot stilts with an extended neck and head built up from their shoulders and two longer poles extending from their arms to make the front legs. Other figures flooded the stage—animals, birds, and perhaps most beautifully, the grasslands of the savanna itself, represented by a whole chorus line of figures, each with a large headdress representing a bed of grass and with flowing floor-length diaphanous robes that as they whirled about the stage seemed literally to bring the earth itself to life.

Then came the real spectacle. The figures summoned by Rafiki to the assemblage no longer appeared from the sides of the stage, but from every part of the theatre, down the aisles, through the balconies and the hanging boxes, across the airspace above us. The entire theatre seemed filled with a dizzying array of birds and animals—the majority of them full-size puppets ingeniously built onto the bodies of actors with poles, wheels, physical extensions, and masks. The figures bore a striking resemblance to the animal originals and yet were also clearly theatricalized machines—four bodies made up one huge elephant and two a lumbering rhinoceros, leaping figures with cutout animal silhouettes represented gazelles, a cheetah was played by a Bunraku puppet manipulated by a cat-clad operator. The central lion figures wore imposing lion masks like headdresses, with fully exposed human faces beneath creating a powerful double focus.

The story itself, the coming of age of the young lion king, was almost lost in the unfolding display of one stunning visual effect or dance scene after another. Even the much-anticipated and demanding stampede scene did not disappoint, but in fact provided one of the most memorable sequences of this remarkable evening. In one of the story's most powerful and frightening sequences, the young lion Samba and his father are lured by the villainous Scar into a stampede of wildebeests, in which the father is killed.

The Disney film created this sequence in a wide variety of shifting perspectives, looking at the hundreds of wildebeests racing through a narrow canyon from above, beneath, almost every possible angle, with constantly increasing tension. Taymor's challenge was to find a theatrical equivalent of this spectacle and her version was, like much of her work, simple, ingenious, and stunning. Large, reddish-earth-colored pieces on the sides of the stage suggested the canyon walls, and the stampede first appeared, as it does in the film, as tiny wildebeest figures dashing from top to bottom of a rotating screen at the back of the stage. Then, as they dashed through the canyon toward us, new ranks of frantically dancing wildebeests poured in from the sides, wearing larger and more threatening horned masks with each new row as they approached the audience, until the entire stage space was filled with savagely dancing figures, while in the distance tiny new figures still appeared.

When I left the production, dazzled and exhilarated, I enjoyed a final turn around the lovingly restored fairy-tale-like lobby space, and as I made my way back out toward the urban reality of modern Forty-Second Street I passed under the huge terra-cotta bas relief bearing at the top the legend "progress." It brought me up short, thinking how appropriate it must have seemed to the first audiences in this bold new theatre, the first erected in the Times Square area, in 1903, almost a century before. They were leaving this lavish new venture after seeing the appropriate inaugural production, a suitably spectacular *Midsummer Night's Dream*. Then, at the dawn of what would later be called the Progressive Era, in a theatre opening a new part of the city to dramatic entertainment, the motto seemed totally appropriate.

What, then, about 1997, when the unalloyed vision of "progress" had taken such a battering in the previous century and when this dazzling new venture could not escape the now much more contradictory emotions that word aroused? For many this unquestionably successful new venture was seen as the long-awaited turning point that would restore Times Square to the position of entertainment capital of America, while others worried about the cultural and social price this might exact. A few voices continued to speak nostalgically even of the crime-ridden old Forty-Second Street, missing its gritty reality, its edginess, and its representation of free speech, even of the most socially questionable type. Others, a much larger group, worried about the "Disneyfication" of the area, turning Forty-Second Street into a kind of entertainment theme park, devoted to consumption and merchandising, centrally represented by the large new Disney store directly connected to the ornate lobbies of the restored New Amsterdam.

From these perspectives, the evocation of progress had a distinctly ironic ring. In the glow of the experience of *The Lion King*, however, I felt few such misgivings. Leaving the theatre amid a delighted crowd, seeing another crowd gathered at the New Victory across the street, and seeing the soon-to-open Ford Center just a few doors down, it seemed to me that the return of the live theatre to this formerly forbidding area was unquestionably a cause for celebration, and that even the heavily loaded term "progress" was not an inappropriate one.

1998 Paula Vogel's
How I Learned to Drive

It has been my great privilege as a late twentieth-century theatre-goer to have enjoyed the career of Paula Vogel from its outset. Paula came as a graduate student to Cornell University during the final years of my service in the theatre department there, and while there she received the first staging of her play *Meg* in December 1976. There is no such thing as a typical Vogel play; indeed what her works have in common is their unconventionality of theme and approach, while individual plays vary greatly in both subject matter and approach. *Meg*, however, showed an interest Vogel would often explore in different ways in gender roles and their personal ramifications and in looking at familiar stories or relationships in a fresh way.

Meg was the daughter of Sir Thomas More, a familiar figure to most theatre-goers in the late twentieth century because of the popular stage and screen retelling of his story, *A Man for All Seasons*, by Robert Bolt. Meg appears as a secondary character in that play, primarily as involved in a love interest of which her father, for religious reasons, does not approve. She does, however, have a key scene in which she has a chance to display her knowledge of Greek and Latin, a rare achievement for a woman of that era, and indeed to best the condescending and self-assured Henry VIII in this ability. It is that Meg who was at the center of the play, causing some to characterize Vogel, rather reductively, as a budding feminist author.

Staging an original play by a student author at the main theatre at Cornell was unthinkable, so *Meg* was premiered in the Drummond Studio, named for the founder of the theatre program there. It was a moderately large black-box space located in the rather dank and uncomfortable basement of Lincoln Hall, the theatre and music building. The entrance to the theatre opened out onto the Arts Quadrangle, meaning a long and cold trek across the Quad from any parking or public transportation, which can create a real challenge in an upstate New York winter. Unhappily the winter of 1976–77 was a particularly severe one, and *Meg*'s opening night audience had to make their way across the snow-covered and windswept Quad, where the wind chill was minus 30 degrees.

In fact the theatre was full and the audience for the short run was enormously enthusiastic. Eight years before, Roger L. Stevens at the Kennedy Center in Washington organized an American College Theater Festival, to bring outstanding college productions from across the country to be presented at the Center each spring. *Meg* was selected to go in April 1977 and won the first-place honors that year, the first of many national awards Vogel would receive and a major indication of her promise.

Before I left Cornell, I heard a staged reading of Vogel's next play, *Desdemona*, an ingenious reexamination of the relationships between the three major women in Shakespeare's *Othello*. I became once more aware of her work more than a decade later, after I had moved to New York City and taken up regular theatre attendance there. Vogel suddenly burst onto the New York theatre scene with a highly successful production of *The Baltimore Waltz* in 1992, a surrealistic but emotionally rich study of a victim of AIDS, based upon the story of the playwright's deceased brother. The production, which won several major awards, showed clearly that Vogel was beginning to realize the promise she had shown at Cornell, but the evening offered me other rewards as well. The star of the evening was Cherry Jones, whom I had first admired on Broadway the previous season in Timberlake Wertenbaker's *Our Country's Good*, and who had immediately impressed me as one of the most promising young talents in New York. The director of *Baltimore Waltz* was Anne Bogart, whose *In the Jungle of Cities* at the Public the previous year had strongly impressed me.

The success of *The Baltimore Waltz* doubtless encouraged the Circle Repertory, a company primarily devoted to new American drama, to present two more Vogel plays the following year, *And Baby Makes Seven* in April and the first fully staged production of *Desdemona* in October. Despite the engaging presence of Cherry Jones in both productions, neither was as well received as *The Baltimore Waltz*, and in any case the Circle Rep phase of Vogel's career was over. The appearance of those three very different and very innovative works in such a brief period remains in my memory, however, as one of the high points in my several decades of attending Circle Rep productions.

The next Vogel play presented in New York was her most successful to date, gaining her a Pulitzer Prize and a host of other honors. This was *How I Learned to Drive*, which was presented at a much newer venture, the Vineyard Theatre. The Circle Rep had been one of the last representatives of the original off-Broadway of the 1960s, primarily located in and around Sheridan Square in the 1960s. When Circle Rep closed in 1996, the center of off-Broadway had almost entirely moved to the East Village, a move of which the Vineyard was a part, although its location, on Fifteenth Street just east of Union Square, placed it on the northern edge of this new theatre district.

Toward the end of the century the off-Broadway theatres were not only changing locations, but transforming spatially and culturally as well, as the differences between the old Circle Rep and the new Vineyard reflected. The Circle Rep building in which I saw *The Baltimore Waltz* was located just off Sheridan Square in a solid brick freestanding building that not only resembled a garage, but still proudly bore its original sign "garage" in the middle of its facade (it is today a jazz bar called

"The Garage"). Circle Rep marked its presence there, as did many off-Broadway houses of the time, by a large banner bearing its logo on a flagpole mounted on the facade. The Vineyard space, on the other hand, was not an adapted space, but a totally new one, created as a $750,000 tax write-off within one of the most important development projects in New York, the massive Zeckendorf Towers on Union Square.

The result was an elegant and comfortable theatre, though one whose internal arrangements reflect that fact that it has been tucked into the back corners of another project. One enters the Vineyard through a door placed in a modest brick portico, the fourteenth of seventeen identical porticos that make up the ground floor facade of the Zeckendorf building, which fills this entire block. Inside is a narrow hallway with the box office on one side, leading to a staircase that descends to a modest lobby. This lobby in turn opens onto the upper row of seats in the 125-seat actual theatre, which extends further down underground to the left. It is a comfortable, but definitely hidden-away, space.

Every new work by Vogel has been a surprise and delight to me, not only because she keeps pushing the boundaries of subject matter (in the case of *How I Learned to Drive* an understanding, even somewhat sympathetic, study of incest and pedophilia), but also by her continually changing utilization of different theatrical styles and techniques (puppetry, dream sequences, cinematic devices, and so on). In *How I Learned to Drive* I was struck by her experimentation with Brechtian devices, which she turned toward the exposure of personal and family relationships instead of the economic struggles so central to Brecht.

The Vineyard stage was, in Brechtian fashion, almost totally bare, with only chairs and an occasional table to suggest different locations—a family dining room, a restaurant, a basement photo shop, and most importantly, the automobile, represented in the style of Thornton Wilder (whom Vogel much admires), simply by two side-by-side chairs facing the audience. Other key elements suggested Brecht as well. Projected on the rear wall was a map of Baltimore in the 1960s and 1970s, when the action of the play began, but as the narrative jumped from time to time and from place to place, other rapidly shifting projections reinforced the motifs of movement and travel with images of road signs, interstate markers, town names, and zip codes.

The show was introduced by a neutral voice over the loudspeakers announcing a course in driver's education, and from time to time that voice would be heard again giving various safety tips on driving and maintenance. This conceit carried over into the structuring of the production, with different sections given Brechtian titles derived from this imaginary manual such as "You and the Reverse Gear."

Basically, however, the play is presented as an extended memory monologue by the protagonist, Li'l Bit, interrupted by illustrative scenes from her memory. This encouraged a presentational style throughout, with much direct audience address. From a part of theatre history quite different from, although not unrelated to, Brecht, Vogel drew another major element of the play. Aside from the central roles of Li'l Bit and her abuser, Uncle Peck, all of the other roles were played by three actors, collectively called the "Greek Chorus"—one male and two females, one middle-aged and one younger, designated as "teenage" in the program, but actually recommended by the playwright as "being clearly of legal age." They deftly indicated changes of roles by shifting their somewhat caricatured delivery and by slight adjustments of elements such as scarves and glasses. Among the many great pleasures of the production was the successful interweaving of this wide variety of production approaches, keeping the audience constantly taken unawares.

According to the author, the work was inspired by Nabokov's classic novel of forbidden love, *Lolita*, but, typically for Vogel, she told this disturbing story not from the point of view of the older man, as did Nabokov, but from that of his preadolescent partner. Both of the actors who played these roles were already familiar to audiences from numerous theatre and film performances, but both added major new luster to their careers in *How I Learned to Drive*. Mary-Louise Parker, though in her midthirties, had a slight, wiry body and pixieish face that allowed her, with simply a turn of her leg or a twist of her body, to convincingly suggest the full range of the character's presumed ages during the play. David Morse exuded a warm and totally trustworthy aura, if slightly tinged with eroticism that made him, as Ben Brantley's review in the *New York Times* was headed, "A Pedophile Even Mother Could Love."

So successful was the production that the Vineyard, committed to continuing its season, moved the play after its first month across Fifteen Street to a commercial venue, the Century Center. A private club, the Century had in 1976 extensively remodeled its interior, adding a 248-seat theatre available for booking, a most convenient location for moving this production. I went to see the production in this new space that fall, not out of a particular desire to see the new venue, but because two new actors were then playing the leading roles, and I was curious to see if they were as effective as the original performers, who had seemed almost perfect casting choices. I was especially interested in seeing Jayne Atkinson in the role of Li'l Bit, since I had recently seen her at the Public as the chilling and grotesque Skriker, a role that seemed far indeed from this one. Moreover, she was a quite different physical type than Parker, more statuesque and projecting a much greater maturity. In fact, she created a very different but still very effective Li'l Bit. While Parker's Li'l Bit was still to some degree caught in her adolescence, Atkinson's was fully mature, more seasoned, more clearly a survivor. Like any good play, *How I Learned to Drive* opened itself to ever-new perspectives as its interpreters changed. I only regret that Cherry Jones, who contributed so much to Vogel's early career, never undertook this fascinating role.

1999 El-Warsha's *Spinning Lives*

In the late 1980s, having devoted most of my research career to Western European theatre, I decided to expand my interests outside that continent, and selected the Arabic theatre as a subject much neglected by Western scholars. I studied the language while at Indiana University in the 1980s and began acquainting myself at first almost exclusively with the Egyptian theatre, traditionally the most significant in the Arab world. I attended my first theatre conference in Cairo in 1993, continued to do research and develop contacts there, and was invited back in 1999 as one of the international judges for the annual Festival of Experimental Theatre there. In addition to attending festival events, I used this occasion to acquaint myself as fully as possible with the Cairo theatre, visiting large and small houses, both national and private. I saw a very wide range of work at that time but by far the most impressive and memorable production I witnessed was *Spinning Lives*, presented by the leading experimental company El-Warsha.

The Festival took place for the most part on the grounds of Cairo's opera house and cultural center, a monumental structure opened in 1988, a gift to Egypt from Japan. On its spacious grounds on the elegant island of Gezira are a number of small theatres, most importantly the

Hanager, and not far away the offices of the Ministry of Culture. The traditional theatre center of Cairo, where the National Theatre is still located, lies in the main business district just across the Nile to the East. Here are also found the National Museum and Tahrir Square, the center of the 2011 uprisings.

El-Warsha (The Workshop), the first independent theatre company in modern Egypt, was founded by Hassan El-Gretry in 1987 and is devoted to developing new works based on Egyptian folk materials and performance practices. They began following the general model of European experimental groups, performing dramatists like Peter Handke, Harold Pinter, and Dario Fo in small theatrical spaces. In 1989, the company made a major shift in direction in their adaptation of the three *Ubu* plays of Alfred Jarry. They moved the action of the play to Mamluk Egypt, performed the work in colloquial Arabic, and staged it in the courtyard of a sixteenth-century house. Most importantly, they told the story through the medium of Egyptian folk culture. The narrator was a professional shadow puppet operator, and his art was woven closely in the work. Since then the group has drawn both its subjects and its means of performance from indigenous material. Most of this work has been presented in large tents, both for ease in touring, which they do extensively, and to create a physical connection with the folk performance tradition that is at the center of their experimentation. The tent they normally use, created by the company designer, is a large, beautiful, translucent, white structure, indeed suggesting some dream abode out of the *Arabian Nights.* It was set up amid the lush gardens of the opera house, whose white floodlit dome and bastions against a moonlit sky added to the striking appearance of the performance space.

Coming out of the graded earthen walkways of the garden and entering the tent, one was at once struck by the different feel of one's movement, since the flooring of the entire interior of the tent was several inches of sand, with an occasional rug. Rising out of this sea of sand were long wooden bleachers for the audience on either side of the tent, with a major open acting area between them and subsidiary areas to either side. El-Gretry, like Ariane Mnouchkine in Paris or Ellen Stewart in New York, personally welcomes audiences to his company's performances, and on this occasion when the audience was seated, he welcomed his guests in English and Arabic, and briefly introduced the evening's presentation, *Spinning Lives* (Ghazl el-Amaar). *Spinning Lives* is by far the most ambitious work yet undertaken by El-Warsha. It is based on one of the world's great epic poems, *El-Sira El-Hillaliyya* (The Hillaliyya Saga) from upper Egypt. It is a massive work, following the fortunes of a major tribe originating in that region over three generations in locations spreading from Arabia to Tunisia. Since it is a constantly changing oral epic, there is no definitive version, but it runs to approximately a million verses, or forty times the length of the *Iliad* and *Odyssey* combined. Astonishingly, the traditional storyteller (*hakawati*) of Upper Egypt is expected to carry this entire work in his memory, as some religious devotees carry the entire Koran.

In 1994 El-Gretry and his company began collecting material from this epic from the last living bards in Upper Egypt. They also studied the storytelling technique of these bards, themselves memorized vast amounts of the epic, and enlisted a leading storyteller, Sayyid al-Dawi, to serve as the narrator for the production. Al-Dawi was said to be the last storyteller who could recite the entire epic, though such a performance would take several months. For each individual recitation in Upper Egypt he would select a small part of the story and present that, always open to elaboration and improvisation. When he joined El-Warsha in 1994 he was sixty-four years old, and still could access the entire epic, although some parts of it he had not performed for twenty-five years or more.

The production proper began with the actors and musicians, in traditional upper Egyptian dress, entering and sitting in two rows in the sand at the feet of the two banks of spectators. Then al-Dawi entered and began to recite the story in a flexible, lilting voice halfway between singing and speech, accompanied by a single musician playing a two-stringed fiddle, the *rababa*. Although I could understand almost nothing he was saying, I was enraptured. I cannot recall ever seeing a performer, with the possible exception of Poland's Richard Cieslak, who exuded such an overwhelming and hypnotic presence. Tall and almost excessively thin, he seemed to glow with the intensity of his recitation.

For perhaps ten minutes he performed alone, and then began to bring other actors into the performance. Although large sections of the work were set, they were always open to rearrangement, elaboration, and improvisation, and so the performance could vary greatly from night to night. The El-Warsha actors had to know the contours of the overall legend, had to have committed long passages to memory, and be comfortable enough within the poetic style to improvise with relative freedom so that they could enter into the narrative whenever called upon by al-Dawi.

Although the storyteller clearly controlled the shaping of the overall narrative, he was supported, after his opening solo introduction, by an almost continual chorus of the seated actors on the two sides and by a small group of musicians, some playing instruments dating back to Pharaonic times—the oboe-like *mizmar*, the ancient double flute called the *arghoul*, the two-stringed *rababa*, and the goblet drum, the *dara-bukka*. Throughout the evening, narrative, recitation, and enactment were continually interwoven, the actors moving into the center singly or in groups of two or three sometimes to engage in extended dramatic sequences and sometimes only to utter a word or a phrase. Neither movements nor vocal delivery suggested realism, the vocal passages being sung or chanted and the movements suggesting dance.

Embedded within both the verbal and bodily materials were examples of or quotations from traditional Egyptian dance and musical forms. Some were at least faintly familiar to me—the spinning dance that in the West is associated with the Turkish dervishes, and the shimmering, sensual eighteenth-century *ghawazi*, surely related to modern belly dancing. Others, variations on circle and line dancing, suggested folk material but not any specific tradition I knew. The songs and chants were even less familiar, but equally impressive as part of the total experience. I had learned to recognize the traditional style of *mawwal* singing, with its extended vowels and displays of vocal virtuosity, but other forms, reportedly derived from a variety of secular and religious sources, while quite distinct from one another even to my untrained ear, were nothing I could identify. Still the overall impression was of a constantly varying web of sonic and visual materials.

Nevertheless the evening did possess an overall narrative frame, even if it was constantly modified by digressions of all kinds—internal monologues, battle and love scenes, descriptive passages, and poetic meditations—and El-Gretry in his opening remarks provided a brief orientation to this overarching story. A central figure in the epic is the warrior hero Abu Zeid, who leads a campaign through Egypt to punish religious dissenters in Tunisia. He has many of the attributes of heroes in other folk legends, including an Oedipal relationship with his father, who casts him away as a child when the baby's black skin causes his father to consider him some other man's child. Abu Zeid is thus forced to make his way alone in the world, which he does by a series of tests of his valor and cleverness. Dramatically speaking, one of the high points of the production was a climactic battle between father and son, carried out through a traditional folk combat, stick fighting. Although ritualized or danced combat with sticks is found in many countries of the world, the tradition in Egypt is documented from very ancient times, with detailed instructions for the activity found in temple carvings from the Old Kingdom.

Training in the performance of this ancient art, like that of other traditional dance and music forms, had been a part of the several years of preparation the company had undergone before presenting *Spinning Lives*, and this central battle had all the passion of a life-and-death struggle with all the grace and control of a classic ballet. To add to the power of the sequence, sections of the translucent tent on either side behind the audience were manipulated to press inward, as if the heavens themselves were pressing closer to watch this epic combat. The contracting white walls almost gave the impression that the tent was a giant living thing, and that every part of the world around us had been drawn into the hypnotic recounting of this epic.

In a traditional coffeehouse performance of this epic, the storyteller could rely upon an audience not only familiar in general with at least the outlines of the complex plot and its many characters, but familiar in detail with certain sequences, even with famous passages and lines. In such a performance there is a strong tradition of interplay between performer and spectator, with the spectator free to comment on the action, suggest other lines of action, and become actively involved in the cocreation of a performed narrative. Today, with this tradition dying out, such an audience has largely disappeared, and El-Warsha could not assume even with a general Egyptian audience, let alone an international festival audience, any possibility of such interaction. Accordingly, although there was much direct address to the audience and a general feeling of skilled improvisation, the performer/audience relationship was still much the same as in a conventional theatre, albeit a quite intimate one. Even so, the feeling of total immersion in the production was certainly a feature of the evening and made me wish for the experience of an Egyptian café spectator of an earlier time, who shared a close knowledge of the founding text with his neighbors and the performing storyteller, and who could actively engage with them in its exploration and expression.

The 2000s

Dollhouse by Mabou Mines, 2003. Photo by Richard Termine. Used with permission.

2000 Moisés Kaufman's
The Laramie Project

Although Anna Deavere Smith's interview stagings, the 1992 *Fires in the Mirror* and the 1994 *Twilight: Los Angeles, 1992* were among the most praised productions of the 1990s, and she has continued to present one-person shows based on documentary theatre with success ever since, she has inspired no really significant imitators. Her particular ability in assembling material and, even more importantly, in re-creating dramatically the creators of this material is clearly a very special combination of gifts, something that no one else has successfully demonstrated. On the other hand, the documentary drama itself, a form that had not been widely seen in the United States since the early twentieth century, enjoyed a major revival in the new century, and Smith's work clearly helped prepare the way for this. The key inspirer of this new vogue, however, was Moisés Kaufman and his Tectonic Theatre Company.

The Tectonic Theatre was founded by Kaufman and Jeffrey LaHoste in 1991, and in its early years presented stylistically and linguistically innovative dramatists like Samuel Beckett and Sophie Treadwell. It first gained major attention, however, with the first work created by Kaufman himself, the 1997 *Gross Indecency: The Three Trials of Oscar Wilde.* The play was drawn from a very wide range of documentary material—letters, diaries, courtroom records, newspaper reports, Wilde's own writings—and ranged in time from the 1890s to comments from Wilde scholars today. The nine actors appeared both as characters, especially in re-enacting parts of the trials, and as researchers/reporters, presenting various documentary material. Unusually for a documentary drama (although the Mabou Mines' *Cold Harbor* used a similar device) the production was staged with a self-consciousness of itself as documentary, with the performers seated at three tables covered with books, papers, and notes, through which they would forage to find a particular passage to read aloud.

The genesis and the production of the group's next, and most famous, production, *The Laramie Project* in 2000, was strikingly similar in inspiration and in construction to Anna Deavere Smith's 1992 and 1994 creations. In 1998 national attention was given to the murder of gay University of Wyoming student Matthew Shepard, and it was widely felt that his sexual orientation was what basically motivated his murderers. The case brought a new focus to hate crime legislation and touched a raw nerve in American society, in this case homophobia, just as the Crown Heights riots touched the raw nerve of ongoing racial and ethnic tensions throughout the nation.

Like Smith, members of the Tectonic company went to the community and conducted extensive, tape-recorded interviews with Laramie residents, some closely involved with the events, and others who were affected only by being part of the community. Like *Fires in the Mirror*, the interviews focused on how this community was dealing with the tragic event that had erupted in its midst. Much more than in the Smith piece, one was aware in these interviews of a note of caution and suspicion. In a town that had been inundated with representatives of the media since news of Shepard's death became public, a group of actors from far-off New York were naturally presumed by many to be yet further outsiders seeking to exploit this local tragedy for their own purposes.

Although this tension was probably never totally overcome, the Tectonic actors sought to reduce their outsider image by spending some eighteen months in the town, taking time to become acquainted with the people they were interviewing and gaining their trust. Eventually around two hundred people were interviewed, including the bicyclist who discovered Matthew's body bound to a fence, mistaking it at first for a scarecrow, and the police officer who took the dying young man to a hospital, possibly exposing herself to HIV by clearing blood from his mouth, but not including Shepard's immediate family or the two now convicted and imprisoned murderers. The shaping of this material was far more complex than in the case of *Fires in the Mirror*, where Smith conducted her own interviews, selected which would be used, and while not adding or changing any actual words, cut and shaped the material and decided upon its order.

The creation of the text for *The Laramie Project* was in the hands of many more people. Although Kaufman had the final word, the entire company discussed which sixty interviews, out of the several hundred collected, would be used, and many members were reportedly highly disappointed when material they had collected and felt highly invested in was not selected. When the final interviews were chosen, Kaufman edited and arranged them, demonstrating that he, like Smith, had an excellent theatrical sense for the telling phrase, the revealing repetition, and the effective contrast between interviews.

The Laramie Project was premiered at the Denver Center for the Performing Arts, coproducer with Tectonic of the show, and its success there encouraged backers to move it to one of the smaller Broadway houses, but these plans did not materialize and it opened instead at the Union Square Theatre on East Seventeenth Street, where I saw it in the spring of 2000. The production was very simply staged, although not as simply as Smith's *Fires in the Mirror.* The setting was essentially a bare stage, although occasional short video clips and slides gave us fleeting images of the town of Laramie, its surroundings, and the crime scene. The specificity of these images, however, was countered by a staging that clearly strove to depict Laramie as a modern "Grover's Corners," with the implications that it could represent any of countless communities in any part of the United States. Clearly the intention was to discourage New York audiences from feeling that this sort of crime could only happen in a distant "Wild West," violent and homophobic by nature.

Wilder's *Our Town* was constantly evoked and nowhere more strikingly than in the opening sequence, where the eight young actors who would perform the sixty roles of the evening were all seated on bentwood chairs placed in several rows, looking out to the audience and recreating the funeral service of Matthew Shepard. The echo of the graveyard scene in *Our Town* was unmistakable, complete even to a couple of black umbrellas, but a very contrasting note was struck by a figure in Western garb and a cowboy hat walking slowly across the rear of the stage and bearing a large sign stating "God hates fags."

The sign invoked the notorious Kansas preacher Fred Phelps, not interviewed, who picketed Shepard's funeral as he did many others, in his campaign against the acceptance of gays and lesbians in the military and the growing visibility of gay people in the culture. In fact, however, the production showed the inhabitants of Laramie as a whole as tolerant of or indifferent to homosexuality and generally bemused and troubled by the tendency of the media to blame the Shepard tragedy on the town's homophobia. In one sad moment, the seated figures all look down and cast a weary collective sigh as an outsider repeats this frequent accusation. The interviews turned up some citizens who were living refutations of this easy stereotype, including even a young Muslim feminist who grew up in the town and is as shocked and confused as anyone about these horrifying events.

The Laramie Project, based on verbal interviews, could obviously not incorporate the piles of books and papers that in the previous *Gross Indecency* served as a constant visual reminder of the derived nature of the text, but a parallel effect was achieved by the device of having most of the actors include, among the three or four interviewed "roles" they performed, their own character as interviewers. The effect was as if from time to time Anna Deavere Smith had spoken to us directly as herself, talking about her experience in collecting certain interviews and her reactions to the situation they represented. This convention even extended to one of the actors appearing in the role of the director/ playwright Moisés Kaufman, presenting the playwright the opportunity to speak directly to the audience in his own words, even if not in his own body.

Partly because of this grounding in the personae of the individual actors, partly because their presentations were not nearly so fleshed out in verbal tics, quirks, and details, and partly because none of the people they presented were known through media depiction to their audience, there was almost nothing of the feeling, so central to the impression given by Smith, that we were watching a master mimic channeling another person's voice and body through her own. The Tectonic Theatre did not give neutral, flat readings of the material. Each played several different interviewees, and these were quite distinct, but even though the actors, like Smith, had spent considerable time with these interviewees gathering this material, they were clearly not attempting to mimic their sources, but to present them more in the manner of traditional stage representations. The emotional impact of the material itself and the fascination with the variety of responses it had elicited created a powerful impression on the audiences of both productions, although their strategies of presentation were extremely different.

No production of the Tectonic Theatre has had so strong an impact upon the theatrical culture as *The Laramie Project*. In focusing neither upon the victim nor the perpetrators, but upon the attempts of a community, quintessentially typical, to try to understand the hidden stresses that this tragic event had exposed, this became perhaps a more powerful and relevant statement for society at large than any of the AIDS-inspired dramas of the previous decade. The play was widely produced across the United States and England, and utilized in many schools to stimulate discussions of homophobia. HBO commissioned a film of it in 2002.

So important a cultural and theatrical landmark had the play become that a decade later the Tectonic Theatre Company returned to Laramie to create a follow-up project. In 2009 Kaufman returned with five of the eight company members who conducted the interviews a decade before to investigate how the events around Shepard's death were viewed ten years later. They interviewed many of the same people but also some important new ones, most notably one of the two convicted murderers, now in prison. The resulting ninety-minute epilogue, entitled *The Laramie Project: Ten Years Later*, was premiered on the tenth anniversary of Shepard's murder, October 12, 2009, and Kaufman, citing the example of the Federal Theatre Project, which often premiered its socially conscious docudramas in a number of cities simultaneously, encouraged theatres, universities, and social organizations to present performances or staged readings of the new work on that date. In addition to this admitted homage to an organization that anticipated the sort of socially engaged theatre *The Laramie Project* represented, this nationwide project, in which more than 130 organizations participated, strongly reinforced the group's insistence that the play represented not a single town in Wyoming but communities across America. The new epilogue was given its first full staging in New York in 2013 at the Brooklyn Academy of Music, where it was presented along with the original play. That production took place just one year and four months before the Supreme Court ruling approving gay marriage brought the country into a new era of the ongoing struggle for LGBT rights. How much the national attention to *The Laramie Project* contributed to the rapid shifting in public opinion on this question can never be known, but it remains a striking document from the period when the country was deeply engaged in coming to terms with the question of its treatment of its sexual minorities.

2001 Stephen Sondheim's *Follies*

During the 1990s I had become particularly interested in the relationship between memory and reception in the theatre, particularly in how previous theatre experiences conditioned new ones, as, most notably, when we see an actor in a new role while remembering him or her in previous appearances. My 2001 book *The Haunted Stage* was devoted to this phenomenon. As it happened, the year that book appeared, I attended a performance that could have been created to illustrate almost every major point in the book, and so its impression upon me was considerable.

It was not, however, my interest in theatrical memory that led me to attend the 2001 revival of Stephen Sondheim's *Follies*, but rather the opportunity to see a work by that composer. I remember clearly when I became a Sondheim fan. It was in the summer of 1973 when I heard on the radio "A Weekend in the Country" from the recently released cast recording of *A Little Night Music.* I fell in love with it at once, bought the recording, saw the still-running New York production, and was totally converted to Sondheim, never since missing an opportunity to see a staging of one of his works, either in the United States or abroad (as when *Sweeney Todd* opened the new National Opera in Helsinki).

That was what brought me on a snowy evening in early March to the Belasco Theatre to see Sondheim's *Follies* for the first time, not yet realizing how deeply it would involve the concerns I had been pursuing for the past decade. The original production of *Follies* in 1971 had taken place in the Winter Garden on Broadway, but although Sondheim's own reputation had grown steadily since that time, New York theatre audiences in general had not, and larger and more centrally located houses like the Winter Garden were by this time given over to less challenging attractions than Sondheim (*Cats* had at this moment just ended an eighteen-year run there and *Mamma Mia!*, still running as I write this in 2015, was preparing to open).

Once a leading venue, the Belasco Theatre was now much less fashionable. Somewhat inexplicably, the theatres located to the east of Times Square have never been as numerous or attractive as those to the west, and are much more likely to be dark. The once-elegant Belasco, on Forty-Fourth Street, suffered especially from the decline of the area in the 1970s and 1980s. Among its few offerings during this era was *The Rocky Horror Show* in the mid-1970s, for which production the handsome lower boxes on either side of the house next to the stage were destroyed and the ones above them heavily damaged to provide a suitably decayed cabaret ambiance. When occasional more genteel productions returned, such as the offerings of Tony Randall's National Actors Theatre, this destruction was masked by heavy discreet curtains hung on either side of the auditorium, giving the place an odd, half-finished look.

When I entered the house in 2001, I had been accustomed for two decades to that strangely masked interior, and was shocked to see that designer Mark Thompson had taken advantage of the depredations to give the Belasco the actual feeling of the abandoned theatre, slated for destruction, where *Follies* presumably occurs. Thompson had ripped all this masking away, revealing (like an ugly scar temporarily obscured by heavy makeup) the ravaged interior of the once elegant auditorium. Further, following the example of Chloe Obolensky, who in 1987 added new cracks and peeling walls to the already distressed Majestic Theater (now the BAM Harvey) in Brooklyn to make it resemble Peter Brook's decaying Bouffes du Nord in Paris, and Paul Clay, who added further decay to the already decaying lobby of the Nederlander Theatre on Forty-First Street in 1996 to provide a suitable venue for *Rent*, Thompson painted new cracks and stains on the doors and walls of the auditorium, making it seem even closer to the brink of collapse.

Although I did not see the almost legendary original Winter Garden production, it is clear that the 2001 performance in these decaying surroundings physically involved the audience in the process of loss that would not have been possible in the original, much more elegant surroundings. As the actors moved through the audience going to and from the stage, we seemed to join them as ghosts in this haunted house, much aware of our own memories and losses. Contributing to this same aesthetic, and in contrast to the elegance and display of the 1971 production, there was something rather tacky and improvised even about the flamboyant Loveland sequence that ended the production, just as the Follies girls this time descended a rather crude, fire-escape-type metal staircase instead of the elegant sweeping stairs of the 1971 premiere, and (it is assumed) of the productions being recalled in their nostalgic memory.

Even the elegant costumes of the evoked Follies girls of the past had, partly by the use of fabric, and partly by that of lighting, a feeling of insubstantiality. The curtain rose on a solitary figure, so costumed and illuminated, a showgirl atop a platform that we could not yet see, either toweringly tall or floating in space. Others followed—various dancers and performers, other showgirls, each moving to her own rhythm but all pale and ghostly, their strange and otherworldly appearance reinforced by Sondheim's haunting music.

In sharp contrast to these visions from the past appeared the show's all-too-realistic four main characters, two former showgirls and their

mates, trapped in loveless marriages and pointless lives. These are recalled to the dreamworld of their youth by a party thrown on the night
before its demolition in the theatre where the girls once performed. In
many ways the 2001 revival more fully fulfilled the haunted quality of
the work as a whole than did the original, in significant measure because while the 1971 performance evoked audience memories of the
great era of American musicals of the Rodgers and Hammerstein era,
stretching back to the last of the variety shows upon which *Follies* itself was based, the 2001 revival also evoked memories of the Sondheim era that had followed the Rodgers and Hammerstein one, including of course the original production of *Follies* itself, now an even
more central part of the nostalgic background than the original Follies
shows. Sondheim's particular skill in musical quotation contributed
significantly to this—with much of the musical theatre tradition of
the past century, including of course his own contributions, evoked in
the score.

One of the features shared by both the premiere and the revival was
the use of veteran performers, who literally embodied the historical trajectory with which the show was concerned. An extra layer of memory,
however, was added in 2001, that of the original creators of the roles. So
that when Betty Garrett, for example, a longtime star of stage and screen
musicals, performed the "Broadway Baby" number, it evoked memories
not only of her extensive career, but also of Ethel Shutta, for whom the
number had been written and who had actually performed as a Broadway showgirl in the 1920s. This same kind of double memory operated
for many of the familiar names in this revival, among them Jane White,
who played Solange, Judith Ivey, who played Sally, and perhaps especially Polly Bergen, who played Carlotta.

In terms of visual images, the number that probably most effectively
captured the basic theme of the show was the "Mirror Song," "Who's
That Woman?" in which the four protagonists confront and dance with
their real and imagined younger selves, a sequence of great beauty and
also enormous sadness. Despite the theatricality of that number, however, it has unquestionably been the song "I'm Still Here" that has become the musical emblem of the show, and which, I have come to realize, suits the show's concerns with ghosts and haunting much more
profoundly than the at first more apparent themes of disappointment
and loss.

What ghosts share most centrally with memory is survival. However attenuated, altered, subjected to the ravages of time, they are *still here*, and it is this dynamic, I would argue, that has made *Follies*, despite the somewhat sordid narrative of its principal characters, a powerful statement of survival of both individuals and of the art they produce, even that most ephemeral of arts, the theatre. The performers who performed this song have significantly added to its resonance. Yvonne de Carlo, who first performed the song in 1971, had then been in show business for thirty years, beginning as a showgirl dancer, achieving her first success as Salome, and going on to a major career in film, television, theatre, and opera. She was still alive, but in retirement, in 2001.

Polly Bergen, who performed this song in 2001, added significant new biographical memories to it. Like de Carlo, she had almost half a century of performance experience in stage, screen, and television, but unlike de Carlo, had fallen into relative obscurity for almost two decades before reemerging, at the age of seventy, to perform in this Broadway revival. Her remarkable comeback added for many in the audience an extra depth to the song, and I recall a *New York Times* interview in which Bergen regarded the number as if it had been written to summarize her own career.

The final twenty minutes or so of the evening provided, as so often in Sondheim, a deeply ironic exploration of human illusion and romantic cover-up of a harsh reality that cannot be faced directly. Each of the four protagonists appears in his or her own dream production number from the golden past—a blue number, a torch song, a jazz saga, and finally a cane-and-kick-line display, but all four, though staged with a lavishness notably lacking the rest of the evening, had a worn and tawdry edge. Even in memory the past was less than ideal, a kind of hollowness was clearly present. When Ben, the last to present his routine, stumbles over his lines and finally collapses in acknowledgment of his unfulfilled dreams, this only brought to the fore what was suggested in the entire sequence, with its rather desperate glittering surface.

And yet, despite this dark undercurrent, as in Sondheim in general, I left the theatre strangely elevated. In part this of course was due, as always, to the sheer brilliance of Sondheim's music, lyrics, and tremendous ability to draw upon an astonishing range of musical strategies of the past to weave a marvelous texture of emotional tones, but it was also in part due to the ability of Sondheim's deeply flawed characters to find a way to live with these flaws and inspire in us a sympathetic understanding.

If this is the most haunted of Sondheim's plays, the haunting, despite the inescapable sense of loss, is not a fearful or destructive one. On the contrary, it provides a strange source of strength and even solace, however insubstantial it appears when faced with the cold light of reality. That is, I think, why "I'm Still Here" resonates so strongly as a statement of the triumph of the human spirit over the destructive forces of aging and the decay of the implacable physical world. What better venue for such a message than a haunted theatre? And the Belasco, like many old theatres, is a famously haunted one.

For many years after his death, the ghost of the impresario for whom the theatre was named, and who lived in an apartment on the top floor, was reportedly seen wandering through his theatre. During its most troubled days, in the 1970s when it housed the shocking *Oh, Calcutta!* and endured the depredations to the interior of *The Rocky Horror Show*, the spirit seemed to have taken his leave, but after the loving renovation of the fabled interior in 2010, sightings have reportedly resumed. Like the indomitable spirits in *Follies*, Belasco is apparently still here.

2002 Big Art's *Flicker*

In the closing years of the twentieth century, I was struck by the ever-greater use of visual technology in the theatre. Like other trends, particularly technological ones, I first became aware of this in German productions, where during the 1990s the work of Frank Castorf in Berlin dominated cutting-edge theatre there by his radical postmodern reinterpretations of classic texts and by his innovative mixing of live video with stage action. As this technology continually improved, this allowed such experimentation to become more and more sophisticated.

In the United States, such work was concentrated in the experimental theatre, where the financial resources were far more limited than in a large state theatre like Castorf's Volksbühne, but even so, improved technology allowed a distinct increase in such work as the century neared its end. The Wooster Group had utilized film and video almost from the beginning, and other important new groups now joined them, such as the Builders Association, founded in 1994 by Marianne Weems, formerly of the Wooster Group, and Big Art Group, founded by Caden Manson and Jemma Nelson in 1998.

By 2002, when I saw Big Art's *Flicker*, both of these companies had established important reputations in the New York experimental scene and were beginning to perform internationally as well. The particular approach associated with the Big Art Group, which they have called "Real-Time Film," was first fully utilized in their third production, *Shelf Life*, which I saw in 2001 in the tiny Kraine Theater, an important new venue for innovative work opened during the 1990s directly across the street from La Mama. Perhaps the most memorable moment of that production was the striking opening sequence. Directly in front of the audience was a band of three live video projections, perhaps four feet high, running almost all the way across the performance space and overlapping so that they formed a continuous visual field. Above them were a set of small horizontal railings supporting small video cameras focused upon four performers, three male and one female, placed behind the projections with only their heads and torsos visible. In the opening sequence, the head and shoulder of the far-right performer were shown on the video screen below him, but his arm, extended to his right, was extended by blending it, in the middle screen, with the video image of the arm of the next performer, clearly recognized as such by a tattoo upon it. That arm image in turn blended into the image of the extended arm and hand of the third performer, pointing toward the live image of the head and shoulders of the final female performer, who could be seen alive above that image. Thus we could see at the same time the image of the impossibly extended arm, reaching all the way across the stage, and could also see, in a kind of Brechtian exposure, the mechanical means by which it was being created.

With *Shelf Life*, Big Art established itself as an important new experimental company, whose rising visibility was suggested by the performance of their next piece, *Flicker*, at P.S. 122, a far more important venue than the Kraine, although not in fact much larger. P.S. 122 was an abandoned public school in the East Village converted in 1970 into a performance venue, Performance Space 122. Under the directorship of Mark Russell, beginning in 1983, it became one of the leading spaces in the city, especially for the solo work of Tim Miller (one of its cofounders), Eric Bogosian, Karen Finley, Ron Athey, Deb Margolin, and many others, as well as presenting important new groups like Mabou Mines (a resident company there), Big Art, and Elevator Repair Service.

As a theatre space, P.S. 122, at the corner of First Avenue and East Ninth Street, left much to be desired. One entered through a small, dark wooden enclosure, isolating the interior somewhat from the weather outside, into a small space with a box-office window to the left, really just a stairwell rather than a lobby, and then ascended three flights of antiquated stairs to attain a long, narrow corridor leading to the rear of the building, where one at last discovered the theatre, a black box that originally served as the school cafeteria, and that contained about 160 bleacher seats facing a performance area, broken up to some extent by rounded fluted metal columns left over from the cafeteria days.

The stage arrangements closely resembled those in the Kraine the year before. *Flicker* also placed a three-segment screen across the space separating the audience from the actors. Atop the screen were stationary live video cameras and behind them were the actors, whose heads, arms, and torsos were visible, as in *Shelf Life*. Although similarly based on mass culture and popular entertainment and utilizing similar technical means, *Flicker* employed a narrative structure quite different from that of *Shelf Life*. The performance was based on two narrative films, which began almost identically and were announced by title cards held up in front of the two end cameras. Both titles announced a terrible tragedy that befell a group of young friends one autumn day.

After this first title, however, the stories began to diverge. The right monitor promises to show the story of three young friends and the unfortunate events on an autumn afternoon, while that on the left announces five young friends on an ill-fated autumn evening. The stories, both drawing heavily upon current commercial romantic and thriller films seeking a teenage market, then unrolled simultaneously. At the beginning the right and left monitors each followed its separate story in a fairly conventional matter, with the middle screen blank, but soon the stories would be pursued on any of the three screens, or in different combinations, so that a visual narrative could expand to all three screens or blend with elements from the other narrative. The story that began on the right followed the deteriorating relationships between its three young protagonists locked in a tragic love triangle. The other story was equally melodramatic but far more physical. There the five young people, on their way to a party through a dark and mysterious wood, were attacked by an ax-wielding psychopath.

Although many groups around the turn of the century, both in Europe and America, explored the combination of live action and live video, the particular approach of the Big Art Group seemed to me quite distinctive. Most commonly live video was used, most notably by Frank Castorf in Berlin, to allow the audience to see offstage and alternative spaces without leaving their seats. At first these spaces were shown only filmically, but later in the 1990s, Castorf's crew, using handheld video cameras, moved freely on and off stage, so that these two spaces began to form a cognitive blend.

Cognitive blending was also a key concern of Big Art, but created in a totally different way. Most important, the cameras did not move, and so their exploration of alternative spaces was created by the actors, who might, for example, suggest that a camera was moving to look out of a window by one actor bringing a window frame close to it, with another actor waving a tree branch behind it. One particularly memorable sequence from the slasher film clearly illustrated the possible complexity of this technique. The actress Amy (her real name was Amy Miller), being chased through the woods by the maniac, in fact ran in place, as if on a treadmill, with her back to the stage-right camera, looking back over her shoulder at the camera and presumably at her pursuer, in the well-established conventions of cinematic point of view. In fact, as the audience could clearly see, her pursuer, of whom we saw only the waving knife on the left-hand screen, was neither running nor anywhere near Amy, but was being filmed on the opposite side of the stage. The middle screen at this point showed only shots of the forest rushing by, produced by other actors moving set pieces rapidly past the middle camera.

In the traditional live theatre, such a run, easy enough to film, would present considerable technical difficulties (one is reminded, for example, of the elaborate treadmills built in major theatres in London and New York a century before to accommodate racing horses). Big Art openly accepted this limitation and revealed the apparent pursuit quite frankly as a constructed illusion. In order to understand the production at all, the audience had to both accept the movement forward of the fictional events and realize that the body experiencing these events was being constructed as they watched in a manner quite different from either the conventional bodies of theatre or film.

In watching this production, I first thought of Brecht, who sought to achieve his alienation effect by setting different semiotic systems in opposition or by exposing (as in the case of lighting) their technical means of production, both strategies for undermining the seamless illusionism of conventional theatre. As I watched Flicker, however, I realized that the availability of contemporary technology had allowed Big Art to take this demystifying or denaturalizing process to a greater extreme, destabilizing the central figure of the actor to an extent never really quite possible in the Brecht theatre. Returning to Amy's run, for example, her running digital body is blended into a very similar running body in the same position on another camera, actually male, but wearing a distinctive red wig and a costume seemingly identical to that worn by the original Amy. This figure in turn blends visually into yet a third running figure, this one another woman (or perhaps the original one) in a blond wig. These foregrounded inconsistencies forced the spectators to give up the traditional assumption in both conventional theatre and film of a unified presented body and to be aware, before all else, of the constructedness of the performance.

Flicker was the central work in what director Manson called his "Real-Time Trilogy," which was concluded by *House of No More* in 2004. Here once again, but to an even greater extreme, the only reasonably coherent story line was that artificially produced by the actors for the video camera. Perhaps inevitably I thought in this context not only of Brecht but also of theorist Philip Auslander, whose influential 1999 book *Liveness* argued that in the contemporary world the digital image was everywhere gaining ascendency over live performance. Actually, however, Auslander was still considering a dynamic of reproduction, even if the copy dominated the original. In fact, rather closer perhaps to Derrida, what the "Real-Time Trilogy" reproduced had no original, but was created directly and digitally as a copy. Process had in a very fundamental way become product.

As I write this, P.S. 122, the host of *Flicker* and of countless important experimental performance works in the late twentieth century, has been closed for two years, undergoing extensive and much needed renovations. When it reopens it will be a far more comfortable and flexible facility. Instead of ascending a crumbling staircase through a warren of halls and landings, audiences will enter an elegant lobby, where elevators will whisk them to two totally renovated fourth-floor theatres, in which even the signature supporting columns have been removed. It promises to be, in short, an impressive updating of an aging facility, not unlike the recent remodeling of the Public.

There are those of us, however, who will remember with a bit of nostalgia the old inconvenient space that was so much a piece, architecturally and emotionally, of the old East Village and whose rough, jerry-built nature provided a significant milieu for works like *Flicker*, which foregrounded the physical process of creation.

2003 Lee Breuer's *Dollhouse*

When I attended Lee Breuer's *Dollhouse* at the recently opened Saint Ann's Warehouse in 2003, I had been attending the work of this innovative director, both on his own and as a member of Mabou Mines for more than twenty years, since the early *animations*. I rarely missed a Breuer production, and always found much to admire as well as almost inevitably choices that seemed to me excessive and self-indulgent. His visual and general theatrical imagination, particularly in his ingenious work with puppets, far outweighed these flaws, however, in my experience, and kept me among the faithful followers of his work.

Unlike most directors, Breuer continued to be equally active both in creating totally original works of his own and in staging major works of the international repertoire, albeit always filtered through his own fecund imagination. Both approaches have produced major contributions to the modern American experimental stage. Among the adaptations of classics, *The Gospel at Colonus* remains for many Breuer's richest work, and his staging of *Lear*, for which he shared the honors with his female protagonist Ruth Maleczech, was a major event of the late twentieth-century American experimental theatre.

Never before 2003 had Breuer attempted the staging of a modern text, however, and since I have always had a particular interest in Ibsen, I was fascinated to hear that he was preparing his own version of that dramatist's often-produced *A Doll's House*, and I attended the production soon after its opening in November 2003. Although Saint Ann's had been in operation for less than two years, I had attended productions there almost as often as any other venue in the city. Remarkably, and almost instantaneously, it had established itself as one of the leading homes of experimental theatre work in the city, and has in the early twenty-first century established the kind of preeminence in this area enjoyed by P.S. 122 in the 1980s or La Mama in the 1960s and 1970s.

St. Ann's actually began more than twenty-five years earlier producing concerts and arts exhibits in an Episcopalian church of that name in Brooklyn Heights. In 2000, that long-term relationship soured and the group sought a new home. Nearby areas in Brooklyn, gentrified in the late twentieth century, were far too expensive, but an area to the north, called DUMBO (Down Under the Manhattan Bridge Overpass), just being noticed by developers and artists, attracted their attention. Like Brooklyn Heights, it was only one subway stop from Manhattan, and although long a grimy industrial area, the neighborhood featured rather exotic cobblestone streets and offered stunning views of Manhattan and the bridges. The group was even able to discover a commodious space in a former warehouse on Water Street that the owner was willing to let them occupy rent-free until plans for the development of the property moved forward. This space was divided into two large spaces, a huge lobby area and at its rear a 499-seat (off-Broadway size) theatre space.

Saint Ann's received an inestimable boost when the Wooster Group decided to present its newest piece, *To You, the Birdie*, an adaptation of *Phèdre*, as the opening production at the new theatre in February and March 2002. The production had important advantages for both organizations. The popularity of the Wooster Group made its small quarters at the Performing Garage increasingly inadequate, and they had been searching for some time for a larger space, while the opening of a work of this reputation immediately established Saint Ann's Warehouse as a major new part of the New York experimental scene. Later that year other leading groups and artists followed—the Builders Association, with close ties to the Wooster Group, Laurie Anderson, and others, solidifying the preeminence of the new venue.

Eating before the show posed a bit of a challenge then, although with the gentrification of the neighborhood this situation steadily improved. The long-established River Café offered great food and views but was expensive, slow, and not very close. Much better was the nearby Rice, a very pleasant Southeast Asian place that also provided in those days the food for the bar of St. Ann's, which was located at the center of a small café-type area at the end of the huge lobby furthest from the theatre area. On the high walls of the lobby the organization gradually built up, in the manner of many off-Broadway houses, an engaging display of posters and large photographs of the many distinguished artists and productions that had appeared there.

Although the performance area did not contain an actual proscenium arch, it was normally utilized in a proscenium arrangement, with rather steeply raked bleachers leading upward from the performing area, and so it was arranged for the Breuer *Dollhouse*, stressing in a manner unusual for Breuer its indebtedness to conventional staging practices. There was indeed a conventional nineteenth-century stage opening, closed by red velvet curtains with gold tassels. To our right, next to the stage, the keyboard of a piano, the almost inevitable accompaniment of classic nineteenth-century performance, protruded through the curtain. When the curtain opened, an empty stage was revealed, surrounded by rich, red velvet curtains, with only an elaborate chandelier hanging above. A stage crew appeared and quickly set up the walls of a lovingly detailed beige and blue miniature Victorian living room, which they then furnished with chairs, tables, a sofa, and even a miniature piano, which actually sat upon the closed lid of the real grand piano downstage right. The pianist took up her position here, a woman of Asian heritage wearing traditional Chinese dress and hair treatment. Throughout most of the evening she accompanied the action in the style of traditional melodrama accompaniment, with snatches of Edvard Grieg in the sentimental passages and ominous chords whenever the presumed villain Krogstad appeared.

Although Breuer claimed that he retained 90 to 95 percent of Ibsen's original text, there was much rearrangement and addition of new material. The production began with a rather lengthy scene between Nora, her friend Kristine, and the Maid, who was clearly pregnant. Their entrance was a memorable one. All three were quite tall, and their appearance tended toward the Nordic, emphasized in the case of Maude Mitchell (Nora) by a bouffant blond wig. All were far too large for this diminished room, and their entrance through the small door on hands and knees, and their attempts to carry on a delicate tea conversation with cups, saucers, tables, and chairs far too small for them, made for wonderful visual comedy. Much less effective was Breuer's decision to have them all speak with a strange accent that presumably was stage Norwegian, but had little resemblance to any Scandinavian accent I had ever heard, in real life or in the theatre. Typical of Breuer, enormously effective original concepts were mixed with puzzling or simply awkward ones like this.

All was redeemed by the entrance of the men, however. Breuer delayed Torvald's appearance until the end of this scene and then brought all three men in the play onstage at once, swaggering through the upstage center door in a group, all in perfectly cut Victorian jackets and trousers, smoking cigars and slapping one another on the back in good-natured male camaraderie. Since all of the actresses were six feet tall or more and the men were five feet tall or less, the contrast was stunning, all the more so as our sense of scale had been tilted toward accepting the actresses as the norm during the opening scene. The striking contrast between the actual physical sizes of the men and women and the inconsistency between this and their social power relationships was of course at the core of this production and inflected every scene. Whether the situation was Torvald pontificating or condescending to Nora, Nora behaving seductively toward Rank, Krogstad threatening Nora, or Kristine making approaches toward Krogstad, in every case the disproportionate size of the actors called attention to the arbitrariness of prevailing social dynamics. This not only emphasized Ibsen's message but often even gave specific lines a powerful extra edge (as when Torvald upbraids Nora for his treatment of Krogstad with the now-devastating line: "Little? You say I'm little?").

The close relationship of Ibsen's drama to nineteenth-century melodrama was especially stressed in the first part of the evening, not only by the piano accompaniment and the stage setting, but by exaggerated gestures, line deliveries, and facial contortions by the actors. Later, however, the production began to segue into another equally exaggerated theatre form, the grand opera. The shift was announced by one of the play's most consciously theatrical moments, the final departure of Dr. Rank. Instead of Rank's own carefully staged exit, Breuer had the maid enter in full Viking dress, complete with Valkyrie helmet, and announce herself with lines from Ibsen's most memorable actual Viking female, Hjordis in *The Vikings at Helgeland*, a touch Charles Ludlam would have loved. She then picked up the dying Rank and literally carried off the small figure to some offstage Valhalla, with accompanying strains of Wagner from the piano.

This striking sequence prepared the way for another, even more elaborate, built upon the famous passage when Nora announces her "change of clothes," which becomes a visual metaphor for the change in self-definition that occupies the final moments of the play. Nora's change of clothes was the most complete I have ever seen, involving even the removal of her luxurious blond hair to reveal a bald head, but that was only the beginning of this remarkable nineteenth-century style transformation scene. The entire setting and performance style underwent a similar transformation. The stagehands from the opening took apart and removed the doll house and its furniture, while curtains surrounding the stage at the sides and rear rose to reveal three walls of arched boxes, suggesting the boxes in a baroque opera house, each box containing male and female puppet figures in elegant Victorian dress.

Nora and Torvald abandoned their melodramatic spoken delivery for a "sung" operatic one (actually lip-synched to accompanying offstage operatic singing of the lines with full orchestral accompaniment), with the puppet figures in the boxes serving as a kind of chorus, the males spotlighted and gesturing during Torvald's "speeches," and the females during Nora's. When Nora made her final departure, she left the bare-chested, diminutive Torvald sitting in their bed, an image strongly suggesting a parodic invocation of Ingmar Bergman's erotically charged reading of this scene. The famous door slam was not heard, however. Instead, Breuer added a brief scene in which Nora and Torvald's young daughter carried one of her male dolls onstage, threatened it with her brother's toy sword, which she had appropriated, and grimly echoed her mother's words: "Here's my ring, give me yours." The final image seemed not only of emancipation but of a shift in power, from the warrior to the Valkyrie.

Whatever one thought of what Breuer had made of the politics of this often-politicized drama, his theatrical imagination and daring made this one of his most successful and famous works. After its New York premiere, it spent most of the rest of the decade touring triumphantly to thirty cities in all parts of the globe, becoming internationally the best-known example of contemporary American experimental theatre. It returned to play at its first venue, St. Ann's, still in its "temporary" quarters, in the spring of 2009 before departing on tour yet again.

2004 Ivo van Hove's *Hedda Gabler*

By the end of the twentieth century I had become a regular attendee of the Berlin *Theatertreffen* and a time-to-time attendee at other festivals, including Avignon, Edinburgh, the Ibsen Festival in Oslo, and elsewhere. I had not yet, however, attended the National Dutch Festival founded in 1986 in Amsterdam, in imitation of the German *Theater-*

treffen, presenting the ten outstanding Netherlands productions from the previous season. I attended this festival for the first time at its tenth iteration, in the spring of 1996 in Amsterdam. I saw an impressive range of productions, among which I most enjoyed the ambitious site-specific work of the company Dogtroep and a powerful mixed-media updating of Camus's *Caligula*, directed by Ivo van Hove, head of the leading Zuidelijk Toneel in Eindhoven. That production, which used live video to create multiple perspectives somewhat in the manner of Frank Castorf during this same decade in Berlin, was awarded the first prize in that year's festival and was my introduction to the work of this major European director.

While in Amsterdam I also made the acquaintance of Linda Chapman, the associate artistic director of the New York Theatre Workshop, also there to attend the Festival, but with a particular mission. The New York Theatre Workshop, founded in 1979 and located just across Fourth Street from Ellen Stewart's La Mama, had during the past decade moved to a position of prominence with its productions of the work of Caryl Churchill, Tony Kushner, the Five Lesbian Brothers, and a wide range of other young dramatists from London and New York. During this same spring it mounted one of its most noted productions, *Rent*, which had just moved from the Workshop to begin what was to be an extended run on Broadway. Linda was in Amsterdam looking for an interesting and innovative continental director that the Workshop could introduce to New York. Prizewinner van Hove was the obvious choice, and he agreed to create a production there the following year, O'Neill's *More Stately Mansions*, opening the fall season in 1997.

The production was reliant much less upon technology than the production of *Caligula* had been, and much more on the physical and vocal demands of its three major actors, who alternated between sitting at the sides of the open, neutral stage, and engaging in often violent and sometimes nude confrontations in the glowing center. Puzzled New York critics spoke of European "deconstruction," but the work's unconventionality and raw power won it an Obie for directing and virtually guaranteed van Hove's return to NYTW. Indeed he has since returned quite regularly, with Williams's *A Streetcar Named Desire* in 1999 and Sontag's *Alice in Bed* in 2000, before mounting his next Obie-winning offering, Ibsen's *Hedda Gabler* in 2004.

The New York Theatre Workshop at that time normally gave the impression of a comfortable but very basic off-Broadway space. One enters the rather small rectangular lobby through a set of glass doors giving onto the street. At one end of this space is the box office and at the other restrooms and a small corner concession stand. Across from the entry doors, there is a door at either end of this lobby giving directly into the two aisles of the theatre. Just under two hundred seats, arranged in continental style with greater space between the rows than is common in New York, slope down toward a large raised stage area, although without a proscenium arch. This standard and traditional arrangement was used for most of the NYTW productions in the opening years of the new century, but more recently both seats and stage have been from time to time removed to create a large neutral black box that can be arranged in other configurations. It was in the winter of 2004, with the productions in October of van Hove's *Hedda Gabler* and in December of Caryl Churchill's *A Number*, that I first experienced these radical interior reworkings of the NYTW auditorium, although there have been a number of such reworkings since, most notably for van Hove's *Scenes from a Marriage*, which required a total rebuilding of the entire space beyond the lobby.

In comparison, the new space for *Hedda* was far less radical, but still quite shocking for 2004. Van Hove's regular designer, Jan Versweyveld, converted the entire stage and auditorium into a vast garret-like interior, with crude, unpainted drywall surrounding the normal seats on three sides, and the main acting area a vast, essentially undifferentiated space in the position of the usual stage, with some rough cabinets suggesting the different interior spaces and a few pieces of worn and seedy furniture scattered about—some simple chairs, a table, an upright piano, and a small sofa covered in white plastic, upon which Hedda and Tesman sat while he incongruously reveled in the "elegance" of their surroundings. The walls were broken only by three industrial metal doors and a set of double glass doors giving onto a walled terrace. Scattered around the room were bouquets of flowers in metal containers. At one point, these became the focus of Hedda's fury and she not only ripped them from their containers and tore them to pieces, but then stapled the remnants to the unfinished walls as pinioned mementos of her wrath.

The audience was allowed into the theatre distinctly earlier than normal, almost thirty minutes before the actual beginning of the play. Elizabeth Marvel, who played Hedda, was seated alone at a worn and battered upright piano center stage, both actress and instrument as stripped down as the surrounding walls, Marvel wearing only an unflattering slip suggesting a rather tacky imitation of that worn by Elizabeth Taylor in *Cat on a Hot Tin Roof*. Marvel was playing a monotonous and unvaried five-note phrase again and again for this entire half-hour. By the end of it, the audience had certainly entered significantly into her universe of entrapment and frustration. This long sequence also provided a powerful visual memory for those (almost certainly a significant part of the audience) who had seen van Hove's *Streetcar Named Desire* at this theatre in 1999, for which Marvel, who played Blanche DuBois, earned an Obie. In that performance Marvel, both clothed and naked, spent almost the entire evening in or near a center-stage bathtub filled with water, serving as the same sort of dominant object for her that the piano did in the current production. Throughout the evening, she would return to the piano and to that five-note motif. Once she even threw herself to the floor in front of the piano and the notes continued to play as if some demonic force continued to produce them.

Very likely taking a cue from Ingmar Bergman's powerful 1998 staging of Ibsen's *A Doll's House*, van Hove, like Bergman, kept his actors on stage for most of the production. When not involved in the action, conducted almost entirely in the better-illuminated area in the center of the acting space, they stood or sat in the darker corners of the set, watching the action but in a rather dispassionate and disinterested way, the maid often smoking a cigarette. Hedda herself at one point listlessly watched an upstage flickering TV screen. The acting was certainly not realistic, but even more strikingly, was not predictable, not even necessarily coherent. Marvel became more and more passive as the evening went on, eventually becoming almost catatonic, but even late in the evening her frustration and boredom would burst forth into violent physical and verbal activity, shouting and rolling about on the floor. Similar surprising mood swings were demonstrated by each member of the company. The normally docile Tesman, like Hedda, could throw himself to the floor in a childish rage, and Thea, or Aunt Julie, would suddenly show unexpectedly sharp edges, a ruthless manipulation of the situation as cruel and destructive as anything Hedda presented, and an open, almost embarrassing interest in sexuality. Who could have expected the prim Aunt Julie to stretch out languorously and distinctly erotically on top of Tesman as he lies on the couch?

In some ways, the Judge Brack of John Douglas Thompson came closer than the others to a traditional interpretation of the role—a suave, slightly decadent, coolly manipulative character, but actor and director gave the character an extra sadistic edge that added a chilling new dimension to the final scenes of the play. As his control over Hedda grew, his sadistic edge became more and more openly expressed. He would drink from a glass of water and spit it directly into her face, sit in one of the room's folding chairs and require her to crawl over and kiss his shoe, and finally, in what became the most often cited image of the production, tower over her, sitting in an almost catatonic state, and slowly pour a can of tomato juice over her head. After this, her gunshot suicide seemed chilling enough, but somewhat anticlimactic.

After winning a second Obie for his *Hedda Gabler*, and at least grudging respect from New York theatre critics, van Hove had clearly established himself as a leading director, perhaps *the* leading director of the New York Theatre Workshop. Since *Hedda Gabler*, van Hove has steadily provided new productions to the NYTW: Molière's *The Misanthrope* in 2007, Lillian Hellman's *The Little Foxes* in 2010, Ingmar Bergman's *Scenes from a Marriage* in 2014, and David Bowie and Enda Walsh's *Lazarus* in 2015. Although all have shared van Hove's generally dark view of human motives and relationships, all have been strikingly updated, and all have departed sharply from a traditional approach. The range of experimentation has been broad—*The Misanthrope* relying heavily upon live video to provide alternative visual perspectives, *Little Foxes* developed with a visual minimalism rather closer to *Hedda Gabler*, and *Scenes from a Marriage* created within multiple performance spaces in which a divided audience witnessed different sequences simultaneously.

The attention gained by van Hove in the New York Theatre Workshop productions attracted the attention of the distinctly more conservative but more formidable Brooklyn Academy of Music, which began offering van Hove work in 2008, and since then has presented a total of four of his productions. New York's other major producer of international drama, the Lincoln Center Festival, joined in the vogue by offering his *Teorama* in the summer of 2012. In a theatre culture whose foreign offerings have traditionally been restricted almost exclusively to works from the British Isles, this is a remarkable record, and clearly the New York Theatre Workshop deserves great credit for undertaking what no other New York theatre within memory has done—finding and promoting a director from the non-English-speaking world with such dedication and consistency that the highly conservative New York theatre eventually recognized and accepted his work. The evi-

dence is clear. As I write this, no less than four major van Hove productions are announced for this season, *Antigone* at the Brooklyn Academy of Music, Arthur Miller's *The Crucible* as well as *A View from the
Bridge* (imported from London) on Broadway, and a new production,
the aforementioned *Lazarus*, by David Bowie and Enda Walsh, at the
New York Theatre Workshop.

Impressive as this record is, it also points to a continuing problem
with the provinciality of the New York theatre. Although van Hove is
clearly a major figure, it is troubling that thanks to the support of the
New York Theatre Workshop, he has received more productions in New
York than all of the other continental theatre directors combined, many
of whom, equally important in Europe and elsewhere, have yet to be
produced in New York at all. Van Hove has now attained the position of
a safe and viable theatrical product, but he remains, unfortunately, a
unique and isolated case. I have often wondered in subsequent years
how different the New York theatre scene might have been had the
New York Theatre Workshop sent its directorial talent scout to Berlin,
for example, instead of to Amsterdam.

2005 Romeo Castellucci's
Tragedia Endogonidia L.#09

In the previous section I mentioned the surprisingly large number of major continental European directors and companies that have never been
seen in New York. High on that list would surely be the Societas Raffaello
Sanzio, based in Cesena, Italy, and headed by Romeo Castellucci. Since
the early 1990s their stunning visual and auditory collages toured widely
in Europe and elsewhere, although never to New York. Fortunately for
adventurous New York theatre-goers, however, Peak Performances, a festival at Montclair State University, has since 2004 regularly brought to
the region Castellucci and other major international figures not seen in
New York.

When in 2004 Montclair State opened a major new theatre, the
Kasser, its executive director, Jedediah Wheeler, who had worked with

artists like Philip Glass and Twyla Tharp, began at once presenting a program focused on major contemporary performance, and often rivaling or surpassing the Brooklyn Academy in its programming. I first attended the theatre in February 2001 to see Robert Lepage's adaptation of *The Threepenny Opera*, the U.S. premiere of which took place there, and not in New York, even though Lepage had for more than a decade been recognized as one of the most important contemporary directors.

By 2004 Manhattan theatre-goers had on the whole, if grudgingly, accepted traveling out to Brooklyn to attend the Brooklyn Academy, although that theatre had found it necessary, ever since the mid-1980s, to run a regular bus service from midtown Manhattan to the theatre before and after each production for the many patrons unable or unwilling to go so far outside their normal theatre world. As the Brooklyn theatre scene has developed, and as Brooklyn residents have increased among the theatre's patrons, this long-standing service was terminated at the end of 2013.

Traveling to Montclair, New Jersey, for theatre presented for most New Yorkers a considerably greater challenge than theatre in Brooklyn, and Wheeler realized from the beginning that if he were going to regularly offer artists like Lepage, a significant part of his audience was almost certain to come from New York. He therefore from the beginning initiated a BAM-styled special bus that ran from Manhattan before and after the weekend performances, and this is the way that most New Yorkers, myself included, have attended the Kasser Theater. The bus left, not from midtown, as did the BAM bus, but from Chelsea, in front of the Maritime hotel, and took about forty-five minutes to reach the theatre.

My first view of the Kasser Theater gave me a bit of a jolt, although it is basically an attractive enough structure. University performance centers having almost always more space than urban ones, it did not surprise me to find the theatre a large free-standing monumental building, much more like European than New York theatres, but its clearly Spanish mission-inspired style, although in a cool modern interpretation, seemed a bit surprising for northern New Jersey. On later trips, when I spent more time looking around the campus, I realized that the mission-style white walls and red tile roofs were utilized throughout the campus and the new theatre fit most handsomely into this century-old architectural tradition. The bus pulled up beside the theatre and we disembarked onto a large plaza, with stairs leading up to a long loggia giving way in turn to a large, attractive lobby with an elegant staircase leading to an upstairs lobby and the balcony. The auditorium seated about five hundred and faced an unusually large stage space, very useful for the impressive visual spectacles of artists like Lepage and Castellucci.

I first began hearing of the Castellucci performances in the mid-1990s, when productions like his 1995 *Oresteia*, his 1997 *Julius Caesar*, and his *Genesis* were more and more spoken of for the beauty, unconventionality, and even shocking quality of their imagery, including techniques like endoscopies, their disregard of conventional structure, and their use of disabled bodies. Although these productions had been seen in major festivals, and a large number of European cities by 2005, I had not yet seen any work of this artist and was eager to see the offering at Peak Performances, bearing the formidable title *Tragedia Endogonidia L.#09*.

This was an impressive introduction to the work of one of Europe's most challenging and imaginative director/designers. *Tragedia Endogonidia* was a major three-year project created by Castellucci, his sister Claudia, Chiara Guidi, and composer Scott Gibbons. They had just brought to completion this eleven-production cycle, ten sections of which were commissioned for and premiered in different European cities, from the history and landscape of which Castellucci drew inspiration for each work. Not since Robert Wilson's monumental *the CIVIL warS* of 1983–84 had any Western director attempted a project of this scope, and in fact only four of the projected six Wilson pieces, also to be developed in and reflect upon different cities, were actually completed. Castellucci's project was on the contrary completed, and the totality was a kind of visceral and Benjaminian look backward over the violent history of this continent. "Endogonidic" is a biological term for an organism possessing both male and female sexual organs and thus capable of ceaseless self-reproduction, an image utilized in the Castellucci work in an endless recycling of elements and motifs and of movement backward and forward between shifting male and female bodies. The cryptic L.#09 placed this work as the ninth in the eleven-work series, the L for its origin in London, where it premiered in May 2004 as part of an international theatre festival.

The production in many ways reminded me of much of the work of Robert Wilson. There was the same emphasis upon memorable visual images, with little or no use of spoken words or conventional narrative structure. There was also a great deal of very slow or static positioning and of minimal and often formal or abstract stage elements. The heavily electronic score of Gibbons, consisting of digitally manipulated human speech, sometimes suggesting low moans or shrill cries, others electronic babble, was far from the hypnotic and more musical repetitions of Wilson's frequent collaborator, Philip Glass, but it was similarly remote from anything like a normal musical background. In the work of both Wilson and Castellucci objects took on the appearance of living beings and vice versa. One difference that struck me at once, however, was that Wilson figures, even when nude (which they rarely have been) remain primarily elements in formal compositions, drained of almost any conventional eroticism. On the contrary, the opening scene of L.#09, though equally formal, was both visceral and distinctly erotic.

The lights went up on a tableau, a tall female figure, standing with her back to us and long blond hair down to her waist, clad in an elegant, embroidered floor-length white dress. Her hands, entwined in a dark rope, were above her head, and she pulled on the rope in an ambiguous manner, so that it was unclear whether she was consciously pulling a kind of alarm (offstage clanking as she pulled suggested this) or struggling to free herself from overhead bonds. Although the stage was otherwise bare, a domestic interior was suggested by a backdrop, which showed a repeating ornate pattern, strongly suggestive of the designs in Victorian wallpaper, but vastly larger in size, as if the woman were standing in a room on a much larger scale. After a few moments both rope and backdrop were drawn out of sight, the stage darkened, and when the light reappeared the woman was standing center stage, next to a thin white plain column, perhaps ten feet tall, its only decoration an ornate Greek tragic mask, hung at head-height with a pair of black ribbons hanging down from it.

If this mask evoked the spirit of tragedy in general, the next image suggested Medea in particular as a small girl, dressed identically to the woman, appeared from behind her bouffant skirts, and with a single sharp cutting gesture, the woman apparently dealt her a deathblow. She then slowly removed her elaborate garments and piled them up in a heap over the supine child, which white pile then slowly moved off stage of its own volition, rather like a Robert Wilson object, leaving the nude woman alone with the column and mask. I now realized for the first time that her face, previously hidden by her long blond hair, was completely black. Perhaps mourning the loss of the child, she collapsed and writhed about on the ground, particularly displaying her bare buttocks to the audience, which she stroked, fondled, and spread. Finally she pulled down the mask from the column and used its bands to tie it across her buttocks, facing the audience, with its grotesque open mouth framing her vulva as she slowly walked toward the rear wall amid a roar of electronic sound.

Her hanging of the mask in the center of the rear wall introduced the next sequence, which was played behind a heavy scrim that blurred the shapes on stage and placed greater emphasis upon contrasts in lighting. The column remained in the center, but attention now shifted to the right, where an open sarcophagus was placed, vertical to the footlights. The woman, now only a blurred figure, moved to its head, and slowly a dark shape, the lid of the coffin, descended, until it dropped into place. Just before it joined the sarcophagus, a brilliant light flared forth from within, as though a powerful source of energy was being contained. The figure of the woman now removed the lid, the light gone, arranged it like a seat across the top of the sarcophagus, and then slid into the open box. When she emerged, we realized that the box was filled with some black liquid that now coated the lower half of her nude body. Walking backward to the scrim, she leaned against it, leaving the dark imprint of her buttocks on it, and then left the stage, leaving also a trail of black footprints.

In a sequence rather suggesting a Robert Wilson knee play, a young clown figure came on with a bucket containing a bloody liver, with which he tried, obviously in vain, to wipe away the footprints and stains on the scrim. The blurred remains of both were superimposed on other blurred remains, apparently from previous productions. The scrim then rose for the second half of the production, the first half of which I found, despite some clear semiotic references, even more opaque. A group of four figures, all in white official or military dress, some with black beards and white military or top hats, arranged a fourth white-clad, black-haired figure on hands and knees center stage, and placed over it an angular tufted shape suggesting a young tree, which proceeded to sodomize the kneeling figure for some minutes as the other figures applauded and two large British flags emerged from holes in the back wall and whirled in celebration.

I was rather relieved when this strange sequence ended and we returned to something more understandable. The stage was vacated, the walls changed from white to black, and the woman from the opening returned to play the sequence with visual values reversed. She was almost invisible now, since her dress and hair were black and only her white face showed clearly. Her hands held a rope that stretched upward, and she disappeared, perhaps pulled up by it. Almost immediately her small double from the opening appeared in the same position, tugging against the same rope, and on that image the production ended, leaving a mixture of powerful images, of varying degrees of transparency, to repeat in my memory during the bus ride back to New York and for long thereafter.

Castellucci and his company have since returned several times to Montclair, although like many other artists who have appeared at that venue, they have yet to perform in New York (as this book was being prepared for press in 2016, they presented a short but stunning series of frangments from the 1997 *Julius Caesar* in the classic rotunda of New York's Federal Hall). Charles Isherwood, one of the reviewers for the *New York Times*, remarked on one occasion that were the Peak Performances to move to New York, it would double the number of major international productions regularly available in the city, a sad but true observation. New York is fortunate indeed to have this ongoing if somewhat inconvenient supplement to its own offerings, but one regrets that the supplement has become so essential to the international theatre offerings of the city.

2006 Rimini Protokoll's *Wallenstein*

Since 1963 the city of Berlin has each spring presented the *Theatertreffen* festival. As my interest in German theatre grew, I attended this festival more and more regularly and have attended annually since 1995, seeing there some of my most memorable theatre. One of the companies I have most enjoyed both at the festival and in other offerings has been Rimini Protokoll, one of Europe's leading experimental groups and a pioneer in the vogue for bringing nontheatrical material, including actors, onto the stage, a major trend in recent experimental work. One of their most striking and original productions in this vein was their 2006 *Wallenstein*, which I attended as part of that year's *Theatertreffen*.

Although the three artists who formed this group had been working together since 2000, and under this name since 2002, I had first experienced their work in 2005, when I attended their *Call Cutta*, an interactive performance experience in which audience members were guided on foot through parts of Berlin with live directions over headphones coming from an operator in India. In 2005, the National Theatre in Mannheim, where Schiller's first play was premiered, organized a major festival on the bicentennial of the dramatist's death, and among the companies invited to participate was Rimini Protokoll, already established as a major new experimental group, though not at all one devoted to revivals of classic drama.

Their production of *Wallenstein* was their first move in this direction, and they used the opportunity to present a classic revival that, despite my considerable theatre-going, was distinctly unlike anything I had ever seen, by working it out through their own approach to a new form of documentary theatre. The production took place in the theatre most associated with their work, the Schaubühne am Halleschen Ufer, located on the banks (Ufer) of the Landwehr Canal, running through the center of the Kreuzberg district. When I first visited Berlin in 1968, this area, snuggled up against one part of the Wall, was one of Berlin's poorest neighborhoods, largely inhabited by immigrants, with very little of theatrical interest. I did one evening, however, attend a performance at a student theatre in this remote area, attracted by a production there of Peter Weiss's *Viet Nam Diskurs*. The director, Peter Stein, was unknown to me then, but I loved the energetic agit-prop approach of the production, so much in harmony with the spirit of the late 1960s.

Between then and 1985, when I returned, although the Wall remained, the Kreuzberg had changed enormously, having become the center of Berlin counterculture and of innovative artistic activity. As far as theatre was concerned, this was largely due to the city of Berlin bringing Peter Stein and his company as a resident company in 1970 to the same theatre where I had seen them as a visiting company in 1968. Their subsequent success there brought this small house to the center of the German theatrical consciousness and made Stein the best-known German director of his generation.

When I returned in 1985, Stein's company had moved to their much larger new quarters to the West in Lehniner Platz, but the theatre remained an important home for visiting companies doing experimental work. Among these was Rimini Protokoll, formed at the turn of the century, and often using the Schaubühne am Halleschen Ufer as its Berlin base. It was here I first saw their work in 2006.

In 2003 this theatre was combined under a single administration with the nearby Hebbel Theatre, dating back almost a century, and a small experimental space, the Theater am Ufer, on the other side of the Canal, to form HAU (Hebbel am Ufer), today the leading sponsor of international experimental performance in Berlin, and the Berlin home for many companies, including Rimini Protokoll.

The theatre itself is a long rectangular upstairs space running parallel to the canal, with an unusually spacious lobby running along the side facing the river. Downstairs, beneath this space, is a casual, very bohemian café, with extra seating outdoors on the canal side (but not, alas, on the canal, which lies on the other side of a busy highway and an elevated railway track). The performance space can be reconfigured in different ways, but it is normally used in a traditional proscenium-style arrangement, with bleacher seats facing a performance area at one end, and that is how it was arranged for *Wallenstein*. The setting at the performance end was fairly simple—its major element was a revolving turntable with six chairs and a table on it and a screen above for projections, and an open space with another table to the left of the stage.

This production was the first time Rimini Protokoll had worked with an established dramatic text. The group's previous work had utilized real-life material and had dealt with various aspects of contemporary social reality. This had made them, however, one of Germany's most lauded experimental groups, and on those grounds they were asked by the committee of the Schiller Jubilee Year to prepare a work for the celebrations in Mannheim. The result, combining their particular aesthetic with Schiller's classic text, resulted in a truly fascinating and innovative theatre experience.

Only a very few lines of Schiller's actual text were spoken, most of them as conscious quotations. The major connection with the original play was of quite another sort. Rimini Protokoll sought real-life contemporary people, none of them actors, with interesting life stories that were in some way parallel to those of Schiller's characters. Their interests, dreams, and stories were then woven into a stage collage presented by themselves. So, for example, Wallenstein, Schiller's betrayed hero, was represented by a real-life politician, a prominent Mannheim conservative who recently lost the support of his own party and was defeated in a hotly contested mayoral election. The play's other central figure, Piccolomini, was represented by a prominent figure in the Mannheim police with a rich and complex personal and political history of negotiating with the shifting demands of allegiance to West and East Germany.

The disillusioned soldier figures of the play were not German, but two Americans, who spoke English throughout, both Vietnam War veterans now involved in antiwar protests. One of them, a musician, delivered a rap denunciation of the war that was one of the memorable events of the evening. The other was a figure familiar to me from American news stories, Dave Blalock, who was a member of a company that, sickened by war atrocities, turned against and killed their commanding officer (a story used to echo the fall of Wallenstein). Later he was involved in a case involving flag burning, which went to the Supreme Court, where he was exonerated. The rest of the cast were citizens of Mannheim. There was a real-life astrologer standing in for Schiller's parallel figure and, perhaps most engagingly, a woman who ran a dating service for married adults seeking extramarital connections, standing in for Schiller's sexually manipulative Countess Terzky. During the evening she even accepted what appeared to be actual business calls on her cell phone and the audience could listen to her side of these arrangements.

The only person whose real life was not in some ways parallel to that of some character in Schiller's play was a Mannheim electrician who happened to be a passionate devotee of the poet and had memorized large parts of this play and of other works. He was thus able to serve as a kind of metatheatrical chorus, providing most of the actual lines from Schiller that were presented during the evening.

Ingenious as this overall system of representation was, there still remained the major challenge of exactly how to work these various characters and narratives into a coherent two-hour presentation, and this was perhaps the most impressive part of the production. The screen over the center of the stage served as a continually shifting orientation for the spectators. On the most basic level, it identified from time to time the scene in Schiller's trilogy that corresponded to our place in the action, and although obviously much of the detailed plot of the original was not included, the evening did essentially follow Schiller's structure in the proper order. These scene indications, often with Brechtian titles to identify the action, were supplemented by a wide range of historic visual material—engravings of scenes from the play in different historical periods, as well as other cultural "Wallenstein" artifacts—decorative plates, beer steins, porcelain statuettes.

Along with these were interspersed photos and film clips depicting moments in the past lives of the various personages onstage, as well as related material, such as visual indications of the Vietnam War and war protests. A significant number of the film clips involved the political career of the politician representing Wallenstein—campaign advertisements and news stories tracing his rise and fall. This visual material as well as autobiographical fragments and anecdotes provided by the performers themselves had been selected and arranged so that there was an ongoing parallel between the scenes and events in Schiller's play and the material being shown onstage or in the slides and film clips. Occasionally the chorus/electrician would provide a specific bridge in the form of a quotation or actual historical or critical material useful for contextualizing the visual elements, but by far the most important part of the ongoing operations of the production was provided by the ingenious montage of projected elements and real-life narration.

Despite its many obviously theatrical elements, I found it difficult to compare this highly original work with anything I had seen before. None of the performers were professional actors, but most of them had significant backgrounds in other kinds of public performance, and all seemed relaxed and confident on stage. Moreover, the author-directors Helgard Haug and Daniel Wetzel had the gift of a Moisés Kaufman or an Anna Deavere Smith of drawing fascinating stories out of their subjects and arranging them in a compelling narrative. Their experiment was far more challenging, however, not only by allowing their subjects to speak for themselves, but even more remarkable, weaving these together in such a way as to provide a contemporary series of parallels to Schiller's dramatic intrigue. I remember excitedly telephoning my wife from Berlin after leaving the show that evening and reporting that I never expected, after almost fifty years of theatre-going, to see something totally new in the theatre, but that the Rimini Protokoll *Wallenstein* had given me that experience.

Looking back a decade later on this and other experiences, I realize that Rimini Protokoll in general and this production in particular illustrated a significant trend in the theatre of the early twenty-first century, particularly strong in Germany, but clearly to be seen in other Western theatre as well, and that is the increasing interest in the utilization of real material on stage. Certain important late twentieth-century trends, such as that of site-specific and documentary theatre, clearly contributed to this development, but the bringing onto the stage of real bodies, with their real stories, while not totally unknown in earlier periods, really became an important part of experimental performance after 2000. The physical incorporation of the audience into this world of real objects, real texts, and real bodies, in what came to be called immersive theatre, provided a further development of this sort of exploration. Even in those more totalizing experiments, however, I have not yet experienced, nor do I expect to experience, a performance that so challenged my expectations grounded in conventional theatre as did this remarkable presentation.

2007 August Wilson's *Radio Golf*

My introduction to the work of August Wilson was not propitious. Between 1979 and 1986 I was teaching at Indiana University, and this restricted my New York theatre-going primarily to vacations there or when passing through coming or going to Europe. Eager to seize every opportunity to attend New York theatre, I would even from time to time go to a show the night I arrived from Europe, weary and jet-lagged, hardly an ideal viewing situation. That was the situation in the fall of 1984 when I attended *Ma Rainey's Black Bottom*, Wilson's first New York show, the same day I returned from several days seeing theatre in Germany's Ruhr Valley. It was clear that this was a major new voice in playwriting, supported by very strong acting, especially by Theresa Merritt as Ma and Charles Dutton as Levee. But seen through a jet-lagged fog, it registered only enough to convince me that I must return to this author at the next available opportunity.

This opportunity did not in fact present itself until *Fences*, with James Earl Jones, which I saw the night after its opening in May 1987 at the Forty-Sixth Street Theatre. In the previous fall my wife and I had moved to New York, where I began teaching at the Graduate Center of the City University. Our first apartment there was in Park Slope, Brooklyn, and so for the first time in my life only a thirty- to forty-minute subway ride separated me from central Manhattan, instead of a lengthy drive from Cornell or an even more lengthy flight from Indiana. As a result I began attending theatre almost nightly, as I had done on my previous visits to New York and European cities.

One of the many pleasures of this steady access to New York theatre fare over the following years was being able to attend each of the new contributions to August Wilson's developing Pittsburgh Cycle, which appeared at fairly regular intervals for the next twenty years. I, like many others, looked forward to each new contribution to this massive project very much as, during the 1960s, I looked forward to each new film by Fellini, Bergman, or Truffaut. All of these shared an artistic interconnection and cumulative effect, but Wilson's project, as it began to emerge, had the extra appeal of presenting in its totality a panoramic view of black life in American over an entire century. Although all of the plays except *Ma Rainey* were set in a single black neighborhood in Pittsburgh, and some characters reappear, each play takes up a different part of that community, rather in the manner of Balzac's series of novels in his *Comédie humaine*. Rather surprisingly, the only other dramatic author I am aware of who has undertaken a similar project has been another leading black American, Ed Bullins, whose "Twentieth Century Cycle," begun in 1969 and still incomplete, now numbers twenty works.

Fences and the following work, *The Piano Lesson*, both won Pulitzer Prizes and made Wilson during the next decade the most-often-produced living American dramatist. Like most theatre-goers of the time, I was fascinated by these blends of traditional American realistic family drama with Wilson's particular gift for poetic expression and a hint of hidden, perhaps otherworldly, forces at work behind these everyday facades. By the early 1990s, although the plays were not created in chronological sequence, the overall outline of Wilson's project had become clear, and added to my anticipation of each new work was that of how various decades, especially those within my own memory, would be reflected in Wilson's dramatic world. This certainly played into my enjoyment of *Fences*, set in the first decade of which I have a clear memory, the 1950s, and of the subsequent decades, from *Two Trains Running*, set in the 1960s, to the final work in the cycle and in Wilson's career, *Radio Golf*, set in the 1990s.

Only one work in the series was not presented on Broadway. This was *Jitney*, set in a gypsy cab station in Wilson's Pittsburgh Hill during the 1970s. Wilson's previous *Seven Guitars* had not been a financial success on Broadway in 1996, and *Jitney*, an earlier work that Mr. Wilson's reputation had led to a number of productions elsewhere in the country, attracted no Broadway producers. Fortunately Second Stage decided to bring the play to New York in 2000. Second Stage was founded in 1979 to give a second showing to plays by contemporary American authors who in the opinion of the theatre's directors had not received adequate attention for their first showing. Normally that first showing took place in New York, but *Jitney* was technically qualified because of its regional presentations. Although located in the heart of midtown, indeed within a block of several Broadway houses, Second Stage is ranked as off-Broadway because it contains less than three hundred seats. In this smaller, but centrally located, space, *Jitney* had a successful run, and reopened Broadway to the four Wilson works to appear in the new century, completing the cycle.

The final play in the cycle and in Wilson's canon, *Radio Golf*, premiered in New Haven in the spring of 2005, and shortly after its opening, Wilson announced that he had been diagnosed with inoperable liver cancer. He died early that October, when the play had not yet been offered in New York. A mark of the high regard in which he was held, however, was that two weeks after his death, a Broadway theatre, the Virginia, was renamed the August Wilson Theatre. A more appropriate house to rename would have been the Walter Kerr, which had presented four Wilson plays while the Virginia had presented only *King Hedley II*, but doubtless Rocco Landesman, who had just that year purchased the five-theatre Jujamcyn group, which contained both houses, preferred to keep the name of the well-known critic and drop that of the wife of the previous owner of the house.

Along with several hundred others, I attended the rededication ceremony on October 17. After a short celebration inside the theatre, which included a number of tributes, a song from *Ma Rainey*, and a moving funeral scene from *Seven Guitars*, all moved outside for the cutting of a red ribbon and the first illumination of the new name on the marquee. Across the long side of the marquee was a huge copy of Wilson's signature, in white letters against a dark background, an arrangement copied on the marquee of the rechristened Stephen Sondheim Theatre four years later. Wilson was the third playwright to be so honored among the forty Broadway houses, and the first African American. His two predecessors were Eugene O'Neill (in 1959) and Neil Simon (in 1977). A representative of the theatre expressed the hope that Wilson's last play would be given its New York premiere in the theatre that now bore his name, but that was not to be. The first show presented in the renamed theatre was the musical *Jersey Boys*, which proved such a great success that it was still running when *Radio Golf* finally came to New York, and indeed continues to run as this is written, a decade later. The Walter Kerr was occupied with another musical, *Grey Gardens*, and so when *Radio Golf* finally came to New York in May 2007, it opened in perhaps an even more appropriate venue, the less popular Cort Theatre, on the unfashionable east side of Broadway, the theatre where *Ma Rainey's Black Bottom* had introduced Wilson to New York almost a quarter of a century before.

Most appraisals of Wilson's cycle consider *Radio Golf* one of its weaker parts, but it, along with *Gem of the Ocean*, presented at the Walter Kerr two years earlier, were among my favorites, since as the first and last plays in the century survey and as the last two actually written, they provide a kind of overarching series of reference to all of the others and are most centrally concerned with the dynamics of memory and memorialization that have become of steadily greater interest to me personally as my theatre-going has extended through more and more years of experience. The central bearer of history in the cycle is Aunt Ester, who, aged 285 when the cycle begins in 1904 with *Gem of the Ocean*, provides a living connection with the African American past. Although her death is reported in the 1980s in *King Hedley II*, her spirit suffuses the cycle and haunts the final play, *Radio Golf*, which on one level is a kind of modern morality play, with its protagonist, Harmond Wilkes, torn between his political and economic ambitions (he is an upwardly mobile real estate developer and a potential candidate for Pittsburgh's first black mayor) and his morality and connections to his roots (a major development by his firm has illegally obtained and plans to destroy the home, and by implication the cultural memory, of Aunt Ester).

Having seen the marvelous interpretation of Phylicia Rashad as Aunt Ester in *Gem of the Ocean* just over two years before, that larger-than-life personage, that house, and that world were clearly in my memory as their erasure was threatened in this work. Those were the central evocations, but the play was full of others. Situations, references to historical events of the past century, even lines and images from previous plays kept sounding echoes of previous works, as did the actual bodies of some of the actors. The two characters who spoke most clearly for preserving the memory of the part were Sterling Johnson and Elder Joseph Barlow, both played by actors whom I had recently seen in *Gem of the Ocean.* In *Radio Golf* Anthony Chisholm played Barlow, the threatened present owner of Aunt Ester's house and the descendent of the troubled Citizen Barlow, whose soul is cleansed by Aunt Ester in *Gem of the Ocean.* In the earlier play, the first Barlow was played by John Earl Jelks, who in *Radio Golf* reappears as a citizen of the neighborhood who repaints the house in order to give it a more presentable appearance.

A great part of the power of the production for me came from the flood of memories it evoked, not only of a quarter-century of experiencing the development of Wilson's monumental project within the theatre, but also of the century of American history that cycle and this play evoked, a good deal of which resonated with my own memories from the Second World War onward. At the center of the play, however, was the tension between a troubled past and a future equally troubled, not least by overly optimistic visions of an assimilated, "progressive" black population. The effective, almost allegorical setting by David Gallo contrasted the run-down threatened neighborhood of Aunt Ester's home with Wilkes's sleek but soulless contemporary real estate office, dominated by a photograph of Tiger Woods, clearly symbolic of the black man who had "made it" in the sport most associated with the economically privileged white upper class. But for audience members in May 2007 an even more potent such symbol was available, since at the beginning of that month Barack Obama had announced his candidacy for president, a major real-life realization of Wilkes's dream of running to be the first black mayor of Pittsburgh. In the enthusiasm and optimism of that moment, Wilson's less than celebratory depiction of such an achievement sounded an unusual cautionary note, but as the dreams of a "postracial" America have steadily faded, the more nuanced racial negotiations of Wilson, in this drama and in his entire cycle, have provided us with a far more complex and informed insight into the ongoing dynamics of race in American culture.

2008 Signa's *The Ruby Town Oracle*

One of the developments that most struck me in the theatre of the late twentieth and early twenty-first century was the ever-increasing interest in the "real," in the "real" texts of the documentary theatre, the use of "real" people onstage by groups like Rimini Protokoll, and the use of "real" scenery and locations in so-called site-specific theatre. This use of elements from the nontheatrical world, at first essentially confined to the performance area, began, in many experiments toward the end of the century, to reach out and involve the audience directly, bringing them into the physical world of the play where they could be offered at least a type of "real" physical experience.

Some of the site-specific work of the late twentieth century moved in this direction, asking the audience not only to observe a nontheatrical performance space, but to move into that space, sharing it with the actors, as the 1987 *Tamara* or Abdoh's 1990 *Father Was a Peculiar Man*. At the beginning of the new century, the British company Punchdrunk, which specialized in such work, called it "immersive theatre," a term that spread rapidly in the United States after the enormous success of their *Sleep No More*, based on *Macbeth*, which they began performing in a multiroom venue in Chelsea, New York, in 2011. Earlier, in 2006, I had experienced their immersive production of *Faust*, where the audience could wander freely through multiple rooms, some with actors and some without, on four floors of an abandoned warehouse in the industrial district of Wapping in South London.

Although these experiments in bringing audiences and actors together in the same space varied in a number of ways, none encouraged the actual interaction of these groups; in that respect all retained the traditional divide between actor and spectator. Inevitably, however, productions began to take place in which this divide was challenged. The first major such production I witnessed was *The Ruby Town Oracle*, created in Germany in 2008 by a pair of Danish and Austrian installation artists, Signa Sørensen and Arthur Köstler, who since 2002 have been developing such work under the combined name Signa.

Ruby Town was presented in Berlin as part of the annual *Theatertreffen* festival of outstanding German-language works held each spring and of which I had become a regular attendee. Most of these productions were presented in traditional theatres, but this was quite impossible for *Ruby Town*, which took place, as the name suggests, in an entire community. This was a kind of a Gypsy slum town, twenty-two buildings in all, trailer homes and crude improvised shacks, mostly dwellings, but also including a couple of small shops, a bar, a barber, an erotic peepshow, and a two-story chapel containing the worshipped matriarch of the community, Martha Rubin (the German title of the production was *The Appearances of Martha Rubin*).

All of the productions I have mentioned above had such extensive spatial demands that they had to be located in areas well outside normal theatre districts, often in old industrial areas where large, little-used, or abandoned structures are not uncommon. *Ruby Town* was created in the Halle Kalk, a large abandoned factory in Cologne, and moved in Berlin to the Lokhalle, a former railway switching station in south Berlin near the Schönefeld airfield, in both cases large empty buildings sheltering the entire makeshift community. Both of these spaces have often been used for recent art installations and experimental performance.

Visitors to the Lokhalle entered through a park that the city of Berlin has created out of an abandoned railway yard and in which this building is the major structure. At its entrance a small wooden structure was erected that served as a kind of border station, manned by some of the German- and English-speaking militia who are in control of this community. We visitors were fingerprinted, issued a visa, and seated within the small building, where we were shown a short orientation film and provided with verbal instructions before being allowed to enter the town itself. The orientation informed us that this "unregulated" community existed on the border between the North State, which supplied food and medicine, along with military occupation, and a presumably antagonistic South State. The population, we were told, was fifty, fifteen to seventy years of age, all descendants of Martha Rubin and most involved in smuggling and other questionable activities. Mysterious radiation in the town had killed all plants and animals and rendered the inhabitants sterile.

Visitors were asked to follow certain rules, such as presenting an ID to the military occupiers if requested, not bringing in any alcohol or communicating devices, and submitting to a medical examination if they remained overnight or participated in sexual activity with any of the inhabitants. Thus warned, we were allowed to circulate freely through the community for as long as we wished, interacting with the inhabitants much as if we were indeed tourists in an alien community. The original passports were issued for twelve hours, but could be renewed or extended, since the community remained open twenty-four hours a day for a period of eight days. Although the community apparently had an agreed-upon backstory concerning its relationship with its neighboring states and the family history of the descendants of the mysterious, quasi-supernatural Martha Rubin, and although a number of events took place during the week, such as a wedding, at presumably planned times, no distinct story or dramatic action seemed to be unfolding, giving this production an even more casual feeling than was the case in each of the other immersive events I mentioned earlier. The experience was more like that of wandering through such simulated historical environments as Colonial Williamsburg or the Plimoth Plantation, where visitors are free to chat with or even to some extent interact with the "inhabitants" of this alternative time and space.

Obviously the experience of each visitor was quite different, especially since, while the majority of these came once and stayed for a few hours, as if attending a regular theatre event, others spent whole days, or even came back several times, developing ongoing relationships with members of the community and even assuming some kind of persona there, though necessarily one of an outsider.

I arrived midmorning, stayed until late afternoon, and departed early enough to take the S-bahn back into central Berlin to attend a more conventional performance that evening. Still, this was sufficient, I felt, to give me a clear feeling of the ongoing "life" of this performance and of the general dynamics of audience participation.

When I arrived in the morning and went through the checkpoint, with about a dozen others, the town was still fairly quiet and I spent the first hour or so wandering through the streets, taking in the general flavor of the settlement. At the northern end was an open space, a kind of town commons, with the community's only two-story structure behind it. I climbed the stairs to the second floor and found a kind of shrine/chapel, the centerpiece of which was a cushioned recess containing a bed piled high with brocaded material. Upon this a woman lay, apparently asleep, wearing an elaborate but faded lace and silk pink embroidered dress with a white silk scarf wrapped around her head. The floral rug before the bed was covered with small plates of food and drink, various small trinkets, flowers, and notes. In a nearby chair was sleeping a younger woman, much more plainly dressed. No one else was in the room, and after observing it a while, I returned to the rather livelier community below. As I walked among the structures, I could observe inhabitants still sleeping and others going about their morning activities, preparing and eating breakfast, washing clothes, and so on. One woman, naked to the waist, was engaged in washing herself. Some acknowledged my presence, others did not, but there was little sense of privacy since the rudely constructed buildings often had spaces between wallboards or at corners in addition to open windows and doors.

I entered into conversations with some of the townspeople (in German) and the occupying soldiers (in English), and began to piece together something of the imagined history and present condition of this village. The soldiers were on the whole brusque and professional, and most seemed contemptuous of the villagers and resentful of their being sent to serve here. There was a distinct feeling of fear among the townspeople and rumors of the community under some major but ill-defined threat. I also heard a bit about the woman I had seen sleeping in the larger building, who seemed a kind of matriarch, seer, and priestess for the community. A number of the inhabitants I met offered me some kind of cheap goods in exchange for my German marks, their own currency being apparently almost worthless. I bought a modest lunch, a wurst on some rather stale bread and a can of Coca-Cola, at the community's single general store, and was offered one actual "performance," a peep show set up in one of the community trailers. When I was seated inside with a few other visitors, a rude curtain was pulled aside and two rather worn-looking young women performed an unenthusiastic and not particularly erotic striptease. At its close they solicited tips from the small audience and indicated that they were available for more intimate entertainment in a neighboring trailer, but at least in my group no one pursued the invitation.

In the early afternoon more visitors arrived and soon outnumbered the inhabitants on the little walkways between the buildings. The main activity seemed to be conversations between these two groups, although there were occasional other actions. At one point the sound of a scuffle drew me to a location where a couple of soldiers were in the process of arresting, and expelling from the community, a person who at least appeared to be a visitor who had presumably broken the rules in some way. The major event that I witnessed occurred about midafternoon, when one of the townswomen rushed up to me and breathlessly announced that Maria had awakened and was speaking to her followers. I assumed that this was the sleeping woman I had seen earlier and turned back toward that chamber, noting that visitors and inhabitants from all over the town were heading in the same direction.

The chamber/chapel was packed with people (perhaps as many as fifty) and indeed the sleeping woman had awakened and was sitting, somewhat groggy still, on the edge of her bed, smoking a cigarette, and responding to questions from both visitors and inhabitants. The inhabitants set the tone by asking advice on personal matters or about the future, very much the kind of query one might direct toward a fortune-teller. One of the young women I had seen in the peep show complained that she had been molested by a soldier and was offered consolation but little advice by Maria. On the whole her responses were vague and in some cases so mystic as to be virtually incomprehensible. After about twenty minutes, she began to sway from apparent exhaustion, and the young girl I had seen sleeping near her earlier, apparently a kind of attendant, ushered the public out.

Friends who attended other days mentioned other formal social events—a wedding, a funeral, an arrest and trial—but clearly the main experience was a much more unstructured one, consisting of individual wandering about and interacting according to one's inclinations, with the inhabitants. Although one could discover a good deal about the history and situation of Ruby Town, there was no story or action to follow. What was offered instead was a kind of commodification of experience itself, a total immersion in a simulated environment, something like a living computer game. In such productions, the narrative so central to drama since the Greeks has been replaced by immersive experience, or if the spectator desires some narration, he or she must create it himself or herself.

2009 The Nature Theater of Oklahoma's *Romeo and Juliet*

Theatre has always employed a significant amount of material from outside the theatre in its creations, but the twenty-first century has seen a particularly widespread experimentation with such material—nontheatrical actors in groups like Rimini Protokoll, nontheatrical spaces and human interactions in groups like Signa, and calculatedly nontheatrical language in groups like the Nature Theater of Oklahoma, so named not for the state, but after a chapter title in Franz Kafka's unfinished novel, *Amerika.*

I first encountered the Nature Theater in September 2005, when they presented a work in progress as a part of the Prelude Festival, a sampling of new experimental work in New York that the Graduate Center of the City University of New York, where I teach, has been presenting annually since 2003 and has been my single best source for discovering such work. The work in progress was called *Poetics*, a movement piece, which, the creators explained, had been constructed entirely by chance, with rolling dice determining the length of scenes as well as the nature and length of the actions carried out by actors during those scenes. John Cage's work on chance art was cited as the inspiration, and indeed the construction of the piece recalled to me Cage's *Theatre of Chance*, created with the Living Theatre, which I had seen in 1960 and which similarly determined movements by rolling dice and other chance operations. *Poetics* had a much more lighthearted feeling and I enjoyed this sample so much that I sought the Nature Theater out at their next offering, *No Dice*, presented by the Soho Rep late in 2007.

As the title promised, no dice were used in this production, but in fact the physical movements were again determined by chance, based this time on a deck of cards, providing a vastly more complex physical vocabulary. At least equally striking, however, was the verbal text, which was not created by chance but by a much more original process. The creators, Pavol Liska and Kelly Copper, constructed the text by combining segments from over one hundred hours of telephone conversations Liska recorded, retaining pauses, interjections, and false starts, but avoiding occasional passages that suggested a more literary or traditional narrative. The result was a text that from time to time suggested a mood or a direction, but which never solidified into a coherent pattern, and which provided a copy of everyday casual speech rarely if ever actually presented on stage. True, Anna Deavere Smith had reproduced interviews, often word for word, but these were relatively well organized, devoted to discussion of a known subject, with few of the hesitations and verbal tics of everyday speech. The new theatrical experience offered by *No Dice* made it one of the most talked-about events of that off-off-Broadway season, and the six-thousand-square-foot space found by Soho Rep for this production, actually a former indoor playground, was completely sold out for the monthlong run of the show.

For their next production, the Nature Theater, while keeping a distinct physical element, placed found speech from everyday life even more clearly at the center of the work, as they have done ever since, and became an even more significant part of the New York, and indeed of the international experimental theatre scene. This was their *Romeo and Juliet*, which I saw soon after its opening in late December 2009 at the Kitchen, a venue in Chelsea that since the 1970s has been a leading organization in New York for the presentation of experimental dance, theatre, and mixed-media performances.

The concept behind this *Romeo and Juliet* could be viewed as a fresh approach to the highly popular docudramas of the previous decade, beginning with the works of Anna Deavere Smith and including the enormously successful *Laramie Project*. Such works clearly looked back to the docudrama tradition of much of the twentieth century, based on significant historical events but drawing its text not from the written records of those events but from transcripts of interviews with individuals more or less involved in the events in question. *Romeo and Juliet* of course recalled this tradition immediately to me, but also struck me by its two important departures from the tradition. First, it dealt with memories not of a specific historical event, but of a widely circulated cultural text, experienced in different ways and at different times by almost all members of that culture. Second, it did not "improve" or regularize the interview material, but presented it just as produced, with the pauses, stammering, interjections, and repetitions of actual speech. The disjointed verbal style was suggested by the headline in the *New Yorker* in 2013 leading off a review of the group's later piece, *Life and Times*, which was "Eight hours of, like, life." Like that of *No Dice*, the text for *Romeo and Juliet* was taken from transcripts of casual telephone conversations. Pavol Liska and Kelly Copper, the creators and directors of the group, called eight friends and simply asked them to recall and recount, to the best of their ability, Shakespeare's plot. Their rambling, disjointed, and often bizarre responses were then woven by the authors into a series of monologues more or less tracking the contours of the play.

I was accustomed to coming into the large open performance area at the Kitchen to find a bank of bleachers facing a more or less open area of the sort required by the dance/theatre pieces I often attended there, so the interior arrangements for *Romeo and Juliet* were surprising in their conventionality. Facing the seats was a very traditional (almost parodic) elevated proscenium stage at the rear of which was a large flat drop, upon which had been painted a light-colored drop curtain framed by voluminous swags of rich dark brocaded blue curtains, all two-dimensional. At the front of the stage was a row of crude but operating footlights, with a large, blocky prompter's box in the center, suggesting a modern tongue-in-cheek version of a nineteenth-century melodrama stage.

Basically the performance consisted of alternating monologues by actress Anne Gridley and actor Robert M. Johanson, both of which suggested in both costuming and acting style the same sort of amateurish, tacky, down-at-heel performance world that the stage itself had prepared us for. Gridley appeared first, dressed in a floor-length orange gown with spaghetti straps over bare shoulders and a black bra clearly visible above the top of the gown. A wreath of fake poppies, with a trailing silk ribbon, sat slightly askew on her pulled-back black hair. She stood proudly surveying the audience, so openly and unjustifiably self-assured that she generated laughter even before she uttered a word. Then she began her first monologue, delivered in an exaggerated pompous vocal and gestural style totally unsuited to the banality of the words. She began: "Uhhh . . . (pause) Romeo and Juliet? The Capulets—and the—(I can't remember the other guys)." And so it continued, with sentence fragments, some relevant and some not, side comments of "or something" or "I can't remember" and occasional sound fillers "Aan-nnd . . ." or "And uhhh . . ."

When Gridley finished this first monologue, Johanson began a second one, equally disjointed, but taking us somewhat further into the action of the original play. When he appeared on stage he cut a much more dashing figure than Gridley. Taller than her by a head, his pale face framed by unruly black hair and dressed in a tight-fitting black sleeveless jacket with a high black collar, tight black trousers, and buckled black shoes, he at least looked rather like a romantic leading man, complete with frequently furrowed brows and glowering eyes. He seemed a walking personification of the process that one of the interviews produced that found its way into the production: "I feel that 'Romeo and Juliet' is the uberplay for high school, and then once you hit college, it becomes 'Hamlet.'" However much his physical appearance may have suggested Shakespeare's haunted prince, however, Johanson soon undercut any solemnity by the same sort of parodic pseudoclassic style as that of Gridley, and of course the same idiosyncratic sort of text: "Romeo, like, gets in a fight with some guy with a very flourish name" or "I know I'm missing a big chunk in the middle." Like Gridley, he did not hurry over the rough passages. Every "um" "aanndd" and "like" was delivered with the same plummy orotund emphasis as any direct words of the bard himself. His bushy black hair also made it even more obvious than it had been in the case of Gridley that both actors were wearing distinct white earphones, and I suddenly realized that these were to guarantee that every "um," "ah," "I mean," and "heh heh" fell in precisely its allotted space.

The text did not hesitate to follow its sources even when their associations led them in strange, anachronistic directions. One passage speculated that had the young lovers not killed themselves, they probably would have eventually gotten a divorce. Even more unexpectedly, the recollection of this tragedy caused some respondents to offer riffs on 9/11 and Anna Nicole Smith. Under the circumstances, the unexpected appearance halfway through the show of an actor in a chicken suit seemed hardly incongruous, although I did wonder just what elements in the delivered text had suggested it.

After a series of alternating monologues, the story of Romeo and Juliet finally reaches what the text calls "that bit in the tomb" where Juliet cries out "Is there not a drop of poison left for me? Or some shit" and "then just—stabs herself." Having reached this point, the two actors for the first time entered into a dialogue, no longer attempting to summarize the action of the play but to comment on their own relationship to it, beginning with comparing their introduction to sex to that of Shakespeare's young lovers. I had the impression that this dialogue was not in fact culled from the interviews but based on improvisations between the actors. The conversation then went on from the personal to the more professional, to the relationship between actors and their audiences and how that related to the general need to be loved. Something of the comic delivery remained and it was entertaining to see the two young actors playing off of each other, but I found this section considerably weaker than the more farcical earlier part of the evening. Finally, however, the self-reflective meditation wound back to Shakespeare's play and the question of how and why this story continues to resonate in a culture seeming so different in its sensibility, even for people like Johanson, who admits in his final lines that he has in fact never read the play.

This less interesting section, however, served to set up a final, totally unexpected and highly effective sequence. After a curtain call in which the two actors (still somewhat in their exaggerated performance personae) received extended and well-deserved applause, the houselights went out, and surprisingly stayed out. Then from the darkened stage came the familiar words of one of Shakespeare's best-known and most-loved scenes, the balcony scene from *Romeo and Juliet*, this time performed by the two young actors without elaboration or pretense, simply offering a heartfelt and moving presentation of those perhaps overly familiar lines. Within the context of the evening's entertainment, however, the lines shone forth with new luster and served as a powerful reminder of why this play and this story continue to haunt our collective memory, however fragmentary and scattered its remnants may be.

2010 The Passion Play at Oberammergau

One of the most famous European theatre events is the passion play performed in the small Bavarian community of Oberammergau every ten years. Its history is a formidable one; it was established in the year 1633 by citizens seeking to be spared the bubonic plague ravaging the region by performing a play on the life and death of Jesus. Although the text has been many times reworked, the play has been performed with only a few minor interruptions through the centuries since that date. More than half a million visitors attend the productions, which run through the summers of each year ending in a zero.

In the summer of 2010 I attended the annual congress of the International Federation for Theatre Research, held that year in Munich. Although the congress is primarily devoted to the sharing of current research, the organizers each year provide opportunities for delegates to attend important theatrical events happening in the host city or region, and so, this being the festival year in Oberammergau, and that city being only a little more than fifty miles south of Munich, in the Bavarian Alps, a bus was chartered to take interested delegates to the town and the performance.

Accordingly, we left on the bus the morning of August 1 for the drive down to the festival city, a pleasant and picturesque trip of just over an hour into the heart of the Alps. The bus arrived midmorning, pulling into a very large parking area already containing dozens of tour buses from all over Europe (private cars parked in another location). These large parking lots were on the edge of the town, and shuttle buses to the theatre were provided, but the distances were small and one could easily walk from the lot into town and the theatre. Since the performance did not begin until 2:30 in the afternoon, there was ample time to visit most of the town and enjoy its picturesque vistas. Having been a tourist center for decades, indeed for centuries, Oberammergau has become almost a parody of the sort of Bavarian village conjured up by fairy tales and Walt Disney movies. Virtually every building in the village is covered with elaborate painted decorations, flags, and banners, with ivy falling in strands from thatched roofs and overflowing baskets of flowers beneath the windows and hanging on hooks from the walls. This is equally the case with private homes and with the ubiquitous cafés and souvenir shops that line the winding streets, the village being almost as famous for its woodcarvings and Bavarian crafts as for its passion play.

I spent the day enjoying the bustling crowds and having a lovely lunch with fellow delegates of Bavarian food, drinks, and cakes at one of the many elaborately festooned restaurants in the town, then went up to walk around the Festival Theatre, located rather to the north of the town center. It resembled less a theatre than a train terminal or aircraft hangar, a huge ungainly rectangular building striped in cream and ochre, with a protruding extension in front of the facade which contained the main entrance to the theatre, under a functional but not very attractive Plexiglas marquee surmounted by a large green upper facade, a white semicircular space at its center containing black bas-relief figures gathered on two sides of a large, simple, unadorned cross. The structure commendably did not attempt to pick up the somewhat kitschy Bavarian village style of the rest of the community, but if anything erred in the opposite direction, offering a rather unattractive jumble of simple geometrical forms that hardly suggested the housing of an internationally known cultural attraction.

Inside, the building was much more attractive and impressive. Originally performed in an open-air space, the play gained a sheltering roof for its audience in 1890, and the audience space has been steadily improved ever since. It is now a huge arched space seating over forty-seven hundred, with comfortable, underfloor heating and excellent acoustics. Perhaps its most striking feature is that the northern end of the audience area has been left open to the sky, and so the actual performance area remains outdoors, as it has been from the beginning of the festival, although of course the stage, like the auditorium, has been many times remodeled and improved. It has traditionally followed the form of a late medieval performance space, with some echoes of both classic and more modern stages. Basically it is a series of neutral architectural forms providing a backdrop to a large central acting area that stretches the full width of the stage. It is strictly symmetrical, with a large, peak-roofed facade at the center, containing an opening that is essentially an inner proscenium stage. On either side of this unit is found first a large open archway, then a two-pillared portico beginning a curve toward the auditorium and approached by a series of semicircular stairs, and finally another large arched entryway in the wall finishing the stage and connecting to the side wall of the auditorium.

The sheer scope of the spectacle was overwhelming. The actors are traditionally not professionals but citizens of the town; indeed one must have lived in Oberammergau for at least twenty years to be eligible to participate. Since the play requires more than one thousand performers (up to nine hundred fill the stage for the mass scenes such as the triumphal entry into Jerusalem and the bearing of the cross through these same streets), this means that approximately one in five of the village inhabitants performs in it. Whenever appropriate, animals were added as well. The scene of Christ challenging the moneylenders in the temple took place amid a crowded and busy street market, complete with donkeys, dogs, caged birds, chickens, and a small herd of sheep. Christ's entry into Jerusalem took place, of course, on the back of a real donkey. The script, which has changed many times over the years, has always dealt essentially with the final week of Christ's life, and the 2010 production consisted basically of sixteen scenes, each depicting a particular episode from that week. The play has always been produced on a single day, usually with one or more intervals between sections, but in 2010 for the first time part of the production was in the evening, so that we gathered for the first section at two in the afternoon for a session lasting until almost five, after the scene of the arrest of Jesus. We then broke for dinner and returned at 8:00 p.m. for another two hours, taking us through the crucifixion and apotheosis.

Having seen other passion plays created in imitation of Oberammergau in the United States, such as the Black Hills Passion Play, which for many years was performed annually in South Dakota, I knew generally what to expect—a respectful and basically realistic, if slightly some-what formal and stylized re-creating of such scenes as Christ praying in Gethsemane and, most spectacularly, the display of the three crucified figures on Calvary. What most surprised me in this passion was the extensive use of material outside of this story in the form of elaborate and highly stylized tableaux vivants displayed regularly throughout the evening on the large inner stage. Indeed the performance began and ended with these tableaux. The first showed the banishment of Adam and Eve from the garden and displayed iconic figures more like those in a child's picture book than a staged scene. In the center of the composition was a huge, dark-clad and dark-winged angel, holding aloft a blazing sword and standing in front of a large painted circle depicting blue clouds stretched across a reddish-orange sky. At his feet was a large brownish rocky element, with a passage through its center that his outstretched wings were clearly barring. Crouching on either side downstage of this rock were the disgraced couple, in simple white garments, and standing over each of them was another angel, these in brown robes, one bearing a large coiled serpent, the other a small but flourishing tree. A narrator and a blue-robed choir of about thirty introduced each tableau, commented upon it, and tied it into the next scene. This first tableau was followed by a second, recalling the rather abstract design over the entrance to the theatre. A large empty cross stood center stage, surrounded by a number of small children. There was no movement in either tableau, no text, only the swelling music of the orchestra. The music that accompanied much of the production was reportedly based on that composed by a local musician in the early nineteenth century. Doubtless like the text it has been considerably modified over time, but it still had the flavor of that period, with passages that suggested Mozart, Haydn, and occasionally Romantics like Weber.

As the play went on, most sections of the play were introduced by one or two tableaux of this sort, all scenes from the Old Testament with presumed particular connections to the section of the passion about to be dramatically presented. Thus the scene in which Judas appears before the Jewish High Court and agrees to betray Jesus for thirty pieces of silver was introduced by a tableau showing a scene from the Old Testament story of Joseph. A young boy stripped to the waist and with his hands tied is presented by his brothers to the Midianites, who are offering them silver coins for him. Only in the final section of the play did a tableau follow the action of the scene. This was the resurrection scene, which began with Roman guards surveying the empty tomb, then showed the arrival of the Marys and their encounter with the angel. Following this came the concluding tableau, an ascendant Jesus in glowing write robes, surrounded by his disciples, angels, the Virgin Mary, and Moses.

Although the tableaux vivants were frozen images with rather the feel of an early twentieth-century children's picture book, there were a number of scenes within the actual production that clearly sought to evoke the visual tradition of the Passion. The most obvious of these was the staging of the Last Supper, clearly modeled on the famous painting by Leonardo da Vinci. The crucifixion scene evoked a whole series of familiar visualizations, from Grünewald to Rubens, and concluded with a downstage pietà, in clear imitation of Michelangelo. Other events of the Passion Week, while often depicted in Western art, had less specific visual associations, and I was aware of no other direct visual quotes. For the most part the costumes followed the custom of standardized period robes and simplified Roman battle dress, but the one notable exception was the Jewish leaders, all of whom wore huge hats, flaring out at the top rather like a caricature of the headgear of Greek orthodox priests. High priest Caiaphas, in flowing white robes with a particularly enormous flared hat, was arguably the most visually striking character in the production.

As we regained our bus and drove back that night through the mountains to Munich, I pondered my impressions of the work. The sheer size and ambition of it was certainly impressive, and the experience had certainly been a powerful one, but it was not, at least for me, primarily either religious or aesthetic. I might characterize it more as a profound sense of an historical dimension. Despite all the changes that the production had undergone over the centuries, the feeling of witnessing this ongoing major performance experience in a space where generations of my predecessors had come to see it created a powerful effect, similar in some ways to when I first saw a production of Molière at the Comédie-Française, or Brecht at the Berliner Ensemble, or attended a firelight Noh production at an ancient temple near Tokyo. It was an experience quite different from attending a production, which I often do, in a theatre filled for me with memories of my own previous visits, but none the less an experience clearly deeply touched by an awareness of the profound historical dimension of this seemingly most ephemeral art.

Coda

I Remember Mama by the Transport Group Theatre Company, 2014. Photo by Carol Rosegg. Used with permission.

2014 The Transport Group's
I Remember Mama

The reader may well have remarked how the operations of memory, clearly central to this writing project from the outset, have become even more prominent in the more recent essays. This is doubtless because a lifetime of theatre-going inevitably engages one in the process of remembering, but it is also because during the last decade or two I have become more and more concerned with the centrality of memory to the experience of all theatre, whether my own or someone else's. My first book of the new century, *The Haunted Stage*, was the outcome of that concern. I began that book with the comment among Ibsen scholars that all of his plays might be called *Ghosts*, and suggested that in fact the dynamics of theatrical memory conjures ghosts of some sort in every new production we witness.

The degree of our conscious awareness of this dynamic of course varies from production to production, but I want to take as the coda of this book of theatrical memory a production that was specifically designed to foreground the process of theatrical memory. As such it succeeded at least in my own case of providing one of the most moving examples of this process in a lifetime of theatre-going. This was the 2014 Transport Group revival of the mid twentieth-century American classic *I Remember Mama*.

The Transport Group, founded in 2001, has specialized in revivals of American plays and in new works commenting on contemporary America. They began with rather conventional proscenium productions and around 2010 began to explore environmental staging, and I was quite delighted with their production in 2011 of a new musical by Michael John LaChiusa, *The Queen of the Mist*, about Anna Edson Taylor, the first woman to go over Niagara Falls in a barrel. The production was created in a space that was simultaneously new and historic, one of the major venues for off-off-Broadway work, especially dance, half a century ago, with the Judson Church on the south side of Washington Square, only a few steps from Eugene O'Neill's Provincetown Playhouse and also from the Sullivan Street Playhouse, home for many years of *The Fantasticks*.

In this historic performance space, where I had seen so much new dance and theatre work in the 1960s and 1970s, a former gymnasium in the basement was converted into an important new black-box theatre, the Gym at Judson, used for the first time for *Queen of the Mist*. The production was a great success, filling the neutral space with a colorful display of nineteenth-century sideshow style display. It was really the pleasant memories of this production, more than the play itself, that drew me back to this space for the Transport's next offering there, a revival of the 1944 hit Broadway comedy by John Van Druten, *I Remember Mama*. The 1944 stage comedy was subsequently converted into a Richard Rodgers musical, an award-winning film, and a long-running CBS television series. I was old enough in the 1950s to see both of the latter and remember them as engaging if lightweight sentimental depictions of American family life as seen in the popular media of the time. Being myself the descendent of Swedish immigrants, I found the gentle ethnic humor brought back some of my own earlier memories.

Even so, there was little in the revival itself to attract me, but the fond memories of *Queen of the Mist* encouraged me to see what this imaginative company might do with this much more conventional fare. It was most fortunate for me that I did so, because the interpretation, totally unexpected and original, turned out to be one of my most memorable theatrical experiences of the decade and a warning never to assume that imaginative actors, directors, and designers might not be able to make stunning theatre out of what might seem a quite conventional dramatic text.

The decision to create the production in the Gym was already a promising one, since the play itself had been conceived for a traditional proscenium stage, a form familiar from countless American family dramas from that era. When I went down the long approach corridor and entered the performance space I was pleasantly surprised to find that the designer had made no attempt to create a conventional theatre in this large open space. Indeed its utilitarian aspect was even more emphasized than in the moderately illusionistic *Queen of the Mist*. Four ranks of conventional gymnasium green scoop lights shared the ceiling with pipes and ducts, some of which ran down the cream-painted but unadorned gymnasium walls. Two rows of red-backed folding chairs, seat numbers pinned to them, awaited the audience along the two end walls, and a single row of the same ran along the two side walls. In the large playing arena at the center, instead of a conventional salon, seven dining room tables, some ovoid, others rectangular, were scattered about the space on the bare, uncarpeted wooden floor, a set of six matching chairs surrounding each table, and each table holding a collection of objects, twenty or thirty small decorative boxes on one table, papers on another, children's toys on a third, and so on. As the evening went on, the actors would gather around one or another of these tables to form large or small conversational groups.

Far more surprising than this unconventional spatial arrangement, however, was the casting, as I realized soon after the production began. The twenty-three roles in Van Druten's play, male and female, were actually performed by ten actresses. This was unusual, but certainly not remarkable in the modern off-off-Broadway theatre, which often has presented four- or five-person versions of Shakespeare, sometimes with only one gender on stage. What was unique about this cast, however, was not that all were women or that most played several roles, but that all were working veteran actresses, the youngest of whom was sixty-five years of age. Several of them were clearly actresses I had seen before, but since no program was handed out at the beginning, it was not until the intermission that the audience was able to gain more information about this remarkable cast, when, going out into the corridor/lobby, we discovered a series of professional headshots displayed with accompanying biographies. Even in more conventional theatre programs, such biographies normally evoke many memories for regular theatre-goers, but here that experience was greatly magnified, with the chronicling of careers that in every case went back decades and covered an astonishing range of New York theatre over that period—straight dramas, musicals, opera, Broadway, off- and off-off-Broadway, not to mention regional work, films, and television.

The theatre memories brought back to me by these listings were almost overwhelming. Here was Barbara Andres, whom I had seen on Broadway in *The Boy Friend* in 1970, and Barbara Barrie, whom I had seen the same year in the premiere of Sondheim's *Company* and as Dave's mother in the wonderful 1979 film *Breaking Away*, which encapsulated for me my experience of the 1970s in Bloomington, Indiana. Here was Alice Cannon, whom I had first seen off-Broadway in the 1960s and as recently as 2000 in the moving Broadway production of James Joyce's *The Dead*, and Lynn Cohen from Andre Gregory's great film *Vanya on 42nd Street*, the series *Sex and the City*, and numerous Broadway and off-Broadway productions. Here was Rita Gardner, the original Luisa in *The Fantasticks* and a frequent Broadway performer in subsequent years, and Heather MacRae, whom I had seen in *Hair* in 1968 and as Charlotte in the various versions of William Finn's *Falsettos* in the 1990s. Here was Marni Nixon, another actress from *The Dead* whose voice can be heard in many of the great film musicals of the century—*West Side Story, The King and I, The Sound of Music, My Fair Lady*. Here was Dale Soules, another veteran of *Hair*, whom I had seen within the past decade on Broadway in *Grey Gardens* and *The Crucible*, and Phyllis Somerville, whom I had first seen on Broadway in 1978 in *Once in a Lifetime*. Only the Transport Group's own Letty Serra, although a longtime author, actor, and producer, did not suggest a number of specific theatre memories to me.

As is generally the case, however, the network of memories aroused by a preliminary look over biographies in the program faded in importance though never entirely disappeared as the living actors developed new impressions and associations in the production at hand. Although the play's tone was relentlessly nostalgic, there was never the impression of any performers of fading abilities. On the contrary, every member of this remarkable company performed her single role or multiple ones with a depth and skill that clearly reflected decades of training and experience. Older and younger characters, men and women, were rendered with equal finesse and telling detail, and this memory play took on a dimensionality that was truly profound both theatrically and emotionally.

I was reminded in a very positive way of the best productions I have seen of Wilder's *Our Town*, written just six years before *I Remember Mama* and looking back, with a similar sentimentalized nostalgia, to the same location, the United States in the opening years of the twentieth century. Both plays, at their best, connect us with our own past and memories in profound ways, and the inspired device of putting this nostalgic evocation into the hands of performers whose own past covers most of that century of memory created an experience that much more profound, especially for audience members like myself whose lifetime was almost the same as that of these remarkable performers.

After the production, an unusually large number of audience members remained in the Gym to express their admiration to the actresses, and in many cases to share theatrical memories with them. I was particularly eager to meet Rita Gardner, who created the role of the Girl in *The Fantasticks*, one of my fondest early memories of New York theatre-going and the memory of which, in 1960, fifty-four years earlier, forms the first chapter in this present book. I told Gardner how well I remembered that production and thanked her (somewhat belatedly) for the experience. She noted that it was her first professional appearance in New York and thus a central experience for her as well. Since then, I thought, she and I had each devoted more than half a century to enjoying that critical relationship between the human beings on either side of the footlights that makes the theatrical experience such a profound human experience.

After the production, I had to walk back to the location of the original Sullivan Street Playhouse, less than two blocks away, where *The Fantasticks* had premiered and played for many years, now converted into luxury apartments. Few of the theatres and cafés that once dotted Sullivan and the next street, Macdougal, have survived into the new century, but the legendary Caffe Reggio is still there, and I ended the evening there, with a cappuccino and dessert, thinking back over the more than sixty years that I had spent seeing so much great theatre in this haunted neighborhood and elsewhere. Inevitably, as my mind went back to that evening when I first saw *The Fantasticks*, the song with which Jerry Orbach as El Gallo opened the show ran through my mind with new reverberations and poignancy: "Try to Remember." To the readers of this book I hope these tries at remembering will prove as pleasurable as they were to me in recording them, and to those who have been fortunate enough to share any part of this fascinating theatrical era with me, I invite them, as did El Gallo, "If you remember, then follow"—which in 1960 the newcomer Rita Gardner echoed: "Follow, follow, follow, follow, follow, follow . . ."

Index